THE RUPTURES
OF
AMERICAN CAPITAL

THE RUPTURES
OF
AMERICAN CAPITAL

Women of Color Feminism and
the Culture of Immigrant Labor

GRACE KYUNGWON HONG

UNIVERSITY OF MINNESOTA PRESS
MINNEAPOLIS • LONDON

An earlier version of chapter 2 originally appeared as "'Something Forgotten Which Should Have Been Remembered': Private Property and Cross-Racial Solidarity in the Work of Hisaye Yamamoto," *American Literature* 71, no. 2 (June 1999): 291–310. Copyright 1999 Duke University Press. All rights reserved. Reprinted by permission of the publisher.

Published by the University of Minnesota Press
111 Third Avenue South, Suite 290
Minneapolis, MN 55401-2520
http://www.upress.umn.edu

Library of Congress Cataloging-in-Publication Data

Hong, Grace Kyungwon.
The ruptures of American capital : women of color feminism and the culture of immigrant labor / Grace Kyungwon Hong.
p. cm.
Includes bibliographical references and index.
ISBN-13: 978-0-8166-4634-0 (alk. paper)—ISBN-10: 0-8166-4634-1 (alk. paper)
ISBN-13: 978-0-8166-4635-7 (pbk. : alk. paper)—ISBN-10: 0-8166-4635-X (pbk. : alk. paper)
1. Minority women—United States—Economic conditions. 2. Minority women—United States—Social conditions. 3. Marginality, Social—United States. 4. Sex discrimination against women—United States. 5. Race discrimination—United States. 6. Feminist theory—United States. I. Title.
HQ1233.H67 2006
305.48'800973—dc22
2006005676

CONTENTS

INTRODUCTION

In her preface to *This Bridge Called My Back: Writings by Radical Women of Color* (1981), Cherríe Moraga begins with a meditation on the stakes of women of color feminist politics:

> I can't prepare myself a revolutionary packet that makes no sense when I leave the white suburbs of Watertown, Massachusetts, and take the T-line to Black Roxbury.
>
> Take Boston alone, I think to myself and the feminism my so-called sisters have constructed does nothing to help me make the trip from one end of town to another. Leaving Watertown, I board a bus and ride it quietly in my white flesh to Harvard Square, protected by the gold highlights my hair dares to take on, like an insult, in this miserable heat.
>
> *I transfer and go underground.*
>
> Julie told me the other day how they stopped her for walking through the suburbs. Can't tell if she's a man or a woman, only know that it's Black moving through that part of town. They won't spot her here, moving underground.
>
> The train is abruptly stopped. A white man in jeans and tee shirt breaks into the car I'm in, throws a Black kid up against the door, handcuffs him and carries him away. The train moves on. The day before, a 14-year-old Black boy was shot in the head by a white cop. And the summer is getting hotter.
>
> I hear there are some women in this town plotting a *lesbian* revolution. What does this mean about the boy shot in the head is what I want to know.

I am a lesbian. I want a movement that helps me make some sense of the trip from Watertown to Roxbury, from white to Black. I love women the entire way, beyond a doubt. (Moraga and Anzaldúa 1981, xiii)

This seemingly quotidian description of Moraga's ride through Boston on public transportation situates segregation, suburbanization, and the concomitant police violence against racialized subjects as constitutive contradictions of the racialized state. In referencing these conditions, Moraga resurrects a historical relationship between white property rights, the protection of a supposedly vulnerable and pure white feminized domesticity, and the criminalization of people of color. Although ostensibly universal, U.S. national identity has privileged white enfranchisement and property— as mutually constituted through a protected "private" sphere— and therefore ensured racialized exploitation and dispossession.

In contrast to normative accounts of U.S. national identity, Moraga presents those formations that are produced by the racialized state yet cannot be accounted for by them. She begins with "Julie," who does not register as "gendered" in any normative way ("Can't tell if she's a man or a woman, only know that it's Black moving through that part of town") because she is only recognizable as a threat to, and a deviation from, the protected institution of domesticity implied by the segregated white suburbs and the police surveillance of those suburbs. In contrast to Julie, who would be invisible when not in the suburbs ("they won't spot her here, moving underground"), the racialized adolescent sexuality of the "Black kid" on the train is marked by his hypervisibility, which makes him vulnerable to spectacularized displays of violence and surveillance from those we can only presume are the police. Moraga's inclusion of the boy of color on the train as an important consideration for any women of color politics marks the ways that men of color are "queered" or estranged from normative masculinity by virtue of the fact that the public sphere is a space of violence and abjection, not self-possession. She thus recognizes the possibilities suggested by the plurality of racialized masculine formations, possibilities that masculinist nationalisms tend to elide. Racialized masculinities do not emerge from the same relationship to property, citizenship, and self-will that constitutes white masculinities. Moraga's rendering maintains that racialized masculinities have the potential for unexpected forms of alliance with, for example, Julie, who is also "queered" from normative gender formations. Moraga emphasizes the difference between herself, with her "white skin" and "gold highlights," which allow her to ride the subway unmolested, and the boy, whose adolescent masculinity and skin color attract the violent and surveilling gaze of the repressive state.

Her explicit emphasis on her "protected" status exemplifies women of color feminist practice in several important ways. First, it highlights the non-analogous but related racializations of these three different formations: herself, Julie, and the boy on the train. That is, while these formations have very different relationships to white domesticity, police brutality, and segregation, they are all linked by virtue of these relationships. Moraga's passage underscores the fact that there already exists a normative reading practice that produces a variety of racialized and gendered meanings—Julie's gender deviance, the boy's threatening criminality, Moraga's invisibility—in order to legitimate racialized dispossession and white property rights, to enact the protection of white domesticity, and to ensure racialized labor exploitation. Moraga's analysis secures an understanding that different racial and gender formations are not produced in isolation, but relationally. Second, with this articulation of her "protected" status, she refuses to narrate "women of color" as a position of ultimate injury. Although she critiques a pathologizing narrative that would define racialized and gendered subjects as deviant and dangerous, she also refuses the project of valorizing such subjects through an identity politics. Rather than merely replacing the privileged subject of cultural nationalism, white feminism, or canonical Marxism with "woman of color" as the purest, most revolutionary subject position, Moraga constantly situates the ways that the category "women of color" completely disorganizes the very idea of a stable and knowable identity. Citing the inadequacies of the single-axis politics of "The Left . . . with its shaky and shabby record of commitment to women, period" and "the white sector of the feminist movement," as well as the white gay and lesbian movement that would call for a "*lesbian* revolution," Moraga situates these movements' tendency to reproduce a nationalist epistemology that would privilege a subject formed through singular identifications. Instead of a politics of identification and singularity, "women of color" signals the need for an analytic that can thoughtfully apprehend the relationship between Julie, herself, and the boy on the train. This need propels Moraga to search for what Kimberlé Crenshaw has usefully termed an "intersectional" analysis—an analytic mode that does not privilege one site of identification over another, but insists on the importance of race, class, gender, and sexuality as interlocking and mutually constitutive. Thus, women of color feminism is not a reified subject position but a reading practice, a "way of making sense of" that reveals the contradictions of the racialized and gendered state.

This passage represents the ways that women of color feminist practice expressed the breakdown of long-existing nationalist definitions of subject and community, at the very moment when the role of the nation-state was being radically reconfigured. For from where does this demand for a new mode of analysis emerge? As Moraga explicitly states, this articulation of need is her way of understanding and intervening into the political economic shift that is reconfiguring Boston ("Take Boston alone") from a "national" city to what Saskia Sassen has called a "global city."[1] In denaturalizing these meanings of "race" and "gender" in Boston in this era, Moraga's preface contests the new political economic order that is mutually constituted by those meanings. The policy of criminalization, the segregated conditions that structure the cartography of Boston, and the privileging of the white domestic space that these processes imply are all signals of this political economic reorganization. These conditions are wrought by the change that Boston underwent in the 1970s and 1980s, as the functions of this formerly industrialized city shifted within a global economy. Postwar Boston felt the stresses of a nationwide urban crisis brought on by the relocation of manufacturing industries overseas and the "white flight" to the suburbs. In the postwar era, federal home ownership programs and highway subsidies created new suburban commuters who worked in the urban core but did not constitute its tax base (Kennedy 1992, 154). At the same time, the industrial base of the New England region—the textile mills and the fishing industry in particular—collapsed: in 1947, 280,000 people worked in textiles, for example, but only 99,000 in 1964 (Kennedy 1992, 158). Becoming a "global city" in response, Boston moved even more completely into a service-based economy of finance, insurance, and law, becoming one of the centers of a global economy rather than a regional or even a national one. One general characteristic of a global city is increased suburbanization and gentrification, as the areas that house the managerial and professional labor of these global economies become bastions of elite privilege through increased police surveillance and the displacement of impoverished racialized communities. Postwar Boston saw several such displacements, as the stable working-class neighborhoods where people of color and immigrants had settled during the era of segregation, such as New York Streets and the West End, were razed in the late 1950s to build an "industrial no-man's land" and "an enclave for the wealthy" (Kennedy 1992, 162, 163). Moraga's analysis marks this shift through her discussion of her own "invisibility" on the train and the hypervisibility of the boy. The shift into service economies focused on racialized women as its labor force while displacing the industrial production that had previously prioritized racialized male labor. In this context, women of color are not subject to scrutiny on the trains, as their presence is explained by their incorporation into a service economy, while the black boy on the train is positioned less as labor and more as the object of state violence and criminalization.[2] While differently racialized and gendered in relation to the shifts in the political economy of Boston, these formations are linked by these changes.

Moraga's preface focuses on Boston to identify the ways the reorganization of cities and economies under globalization leads to an increase in the repressive role of the nation-state, in the form of police surveillance and the displacement of impoverished racialized communities. Moraga's preface articulates the need for more complex, intersectional analytics that might understand segregation, suburbanization, and police violence not only as signals of the fundamental contradictions of the nation-state but as inherent to capital's global phase. She situates women of color feminist practice as a means of exploiting these contradictions by displacing the singularly formed subject of the nation-state in favor of a contradictory, multiply determined subjectivity, articulated through an intersectional analysis.

This strategy fundamentally centers *culture.* Moraga's preface calls for a women of color feminism that can address a "14-year-old Black boy . . . shot in the head by a white cop," a feminism that takes her from racialized ghetto to white suburb. What that means for Moraga is a movement charged with the task of "mak[ing] sense of." When this passage stresses the importance of a *reading practice*—a movement that "makes sense of" the links between segregation, criminalization, and the privileging of white domestic space—it is asserting that the contradictions inherent to the global reorganization of capital can be apprehended through culture, through the displacement of nationalist modes of knowing. Culture thus becomes the site of struggle, where newly naturalized meanings are both established and contested: How might we counter narratives that would situate the boy on the train as a violent threat, rather than as a recipient of violence? What does Julie's incomprehensibility within a normative gender regime say about the racist underpinnings of that regime? Culture in this context does not refer only to individual works of cultural production, but encompasses a system of meaning-making, a system ordered by relations of power. Moraga's preface evidences neither a determinism that makes culture a "reflection" of the material world nor an aestheticization that makes culture unrelated to social relations. Women of color feminist practice never posited culture as a separate sphere transcending or disconnected from a material order but rather understood culture as itself always a material and social practice.

For Moraga, to "transfer and go underground" implies an epistemological shift as well as a spatial one. Traveling from one part of town to another in that particular moment ("Boston, Massachusetts—July 20, 1980") is not simply moving through undifferentiated, abstract space but through variegated heterotopic spaces rife with a proliferation of meanings, histories, and material circumstances. These spaces mark safety and danger, visibility and invisibility, surveillance and punishment differently for differently racialized and gendered subjects. To "make some sense" of these formations is to understand that they exist as a deviation from the national ideals of domesticity, property, and individuated subjecthood, insofar as they tell of the violences committed in the defense of such ideals. As such, it is also to understand that women of color feminist practice emerges to name that which cannot be narrated through those ideals. Transferring and going underground means that another analytic emerges to "make sense of" that which is pathologized or rendered invisible by the epistemologies of nationalism. As such, women of color feminist practice must be situated *within* a genealogy of liberal capitalism, as naming the crises and erasures of that genealogy. Yet women of color feminist practice marks the forms of racialized and gendered difference that such a genealogy depends on but cannot account for. Moraga's testament that something will emerge to "make sense of" these heretofore inarticulable experiences is a promise that violence, dispossession, and pathology will not exhaust the meaning of their lives and struggles. Further, women of color feminism's naming of the crisis and ruptures of this genealogy of U.S. nationalism allows it to make links with those formations—such as racialized immigrant women's culture—never hailed by such nationalist inclusions in the first place.

I begin with this moment from *This Bridge Called My Back* because it cogently reveals the epistemological ruptures that marked a key transition in American capitalism, a transition I argue can be apprehended only through the formations that emerge to mark its contradictions. In the first part of this book, I address the national phase, in which the social relations of capitalism within the history of U.S. liberal democracy endowed the abstract citizen with the right to property. The U.S. nation-state attempted to resolve the contradictions between state and capital from the late nineteenth to the mid-twentieth century by systematically rendering racialized subjects vulnerable to labor exploitation, dispossession, and state-enforced violence by denying access to a privileged citizen-subject formation. Racialized citizenship was managed, of course, through actual legal enfranchisements such as the 1790 Naturalization Act, which restricted citizenship to "free white persons." Yet these *legal* enfranchisements were mutually reinforced through a privileged subject position, established through culture: what political theorist C. B. MacPherson has called the "possessive individual." As I argue in chapter 1, although organized around whiteness and masculinity and based over and against racialized enslavement, the possessive individual was posited as ostensibly universally available. Examining late nineteenth- and early twentieth-century texts such as Mark Twain's *The Adventures of Huckleberry Finn*, Henry James's *Daisy Miller*, and Booker T. Washington's *Up from Slavery*, this chapter posits the importance of *narrative form* as a site where the possessive individual was unevenly constituted as a universal national subject, while the nation-state categorically expelled or excluded these racialized workers from the category of citizenship. U.S. narratives of development—whether through the novel form, as in Twain's and James's texts, or in the autobiography, as in Washington's—posited differences and particularities as that which could be transcended on one's way to becoming the possessive individual. My analysis takes the conventions of genre—in this case, the genre of the novel or autobiography—as positing normative modes of affiliation and subjectification, and, in so doing, disavowing racial and gendered subordination through the promise of universal incorporation through possessive individualism.

Women of color feminist practice emerged as the trace of that which had to be erased for this promise of incorporation to remain coherent. Women of color feminist practice marked the return of the repressed of possessive individualism, and thus emerged as the *crisis* of capital's national phase, at the very moment when capital was transitioning from its national to its global phase. It did so by suggesting modes of subjectivity and collectivity unimaginable under nationalism. My discussion of the writings of Hisaye Yamamoto and Toni Morrison in chapter 2 explicates exactly how these alternative subjects and communities were constituted.

We may understand women of color feminism's emergence in the 1970s and 1980s as one register of the shifts in the restructuring of the global political economy after World War II. This restructuring was marked by the United States' displacement of Britain as the leading world economic power after World War II. The hegemony of the United States was based on neocolonial policies that, unlike formal territorial colonialism, operated through economic and cultural institutions, rather than through political governance. After the advent of worldwide movements for decolonization, U.S.-controlled financial institutions such as the World Bank and the International Monetary Fund (IMF) shifted to neoliberal policies that no longer depended on formal colonial ties but exploited the establishment of postcolonial nation-states. The increasing militarization of the world, the "development" policies dictated by U.S.-controlled financial institutions, and the violence brought about by capitalist development have violently displaced laboring populations, some of whom are rendered absolutely immobile and fixed to a certain locale, while others are forced by necessity to migrate, depending on the needs of capital. At the same time, economic restructuring turns postindustrial nations like the United States into service economies, dependent on cheap, easily exploitable labor. Transnational immigration to the United States from the 1980s onward can be seen as a feature of this process.

Therefore, in the second part of this book, I investigate what I call capital's global phase. I argue that late twentieth-century capital has its own universal mode: paradoxically, a universalized fetishization of difference. This fetishization of difference is most clearly articulated through the rise of consumerism. I examine the history of U.S. consumerism, which stretches back to the Fordist era, in order to excavate the prehistory of contemporary U.S. neocolonialism. In chapter 3, I examine the emergence of consumerism in relation to the bureaucratized and rationalized governmentalities of the early twentieth century, governmentalities that expressed imperialist and Fordist relations of rule as forms of "abstract space." Through an examination of John Dos Passos's *U.S.A.*, I posit culture as the site where

recalcitrant subjects who could not be subsumed to the totalizing epistemology of abstract space emerged. These recalcitrant subjects, who could
not be incorporated as the working class and were therefore "unorganiz-
able" under the models of labor organizing that emerged in the Fordist era,
operate more as a prehistory for the racialized immigrant women's culture
of the post-Fordist moment than the white working class. While post-
Fordism jettisoned the burdensome bureaucracy of Fordism, it retained consumerism as its organizing logic. Under global post-Fordism, commodity
culture and consumerism become the key abstractions. In other words,
unlike in the earlier era, when racialized populations were ostensibly recruited, however unevenly, for U.S. citizenship and abstract labor, in this
later era they are enlisted for capitalism precisely due to their capacity for
exploitation because of their differentiated—noncitizen, female, temporary—status. Because of the logic of differentiation that signals capital's
global phase, racialized immigrant women workers are disconnected from
the liberal institutions of citizenship and civil rights that were the sites of
contradiction in the 1960s and 1970s. Therefore, these workers do not organize their claims only against the state, but they do so in a variety of ways
and in a variety of sites. We therefore need to understand "labor struggles"
differently, as they emerge around racialized and gendered contradictions.

In this era, race and gender might seem to have been transformed into
yet another kind of commodified difference. Whether it's the various consumerist deployments of race—the use of racialized youth culture, most
obviously and extensively hip-hop, to create new consumer markets and
demographics—or the corporate policies that specifically and explicitly target racialized women as vulnerable labor in their production plants,[3] racialized and gendered difference equals profit in a global economy. As such,
an important site of struggle in this era is commodity culture and consumerism. While capital in its global phase attempts to cast difference
itself as ahistorical and commodified, I argue in chapter 4 that racialized
immigrant women's culture, like the work of Helena Maria Viramontes and
Jessica Hagedorn, brings to light both the varied, contested, and uneven
modes of incorporation into consumer culture and the *labor* that is held
at a distance from the consumerist subject. Racialized immigrant women's
culture attests to the ways this ostensibly universal global subject necessarily must erase the histories of exploitation and differentiation that occasioned its emergence, and, in so doing, it resurrects these erased and lost

histories. These texts demonstrate the unruly and heterogeneous inhabitations of this supposedly universal condition, revealing the different histories of struggle that racialized immigrant women bring with them.

Tracing the transition in capital in the twentieth century through its crises and contradictions allows me to articulate "women of color feminism" and "racialized immigrant women's culture" not as identity categories but as analytics. Women of color feminist practice is often misunderstood as an incorporative category that can be used to describe the experiences of any racialized woman. I try to work against such homogenizing tendencies by situating these two formations within two historical phases of capital, which allows me to understand them as *differentiated,* rather than as similar or analogous. I do not seek to argue that racialized immigrant women are "women of color" by highlighting presumed similarities between these formations and obscuring their fundamentally non-analogous natures. Taking up these formations to write a history of the transition from capital's national phase to its global phase requires quite the opposite: I read women of color feminist practice as a *methodology* for comparative analysis that allows us to relationally understand the possible links between very disparate formations.

I'd like to take a moment here to explore the implications for a relational analysis that creates models for coalition between these two divergent formations without occluding important differences. I have argued that women of color feminist practice marks the ways in which models of struggle that simply center on the nation-state are no longer viable. In other words, women of color feminist practice identifies the state as a site of violence, not resolution, and in so doing, it displaces rights-based struggles, such as appealing to labor laws or engaging a discourse of civil rights. Further, unlike single-axis forms of organizing, such as the mainstream white feminist movement, traditional labor organizing, or race-based movements, women of color feminism's insistence on difference, coalitional politics, and a careful examination of the intersecting processes of race, gender, sexuality, and class, which make singular identifications impossible, displaces a U.S. nationalist subject formation based on homogeneity, equivalence, and identification. Women of color feminist practice therefore addresses the manifestations of the nation-state (as repressive apparatus, as guarantor of unequal property relations, as privileged possessive individual) within its new role in capital's global phase. In other words, women of color feminism is a historical formation that I am relationally linking to racialized immigrant women's culture, but it also provides the methodology or reading practice through which these links can be made. I take women of color feminism's theorizing of "coalition through difference" as a comparative race methodology for opening up a way to apprehend what Angela Davis has called "unpredictable or unlikely coalitions grounded in political projects," which can emerge when coalition is not imagined only through similarity or identification, but through difference, contradiction, and contestation (Davis 1997, 322).

In this introduction, I do not provide an extended reading of racialized immigrant women's culture as I do with women of color feminist practice, leaving a more lengthy discussion of racialized immigrant women's culture to chapter 4, but I do want to suggest some implications for understanding them relationally. Understanding women of color feminist practice as documenting the transition from capital's national phase to its global phase allows us to regard the experiences of U.S. women of color as part of the worldwide proletarianization of racialized women. As a 1979 pamphlet created by the black feminist socialist Combahee River Collective notes, the murders of the twelve black women, as well as the dismissive response of the police and the press, can be contextualized within the general devaluation of black women's lives that is the ongoing legacy of centuries of racialized capitalism—what they in their "Black Feminist Statement" describe as an indication of "how little value has been placed upon our lives during four centuries of bondage in the Western hemisphere" (Combahee River Collective 1981, 212). This astute analysis of the devaluation of black women's lives points to the devaluation of racialized women, as global capital fixes on racialized women as the cheapest and most vulnerable form of labor. These are the conditions in which it becomes important to understand the relationship between older formations, like women of color feminism, and later ones, such as racialized immigrant women's culture.

One important index of the reorganization of economies are new patterns of migration and immigration. These patterns have reshaped racialized communities in the United States, creating the need for new intersectional and comparative modes of analysis and organizing. The emergence of the global city has accompanied the U.S. economy's shift to service labor, resulting in an economy that is now more dependent on racialized immigrant women as the labor base. In the late nineteenth and early twentieth

centuries, immigration laws and policies recruited itinerant male labor—
Chinese "bachelors," for example, or Mexican bracero workers—but currently, racialized women, through the immigration rubric of "family reunification," make up the majority of new immigrants. Chandan Reddy notes
that "since the 1980s the state has actively worked to produce a racialized
and gendered labor migration through the rubric of family reunification"
(2005, 109). A new workforce of racialized immigrant women fills those
labor needs historically filled by racialized women—such as domestic
work—while also filling the new labor niches demanded by more recent
developments, such as the return in the 1980s of sweatshops to the United
States. The importance of subcontracting and sweatshops to new modes
of global production and flexible accumulation now ensure that older categories of "core" and "periphery" nations no longer cohere, as the kinds of
work being done and the workers employed to do the work are increasingly
the same the world over (Bonacich and Appelbaum 2000). We cannot
understand these processes without examining earlier racial formations, like
women of color feminism alongside later ones, like racialized immigrant
women's culture.

Yet women of color feminism's attention to difference reminds us that
these processes happen unevenly and disparately, producing struggles that
are sometimes in contestation. Texts by women of color feminists of the
1970s and 1980s mediate the racialized criminalization, state violence, and
racialized property dispossession that were the logical extensions of the U.S.
nation-state's history of what legal scholar Cheryl Harris has called "whiteness as property." In distinction, racialized immigrant women's culture
attests to the existence of historical unevennesses in an attempt to displace
a homogenizing global commodification. Moraga, in her new foreword to
the twentieth anniversary reissue of *This Bridge Called My Back,* explicitly
remarks on the sometimes contentious relationship between the older formation of women of color feminism and later formations, like racialized
immigrant women's culture, by pointedly naming the immigrant, refugee,
and indigenous women's struggles that remained unaddressed in the 1981
volume. She asks, "What then is the racial women of color response to these
times of armored embattlement?" (Moraga 2002, xvii). This query is one
I take very seriously in this book; this is why one of the goals of my project is to theorize the different but related emergences of the women of
color feminist practice of the 1970s and 1980s and the racialized immigrant

women's culture of the displacements and migrations from the 1980s onward. Like Moraga, I maintain that the earlier formation of women of color
feminism from the 1970s and 1980s does not specifically address the conditions that occasion racialized and gendered immigration to the United
States in the decades following. Yet also like Moraga, I insist that there are
ways to bring together these different, yet aligned, struggles. In so doing,
I situate the insistence of women of color feminism on intersectionality and
difference as an important comparative race methodology that will allow
us to make these links.

Women of color feminist practice emerged to name the contradictions of
the racialized nation-state by deploying tactics that exceeded nationalism's
scope: intersectional analysis, an attention to difference, and a critique of
identification with the normative race, gender, and sexual institutions of
the state. These analytics align women of color feminism with other formations—such as racialized immigrant women's culture—never hailed by
nationalist inclusions. To restate, because women of color feminist practice attests to contradictions of liberal institutions of nationalism—in other
words, that the very rhetoric of inclusion and universality ensures racialized and gendered dispossession—there exists the possibility of affiliation
or affinity between women of color feminism and racialized immigrant
women's culture. This project thus concerns itself with the possibilities of
forms of coalition that are not necessarily based on conscious identification or sentimental sympathy between members of racialized groups, and
are thus not contradicted by the existence of racisms or chauvinisms. Rather,
this project highlights solidarities that might arise *through* a variety of disidentifications and contestations.

For the purposes of this book, women of color feminist practice as represented by what Chela Sandoval calls a "particular and eccentric" group
of writers and activists is an illustrative—but by no means the only—example of the variety of culture-based oppositional formations that have
emerged to comment on and contest capital's global phase. As Roderick
Ferguson has argued, for example, queer of color critique's intersectional
analysis, like that of women of color feminism, emerges from black lesbian
feminism (2004, 111). Further, while I focus on an explicitly termed "women
of color feminism" that emerged in the 1970s and 1980s, intersectional analysis, the use of difference as an analytical category, and coalitional organizing
and thought did exist prior to this moment. As Angela Davis reminds us,

there is a long tradition of women of color organizing that predates the
1981 publication of *This Bridge Called My Back,* a tradition that encompasses anti-imperialist and anticapitalist organizing by third world women,
as well as black women's critiques of masculinism in the civil rights movement (Davis 1997, 310).

Rather than claiming women of color feminist practice as a representative
or incorporative category, I look upon a discrete and historically situated
formation of 1970s and 1980s women of color feminist practice to examine an epistemic crisis that marked a transition in capitalism. In a manner
of speaking, this project is a response to a call made by Chandra Mohanty
and M. Jacqui Alexander in the introduction to their coedited anthology,
Feminist Genealogies, Colonial Legacies, Democratic Futures. Mohanty and
Alexander call for projects that excavate the genealogies of third world
women's feminism to provide enduring legacies for current work that can
address the forms and structures of transnational capital in the contemporary moment. Their volume collects work on feminist movements emerging
in a variety of localities: the Caribbean, Africa, Asia, and North America,
including essays on Chicana and black feminisms. Yet an extended study
that centers U.S. women of color feminist practice and racialized immigrant women's culture to delineate the constitutive contradictions of race
and gender in the transition in *U.S.* capital from national to transnational
has not yet been produced. Toward such a project, I examine women of
color feminism and racialized immigrant women's culture as part of such
a larger project on "third world women's feminism" and delineate a very
specific genealogy of epistemic crises around American modernity that these
formations bring to light. Because I am primarily concerned with these epistemic crises, I have not organized each chapter around a reading of particular women of color texts. I imagine this book not as a historical study of
women of color feminism and racialized immigrant women's culture, but
as an attempt to track and describe American modernity through these
racialized and gendered formations. This is not to imply that women of color
feminist practice and racialized immigrant women's culture are unimportant
in and of themselves, but rather to explain exactly why these formations
are as significant as I claim them to be. This book provides a genealogy
for why an explicitly named women of feminist practice emerged when it
did, what it was addressing, what has emerged in its wake, and what might
emerge from it still.

I focus this project on the epistemological crises and emergences that bear witness to the transition from capital's global phase to its national phase so that I might highlight the contemporary reconceptualization of the stakes, sites, and aims of progressive, anticapitalist, antiracist, and feminist struggle. In the context of our new world, we cannot unthinkingly deploy the strategies that were invented in the era when the nation-state was the preeminent mode by which capital organized itself. As I have noted, in the global era, "race" itself has become commodified. As Kara Keeling has argued, the race-based movements of the 1960s and 1970s insisted on articulating a racialized differentiation that radically intervened into the homogenizing tendencies of the Fordist modes of production—and the corresponding definitions of social organization—that were their context. Yet in the current era, global capital reproduces itself exactly by manipulating racial, gender, and sexual difference for the purposes of accumulation. In other words, if "Asian American" or "Chicano" or "African American" are categories that assert racialized subjectivity as a critique of white supremacy and the corresponding logic of assimilation, they are now equally ways of identifying and producing consumer bases, or alternatively, pools of exploitable labor. If the idea of "black is beautiful" is a radical challenge to ideologies that based material inequalities on the notion of white superiority, it is now also a way of selling images of a fetishized blackness to white suburban teens. If, as Keeling argues, shifting to differentiation as its primary logic is late capital's response to the success of race-based movements, we can note that the project of these movements has become incorporated into the project of global capital today. In other words, we cannot limit our definition of racialized subjectivity to that of the hero of a privileged historical narrative, the telos and resolution of which is the eventual and complete attainment of the rights and privileges of the propertied subject of the nation-state, for this narrative sustains, rather than disrupts, the logic of global capital. Yet we cannot relinquish a critique of the state because the nation-state still has powerful, albeit different, functions and roles in capital's global phase. A complete dismissal of the nation-state risks erasing the violence done to racialized communities through the very institutions of the state. Therefore, while some scholars, most notably and polemically Masao Miyoshi, have pronounced the death of the nation-state,[4] I would contend that global capital does not relinquish the nation-state form, including the racialized and gendered violence and dispossession upon which it was based. Rather, the nation-state plays a different role, and poses new sets of contradictions that remind us that gender and racialization are still fundamental to the modes of rule and to oppositional struggles. As such, contemporary conditions demand a new set of strategies that address the nation-state, but in its new role within capital's global phase, a set of strategies that recall a long genealogy of those subjects, communities, practices, and knowledges subordinated by nationalist epistemologies. In this book, I trace a genealogy of the occluded knowledges that emerge to attest that, as M. Jacqui Alexander suggests, "the international [is] not one-sidedly pernicious" (1994, 23).

In some ways, my project might seem like a version of Marxist "long wave" analysis, which looks at shifts in capital over an extended historical period.[5] Long wave theorists take up a tendency inherent in Karl Marx's work, insofar as Marx's project was not only to provide a formal analysis of capitalist relations, but to advance this analysis as a way of narrating the history of the emergence of the modern world through the shift from feudalism to capitalism, and to advance a theory for capitalism's inevitable demise. Long wave theorists take up this project by tracking the fluctuations and cycles of capital over an extended period of time, identifying recurrent patterns to describe how capital eventually will no longer be able to overcome its internal contradictions. Many of these theorists do so to query whether the contemporary period—what Ernest Mandel would call the era of "late capitalism"—is part of a longer pattern of boom and bust or is a signal of ultimate decline. I share with long wave theorists the impetus to challenge neoliberal assertions of capitalism's ability to self-sustain. Yet like many critics of this intellectual tradition, I find their narrative of capital forecloses the possibility of a diversity of sites of contradiction.

Within this tradition, David Harvey's volume *The Condition of Postmodernity* is a useful point of entry because it inserts an analysis of culture into the narrative of capitalist development articulated by long wave scholars of political economy. Harvey examines the cultural formations of modernism and postmodernism as reactions to shifts in the experience of time and space that occur with changes in modes of capitalist production, and in particular with the shift from Fordism to post-Fordism. As my project also traces these shifts, it is indebted to Harvey's work, which argues for the need to study culture within Marxist scholarship. Yet Harvey's work is marked by the totalizing tendencies of long wave Marxist analysis. Harvey sees capital as having one main contradiction, and presumes that this contradiction can be best apprehended through political economic analyses. For Harvey, such a contradiction is overaccumulation, an inevitable result of capitalist accumulation, which occurs when surplus labor and capital cannot be brought together for a socially productive purpose. The British economic crisis of 1846–47, the subsequent global economic crises, and the political reactions of 1847–48 mark this first crisis of capital. Attempting to overcome this crisis, capital shifted into a Fordist and Keynesian mode, which was itself eventually overcome by capital's intrinsic contradictions. At that point, capital shifted into the post-Fordist mode. Each of these shifts precipitated cultural movements—modernism and postmodernism—that tried to come to terms with the resultant changes in the experience of time and space engendered by such changes in the world economy. In this way, Harvey makes culture a secondary or reactive formation: the cultural movements of modernism and postmodernism are wrought by capital's struggle to overcome its contradictions, rather than being themselves capital's contradictions.

Yet as I argue in the chapters that follow, capital's contradictions are multiple; they do not arise only from one totalizing structure of accumulation and overaccumulation. As I argue in the first part, in the earlier era when capital reproduced itself through the racialized and gendered institutions of the nation-state, workers were recruited and disciplined through the ostensibly universal category of citizenship, understood not only as a strictly legal category but as a subject formation articulated through culture: possessive individualism. Racialized and gendered difference is absolutely necessary to the hierarchization of workers and the extraction of capital in this era; in this way, race and gender are constitutive to the operations of capital. Yet such articulations of difference are foreclosed by the notion of a universal and homogeneously inclusive citizenship. A "women of color" formation emerged to name race and gender as constitutive contradictions of capital's national phase, attesting to the possibility of alternative models of subjectivity and collectivity. In the second part of this book, I argue that in the post-Fordist era, capital also reproduces itself through racialized and gendered difference, but not through the extension of an ostensibly universally available form of citizenship. "Difference" instead becomes articulated as a kind of commodification. Yet as I argue, racialized immigrant women's culture attests to other sites of difference—emerging from the histories of neocolonialism and labor migration—that cannot be subsumed to the logic of commodification.

Therefore, unlike Harvey, I posit political economic processes as in themselves multiply constituted by race and gender, and assert that these processes are not only reflected by but are established and contested through culture. Because race and gender are not secondary processes, but are constitutive contradictions, centering formations like women of color feminism and racialized immigrant women's culture necessitate a displacement of a totalizing "systemic" tendency inherent to such analyses. Racialized and gendered difference is intrinsic to capital's reproduction, but it is also erased and disavowed. Naming race and gender as constitutive processes thus requires tracing the history of this erasure and disavowal. In other words, I trace a transition in twentieth-century capital through the epistemological ruptures and crises—marked by women of color feminism and racialized immigrant women's culture—that bring this transition to light. Women of color feminist practice and racialized immigrant women's culture emerge as the return of the repressed of capital, naming the *erasures* at the very moment of articulation. As such, the histories of race and gender must emerge in culture, where the impossible is imagined. While literature's emphasis on the imaginative and the nonfactual has been often turned toward an aestheticization of culture, women of color feminism and racialized immigrant women's culture seize the imaginative function of literature and culture for different ends, revealing and intervening into the dynamics of power that subtends the production of knowledge. Culture thus has a mutually constitutive, rather than a deterministic, relationship to capital. Therefore, while I discuss culture in relation to capital so I can posit culture as a material force rather than a transcendent, autonomous, aestheticized separate sphere, I also resist positing culture as merely reflective of, or entirely determined by, "real" social formations.

With this in mind, I now turn back to some of the major texts of the women of color feminist practice of the 1970s and 1980s to explicate exactly how and why this formation seizes culture as a site of struggle, and how this helps us understand culture as a social force. Yet even while I focus on this particular "women of color" formation that emerged in the 1970s and 1980s, I do not seek to further reify this formation. The formation of women of color feminism that I reference has a history of being understood as representative of all women of color feminist practices. The foundational texts of this formation are now well known: Toni Cade's edited collection *The Black Woman*, Angela Davis's *Women, Race, and Class,* Audre Lorde's *Sister Outsider* (including, most famously, the essay "The Master's Tools Will Never Dismantle the Master's House"), the Combahee River Collective's "Black Feminist Statement" (colloquially known as the "Manifesto"), Barbara Smith's *Home Girls,* as well as Moraga and Anzaldúa's *This Bridge Called My Back.* Because these texts are now so canonical, other feminist formations become occluded and unstudied; scholars are right now working to correct this bias.[6] I would posit my project as different from, but complementary to, the work of such scholars because I argue that this now-canonical formation never meant to be representative of all women of color feminisms, and that indeed, it worked against such a representative logic. For even the most cursory perusal of this work reminds us to sustain the sense of historical contingency that these works express. In other words, even these theorists most associated with this particular "women of color" formation did not imagine this category as stable, fixed, or preexistent. For Moraga in 1981, for example, the notion of women of color feminist practice was in no way a given. Her language in the passage that opens this introduction is one of desire, not fulfillment, of "[wanting] a movement," rather than of actually having found one. Throughout the preface, Moraga stages women of color feminism as a process or practice, rather than as something already existing and accomplished. Even in 2002, when the release of a new edition of *This Bridge Called My Back* might have led the authors to reify a women of color feminism, Gloria Anzaldúa warns in the foreword against a sense of complacency that might treat women of color feminist practice as stable and knowable: "Yet despite *Bridge*'s great impact on international feminisms, despite the discussions it provoked, the theories it has inspired feminists of color to generate, the activist organizations it has motivated, despite its growing legacy, there's even more work to be done" (xxxiv). Anzaldúa resists capturing women of color feminism as a fait accompli, instead defining it by describing the further work it inspired. She stresses the ongoing nature of the work that the original volume itself expressed as a process.

As I have said previously, many of the foundational texts of "women of color feminism" are well known. Many useful analyses of these women of color feminist works have already been written.[7] Rather than repeat such analyses, I focus on women of color feminist practice to explore how and why it seizes culture as the site for articulating the radically disjunctive epistemological practices of "intersectionality" and "coalition through difference." I have previously referenced my argument in chapter 1 that developmental narratives produce identification with the abstract propertied citizen of the U.S. nation-state, the possessive individual, subordinating difference by positing this subject formation as universal. Quite in distinction, women of color feminist practice fundamentally displaced such singular identifications or universal notions of subjectivity. Rather, women of color feminist practice stressed the notion of intersecting and competing axes of identification and disidentification. The Combahee River Collective's famous description of their project in their "Black Feminist Statement"— that "we are actively committed to struggling against racial, sexual, heterosexual, and class oppression and see as our particular task the development of integrated analysis and practice based on the fact that the major systems of oppression are interlocking" (Combahee River Collective 1981, 210)—advanced their theory of intersectionality, summarizing their critique of the gendered, racialized, sexualized history of the state, and their analysis of the ways that single-axis politics ultimately has normative investments in this history.

Through the contradictory and multiple identifications and disidentifications implied by intersectional analyses, women of color "identity" politics critiqued the process of singular and linear identification that is the hallmark of nationalism. While we can trace the coining of the term "identity politics" to women of color feminist practice, what it meant to those who used it the 1970s was quite different than how it is understood today. Today, we understand identity politics as signifying a process whereby one singular identification—race, class, gender—is prioritized over all else. But identity politics as imagined by women of color feminists was fundamentally critical of a unitary and reified notion of subject formation. Miriam Harris quotes Barbara Smith, referring to the Combahee River Collective's assertion of the importance of identity politics in the "Black Feminist Statement," as saying, "I think we came up with the term 'identity politics.' I never really saw it anywhere else and I would suggest that people if they really want to find the origin of the term that they try to find it in any place earlier than in the Combahee River Collective statement" (Harris 1997, 130). The passage Smith refers to in the "Black Feminist Statement" states, "This focusing upon our own oppression is embodied in the concept of identity politics. We believe that the most profound and potentially the most radical politics come directly out of our own identity, as opposed to working to end somebody else's oppression" (Combahee River Collective 1981, 212). In the context of the "Black Feminist Statement," as in many women of color feminist texts, because "women of color" as a subject position mediates a variety of contradictory and competing identifications and disidentifications, "identity" is not singularly formed but is multiply determined, and as such, is always unstable. As Kayann Short argues, identity politics as expressed by women of color feminist practice fundamentally undermines any singular notion of identity, rather than reaffirming it. Short argues that "the phrase 'identity politics' itself indicates how the concepts are coterminous: neither 'identity' nor 'politics' can assume a stable position prior to the other; instead, the two concepts are mutually informing" (1994, 13). Therefore, as Chandra Mohanty argues, women of color is not an essentialist or biologistic category, but rather refers to "imagined communities of women with divergent histories and social locations, woven together by the *political* threads of opposition to forms of domination that are not only pervasive but systematic" (Mohanty, Russo, and Torres 1991, 4). While the term "woman of color" has been often used as a demographic category ostensibly subsumed under an ultimately all-inclusive national citizenry, or a subset of a universalizing notion of "woman," or of a singularly racialized community, I would posit that this mode of incorporation is exactly that which "women of color feminism" was conceptualized as rendering impossible.

This intersectional subjectivity also implies different, coalitional understandings of community formation. While not all of the texts associated with women of color feminism explicitly and consciously address differently racialized women, they are often characterized as "women of color feminism." I understand this categorization as valid because intersectionality implies coalitional politics. In other words, even those texts that only focus on African American racial and gendered formations implicitly lend themselves to coalitional and cross-race politics because they maintain that African American subjectivity is not stable and unitary, but is formed through multiple and contradictory identifications. In other words, because black feminism envisions "African American" not as essential and unchanging, but as always already a coalition of different, sometimes competing formations, it implies the possibility of alliances among a variety of racial, gendered, sexualized, and national differences. The articulation of this differentiated notion of coalition is crucial to understanding the interventions of women of color feminist practice. Rather than imagining the category of "women of color" as monolithic, these theorists highlighted the contestations and conflicting interests among racialized women. Therefore, in an introduction to one of the sections of *This Bridge Called My Back*, Moraga and Anzaldúa list the differences of class, geography, and skin color that form the women who have contributed to the book. Yet from these differences come the possibility of coalition and solidarity; they note, "We learned to live with these contradictions. This is the root of our radicalism" (1981, 5). In other words, these contradictions and conflicts are not the obstacle to coalition, but are the basis from which to imagine a political practice. In Lorde's famous formulation, "[C]ommunity must not mean a shedding of our differences, nor a pathetic pretense that these differences do not exist. . . . It is learning to take our differences and make them strengths. *For the master's tools will never dismantle the master's house*" (1984, 112).

In putting forward these different modes of subjectivity and community, women of color feminist practice displaced a model of "inclusion" that might prioritize articulation or visibility within national epistemologies: articulating modes of subjectivity and community that are different from those privileged by the U.S. nation-state means bringing to light the ways that racialized property relations disavow the conditions that occasion the emergence of alternative modes of knowing, other ways of organizing human life. Therefore, women of color feminist practice embeds into the very foundation of the articulation a sense of the *dangers* of articulation. When Moraga and Anzaldúa maintain that one of the "major areas of concern for Third World women in the U.S. in forming a broad-based political movement" is "how visibility/invisibility as women of color forms our radicalism" (1981, xxiv), they are not suggesting visibility as an easy remedy for the condition of invisibility, but are implying a dialectical relationship between the two. In other words, for women of color feminist practice, visibility is a rupture, an impossible articulation. If, as Mitsuye Yamada posits later in the volume, "invisibility is an unnatural disaster," so, too, is visibility unnatural; it is also a kind of violence. In the passage from Moraga's preface, for example, visibility is not inclusion, but surveillance, as the hypervisibility of the boy on the train subjects him to a racialized state violence.

Visibility for women of color feminism also manifests itself as tokeniza-
tion. The very genesis of *This Bridge Called My Back* demonstrates the pit-
falls of visibility. In the section of the introduction entitled "How It All
Began," Moraga and Anzaldúa recount the "seed that germinated into this
anthology" (1981, xxiii): a narrative of Anzaldúa's tokenized status at a
women's retreat run by white feminists. Scholars of women of color feminism such as Norma Alarcón and Chela Sandoval have commented on
the ways that mainstream white feminism performs this action of erasure
and containment. These scholars have specifically situated the interventions of women of color feminist practice in relation to white feminist
movements, noting the ways that Anglo-American feminism implicitly
valorizes "an autonomous, self-making, self-determining subject who first
proceeds according to the logic of identification with regard to the subject
of consciousness, a notion viewed as the purview of man, but now claimed
for women" (Alarcón 1990, 357). Indeed, Sandoval argues that white feminism, with its investments in liberal notions of subjectivity, is that which
manages and thereby objectifies women of color feminism: "The theory
and method of oppositional consciousness and social movement documented here—and enacted by an original, eccentric, and coalitional cohort
of U.S. feminists of color—was contained and made invisible through the
means of its perception and appropriation in the term of what became during the 1970–80 period a hegemonic feminist theory and practice" (Sandoval 2000, 42–43). In other words, white feminism's appropriation of
something called "women of color feminism" ironically further occluded
the contradictory subject formation that "women of color feminism" was
trying to name. In contrast to Anglo-American feminism's reification of, in
essence, the possessive individual, Sandoval sees women of color feminism's
articulation of a multiply constituted subjectivity as a fundamentally contradictory state. In affirming an impossible and inarticulable subject position,
women of color feminist practice undermines the very idea of a knowable
subjectivity. As important as women of color feminism's critique of white
feminism is, I would situate this critique, as Moraga and others have, as
only one mode of incorporation, alongside hegemonic versions of oppositional race-based nationalist movements, and hegemonic Left or socialist
movements. In response to these movements, women of color feminism
resisted the privileging of a normative category, whether it be "citizen,"
"woman," or "black," which disciplines and erases racialized and gendered

difference. Instead, women of color feminist practice built a political and intellectual practice around the very excesses that cannot be categorized and thus can only be named in fragments. As we have seen in Moraga and Anzaldúa's characterizations, "women of color feminism" names a futurity, an inchoate and fragmented formation always in jeopardy of being lost. Women of color is an epistemological formation, one that tenuously recovers that which is always fragile and threatening to collapse into incoherence or inaccessibility.

Consistently in my readings of women of color and racialized immigrant women's texts, I find a thematizing of the fragmented and difficult to recover articulation that is not remembered whole but rather points to the erasures inherent in regimes of knowledge. For example, even Angela Davis's use of a more academic and rationalized essay form contains a moment that points to the failure of this genre, a moment where she has to speculate on why certain epistemological lacunae exist. In her now canonical essay "Rape, Racism, and the Myth of the Black Rapist," Davis notes that most rapists remain anonymous, and she questions why this absence of knowledge exists. She notes that "the anonymity surrounding the vast majority of rapes is consequently treated as a statistical detail—or else as a mystery whose meaning is inaccessible" (1981, 199). She both suggests an answer to this question—that this anonymity hides the prevalence of white male rape of white women and women of color—and points to the ways her hypothesis cannot be "proven" because of the very structures of racist power that produce this epistemological erasure in the first place. As such, Davis turns to a different, more speculative mode of expression, writing,

> But why are there so many anonymous rapists in the first place? Might not this anonymity be a privilege enjoyed by men whose status protects them from persecution? Although white men who are employers, executives, politicians, doctors, professors, etc., have been known to "take advantage" of women they consider their inferiors, their sexual misdeeds seldom come to light in court. Is it not therefore quite probable that these men of the capitalist and middle classes account for a significant proportion of the unreported rapes? (1981, 199)

Her use of an interrogative mode of address, rather than an expository one, marks her shift to an *imaginative* mode of writing that illuminates the ways her argument cannot be categorized as either "fact" or "fiction." Her argument cannot be proven through the documents, archives, and genres that produce "fact," but instead it points to the racialized and gendered hierarchies of power maintained by the deliberate erasures of those structures. Here, where no documentation exists to "prove" her argument, Davis relies instead on colloquial, unwritten knowledge that must exist without an author, as seen in her use of the passive voice in the passage "white men . . . *have been known* to 'take advantage'" (my emphasis). Davis also relies on other archives of knowledge and memory, highlighting the existence of the colloquialism "take advantage" and thus referencing an entire terrain of discourse created by working-class black women who produce their own vocabularies to record their experience of white male predation. That such records do not exist as statistics and data, Davis asserts, does not mean that they do not exist at all. Yet the recovery of such archives is complex, which Davis underscores by pointing to the difficulty of access at the very moment of articulation. In this moment, Davis's essay is a paradigmatic example of how women of color feminist practice theorizes "culture" as a site to express that which is unspeakable.

This conceptualization of culture allowed women of color feminists to seize culture as a site of material struggle. Cherríe Moraga writes, "I want a movement that makes sense of." A movement for her means a struggle that happens on the level of epistemology and culture. It means contesting and displacing the narratives that legitimate exploitation and violence, and finding a *new* way to make sense of historical and social conditions. I would like to now turn briefly to a discussion of just this kind of "movement." One important early women of color feminist project was the Combahee River Collective, a Boston-based black socialist lesbian feminist organization that included writer, editor, and publisher Barbara Smith, cofounder of Kitchen Table: Women of Color Press. One of the most catalyzing projects for the Combahee River Collective was a pamphlet entitled "Why Did They Die?" which addressed the sexual assault and murder of twelve black women in the Boston area in the first six months of 1979. Working alongside other community groups, the Combahee River Collective produced 26,000 copies of this pamphlet in English and thousands more in Spanish and distributed them for free; a version of the pamphlet, with an added introduction, was reprinted in the October/November 1979 issue of *Radical America*. Containing an analysis of the murders, a list of measures a woman could take to protect herself, and a poem by Ntozake Shange, this pamphlet was an interdisciplinary, multi-axis organizing tool that also could be seen as Barbara Smith's first participation in an anthology or collected volume. Clearly a document produced to instigate an immediate and material social change as a part of a coalitional movement, this pamphlet does not differentiate arbitrarily between "social movement" and "culture," as we can see by the fact that its primary project is to ask "why."

We could read each of the "genres" represented in the pamphlet—the critical analysis, the poem, even the list of safety measures—as different yet interlocking ways of addressing the question of why these women died. The central aim of the critical analysis is to investigate the complicity of the racialized state in these women's murders, an investigation that demanded the deployment of an intersectional analysis. The pamphlet notes the complicity of the police in the devaluation of black women's lives revealed by the murders: "The mother of a fifteen-year-old girl, one of the first two victims, says that when she reported the disappearance of her daughter to the police, they hesitated to file a report, claiming that the girl had probably gone off with a pimp" (Combahee River Collective 1979, 41). The Combahee River Collective calls into question the deployment, by the police, of long-held racialized narratives about African American women's promiscuous and therefore indefensible sexuality. In so doing, this analysis points to the ways the state legitimates the devaluation of racialized lives through exclusion from the normative institutions of domesticity, femininity, and "proper" sexuality. The Combahee River Collective uses this analysis of the state to underscore the difficulties of forging alliances with white feminists. They highlight the differing relationships to protected, normative femininity that comprise the experience of black and white women. A precursor to Angela Davis's important argument in her essay "Rape, Racism, and the Myth of the Black Rapist," the Combahee River Collective argues that this investment in normative white femininity racializes black men as well as black women: the pamphlet notes that "when eleven white women were raped in another part of Boston, all describing their assailant as a Black man, the press and the city officials were quick to recognize their plight and a great deal of attention was drawn to their situation" (42). Yet they simultaneously critique the ways that "Black male paternalism" similarly invests in notions of patriarchally organized domesticity (42). The strategy suggested by "a number of male speakers" at a memorial rally for the murdered women, they note, was "a plea to Black men 'to protect their women,'" to which the Combahee River Collective responded by "asserting that it is women organizing together that will create the conditions in which women will be free of fear" (42). In advancing this important analysis, the Combahee River Collective reveals how a singular focus on "race" or "gender" unwittingly reproduces the normative narratives of the state and is therefore inadequate to addressing violence against black women.

Shange's poem, entitled "with no immediate cause," extends the critical analysis's discussion of state complicity by pointing to its epistemological implications. Shange remarks on her impotence to stem the crushing tide of misogynist violence that she knows occurs, despite her inability to "establish immediate cause" as the "authorities require [her] to" do:

> every 3 minutes a woman is beaten
> every five minutes a
> woman is raped/every ten minutes
> a lil girl is molested
> yet i rode the subway today
> i sat next to an old man who
> may have beaten his old wife (49)

This poem cites statistics ("every 3 minutes a woman is beaten"), but not merely to dismiss them out of hand. Indeed, the poem attests that these statistics are partly how the narrator knows that violence against women is ongoing. Yet the poem ultimately also contests a simple faith in such a positivist epistemology, noting later that these statistics are not enough to "establish/immediate cause" and thus enlist the "authorities" for protection. Marking the ways that this knowledge doesn't count as "proof" and does not alleviate her impotence ("but i sat there"), Shange describes a mode of knowing at the same time that she marks that which is erased by that mode of knowing. Shange makes her critique of the state as complicit with misogynist violence by exposing the epistemological underpinnings of state power. In so doing, this poem suggests an *alternative* epistemology, that of simultaneous knowing and unknowing.

Of all of the many compelling aspects of this pamphlet, I find especially moving a photograph reproduced in *Radical America* that depicts a banner held by a demonstrator at one of the many rallies to protest the murders.

The banner reads, "[W]e cannot live without our lives."[8] Upon first en-counter, this may read like a tautology. Yet when we understand that it attests to the ways that even the most basic guarantee of a liberal demo-cratic society—life—is not extended evenly or protected universally, it is not so tautological. Or perhaps it tells us that tautology is the proper mode of expression for those who live daily with the bad faith promise of univer-sal inclusion, and the legacies of violence that such a promise has both insti-gated and occluded. This book is driven by a similar need: to identify modes of sustaining life that do not take recourse to such dangerous universalities.

PART I

chapter 1

THE POSSESSIVE INDIVIDUAL AND SOCIAL DEATH: THE COMPLEX BIND OF NATIONAL SUBJECTIVITY

From the wilderness romance of settling the frontier, to the faith in American ingenuity that narrativized U.S. capitalism and the industrial revolution, the "progress" narrative was arguably the most important explanatory paradigm through which the various tensions, contradictions, and contestations around the U.S. nation-state in the nineteenth century were articulated and negotiated. In this era, the contradictions of capital manifested themselves via the nation-state, as the nation-state became the central locus of political, economic, and cultural contestation. In this chapter, I read U.S. narratives of development as expressing a variety of struggles around U.S. nationalism. I do so by examining the implied subject of this narrative, which I identify as the propertied subject, an individuated subject formed through the ability to exert will. Using political theorist C. B. MacPherson's notion of "possessive individualism," I argue that subjectivity in this era is defined by the ability to own, and what the subject primarily owns is the self. That he "owns" himself, or in other words, is self-possessed and self-determining, is demonstrated through the exercise of will. This subject is the propertied subject, the citizen-subject of the nation-state. Contradictions between U.S. capital and the U.S. nation-state were assuaged, experienced, and exacerbated via the contestations over subjectivity, as it was exactly the possessive individual that mediated these contradictions. As Lisa Lowe writes, "[I]n a racially differentiated nation such as the United States, capital and state imperatives may be contradictory: capital, with its supposed needs for 'abstract labor,' is said by Marx to be unconcerned by the 'origins' of its labor force, whereas the nation-state, with its need for 'abstract citizens' formed by a unified culture to participate in the political sphere, is precisely concerned to maintain a national citizenry bound by race, language, and culture" (1996, 13). As Alexander Saxton, David Roediger, and others have argued, in the late nineteenth century, the differentiation of laboring forces enabled U.S. capital to undercut class solidarity by creating a white working-class identity over and against racialized workers.[1] At the same time, the nation-state's need for a homogeneous citizenry barred these differentiated racialized populations from citizenship. If U.S. capital needed to differentially incorporate laboring populations, and the nation-state categorically expelled or excluded these racialized workers from the category of citizenship, the possessive individual as the ostensibly universally available subject was supposed to resolve and homogenize these differences. It was through culture—in particular, through narratives of development—that these particularities and differences were posited as that which needed to be transcended for one to become the possessive individual.

Yet this properted subject is unstable, as it must negotiate the basic contradictions of liberal humanism. Although this subject is ostensibly universal, it depends on an enslaved antithesis, fundamentally defined as without will. In the late nineteenth century, the patently unfree and dispossessed status of slaves required the foreclosure of the enslaved from the subject position of the possessive individual—a condition that Orlando Patterson has called social death. I identify the U.S. narrative of development as an important technology of subject formation in this era, one that attempts to resolve the contradictions inherent in the properted subject. The "imagined community" of properted subjects that the U.S. narrative of development attempts to call into being is always inherently unstable, and these instabilities emerge in the texts I examine. For the purposes of my argument, then, *property* references not only the actual objects that are owned, but the way that social relations are organized around ownership, and the narratives by which these social relations are both legitimated and contested. This process, as I demonstrate below, necessitates the occlusion of a variety of other subjects, formed through capital's uneven economic development, and modes of relation between these subjects.

A discussion of nineteenth-century narratives of development may seem far afield from an analysis of women of color feminism of the 1970s and 1980s. Yet for the purposes of this project, it is important to construct a genealogy from which women of color feminism emerged, in order to appreciate the ways that its articulation of subjectivity ("intersectionality") and its imagining of new forms of community (coalition through difference) emerged out of, but in contradiction to, this history of racialized citizenship. In other words, possessive individualism became the narrative through which subjects were imagined and thus sutured to the nation-state. In this era, this version of subjectivity was so compelling that only those contestations around nationalist subjectivities that contended with the narratives of the possessive individual registered as legible or comprehensible, as I demonstrate through my reading of Booker T. Washington's *Up from Slavery.* The propertied subject was understood as the ostensibly universal subject of the nation-state, yet it inherently privileged whiteness and bourgeois domesticity. As such, as I argue in chapter 2, the U.S. state, an ostensibly neutral institution, operated in actuality as a *racial* state. By privileging the (white male) propertied subject, the U.S. state legitimated and naturalized the dispossession of racialized subjects through such mechanisms as segregation and internment. Thus, when women of color feminists attempted to imagine a social movement that challenged the material circumstances wrought by white property rights, such as labor exploitation, segregation, or police violence, this movement had to imagine modes of subjectivity and collectivity differently. To articulate this genealogy of women of color feminism, I begin with a discussion of possessive individualism as an institution of whiteness and masculinity, subtended by bourgeois domesticity.

In this chapter, I examine a variety of developmental discourses about the United States, from Frederick Jackson Turner's famous historical narrative about Manifest Destiny and the settling of the frontier, to novels like Mark Twain's *The Adventures of Huckleberry Finn* (1884) and Henry James's *Daisy Miller: A Study* (1879), to autobiographies like Booker T. Washington's *Up from Slavery* (1901), to underscore the material inequities that U.S. narratives of development needed to negotiate in their attempt to constitute this propertied subject. It is not my intention to exhaustively analyze these complex texts, around which a significant body of critical scholarship has already accrued. Rather, I refer to these texts insofar as they allow me to demonstrate the thorny project of narrating self and subjectivity as the possessive individual in the nineteenth century. In this discussion, I argue that U.S. narratives of development differ crucially from the European version—specifically, the bildungsroman—in their emphasis on establishing the American individual through a break from society, rather than a resolution to societal structures. This chapter thus explores the tendency of the nation-state to both depend on and disavow racialized differences.

Twain's quintessentially American novel, written twenty years after the end of the Civil War but set prior to it, maps U.S. sectionalism and the incorporation of the U.S. South into the Union after the Civil War onto Huck's narrative of moral development and his dilemma about whether to free the escaped slave Jim. The seizing of power by the industrial U.S. North and the subsequent economic marginalization of the U.S. South becomes erased through the recoding of the Civil War as a moral victory over the evil institution of slavery, a quite common Civil War narrative. As we well know, faced with the decision to turn Jim in, Huck chooses "correctly," departing from the demands of what is characterized as a racist society, and in so doing he exemplifies the individuated and secular propertied subject by establishing his ability to exercise will. Yet this text's need to resolve Huck's moral dilemma around the question of slavery bears the traces of sectional and regional contestations and attests to the instability of national identity at the time. In contrast, James's text registers his era's complex anxieties around masculinity and sexuality by staging "society" as distinctly feminizing and European, something the protagonist must break from if he is to become a true (read "masculine" and "American") individual. *Daisy Miller* is a cautionary tale about the stultifying and feminizing effects of choosing "society" over individuality, as James's protagonist Winterbourne finds the comforts of society too difficult to give up. As different as these texts may seem, I argue that they both depend on the production of a form of American individualism.

This version of American individualism is what C. B. MacPherson (1962) has termed "possessive individualism," a conception of the self based on one's ability to own property privately and dispose of it as one chooses. Basing subjectivity on property ownership defines subjects as atomized, individuated beings whose most basic right is to exercise their own free will. Unlike Henry James's protagonist, who presumably owns many, quite lovely things, the poor, rural boy Huck doesn't seem to "own" anything. Yet I would argue that because these narratives give each character a choice, and therefore ascribe to him the possibility of free will, they imply that the characters each have "property in his own person"—they have the *capacity* to own that is the foundation for the propertied citizen-subject and the nation-state founded on a system of private property ownership.

Furthermore, although these texts depart from the mold of the classical bildungsroman in emphasizing a moral imperative to *break* from societal norms rather than resolve oneself to society, they reproduce the "canonical nationalist project of reconciling constituencies to idealized forms of community and subjectivity" (Lowe 1996, 100) by narrating an internalization of American individualism through development into a mature, independent subject. Maturity in the American narrative of formation is articulated through the ability to choose, to exert one's will, to have "property in his own person." The possessive individual is therefore constituted through this narrative of development.

These texts thus respond to a variety of crises by reasserting the primacy of the propertied subject. The self-possessed citizen-subject was defined against those who could not own themselves because they themselves *were* property in a system of chattel slavery. As such, because this propertied subject is defined over and against those without the fundamental right to property—those incapable of exerting their will and thus unable to assume the "self-ownership" that marks subjectivity—this subject is rife with contradictions. Although this propertied citizen-subject is ostensibly unmarked and universal, property depends on racialized and gendered difference. While citizenship is supposed to imply equal protection of property rights by the state, citizenship is differentially available and applicable. These contradictions emerge in African American thought, which grappled with the complex legacies of "object" status, or what Orlando Patterson has termed "social death." I examine Booker T. Washington's *Up from Slavery* as an example of the contradictory subjectivity implied in writing out of the situation, to use Patricia Williams's phrase, of "being the object of property" (1991, 216). Washington's uplifting autobiography claims to offer a solution to the "problem" of how to incorporate African Americans as citizens after centuries of enslavement. Narrating his progress from slave to educator and leader, Washington uses his life story to demonstrate African American fitness for incorporation into American modernity. Yet because that modernity was dependent on conceptions of African Americans as devoid of will, Washington's narrative must paradoxically articulate his life story as both a triumph of the will and a submission of the African American will to white power. Washington's narrative then articulates a subject position that is both the agent and the object of will, both the propertied subject and the unpropertied object.

The differential access to the propertied subject structures relations of rule and the distribution of resources and life chances into the twentieth century, and is the history of contemporary conditions of racialization. As I will argue further in chapter 2, this condition of differential relationship to property relations is what makes it fundamentally impossible for racialized subjects to "own," because to be racialized is to not own oneself. This condition of social death is what "dispossession" means—not only the actual denial or lack of property, wealth, or assets, which is certainly the case, but the fundamental condition of not being able to own that is both produced by and legitimates the denial or lack of actual property. Given this, I describe "racialization" as the process by which the differential incorporation of laboring subjects by capital leads to a distanced, contradictory relationship to the state, and to nationalist notions of subjectivity that attempt, unsuccessfully and violently, to resolve and erase these differences.[2]

"Culture" is not an innocent category, but one that has been constituted by struggles around national identity. U.S. narratives of development produce an abstract, ostensibly universally attainable subject by narrating the transcendence of social constraints through the exercise of will. The subject of this narrative moves from his embeddedness in the particularity of his social situation to become a mature self-determining subject who is the master of his own fate. In this way, U.S. narratives of development suggest that anyone in any circumstance can transcend their material social relations and become the mature, self-possessed propertied subject. Yet the promise of universal incorporation offered by these developmental narratives is contradicted by the material histories of racialized and gendered difference upon which the property system is based.

In this chapter, I examine a variety of developmental narratives, including the novel, the autobiography, and the historical narrative, to understand the ways they imagined Americanness to be defined by rugged individualism. These narratives posited Americans as not content to reproduce tradition, but instead bent on building a new society out of frontier wilderness. Frederick Jackson Turner's landmark history, "The Significance of the Frontier in American History," for example, narrates the development of U.S. society as characterized by the perpetual taming of the savagery of the "great

West": "Thus, American development has exhibited not mere advance along a single line, but a return to primitive conditions in a continually advancing frontier line, and a new development for that area. American social development has been continually beginning over again on the frontier. This perennial rebirth, the fluidity of American life, this expansion westward with its new opportunities, its continuous touch with the simplicity of primitive society, furnish the forces dominating American character" (1894, 28). Like *Huck Finn* and *Daisy Miller,* Turner's historical narrative posits a particularly American identity that emerges from an iconoclastic renunciation of the previous social norm in favor of a new social order. Turner's narrative articulates American history as the repetition of the fabled originary moment of rupture from European tradition, and thus implicitly depends on and replicates a notion of American exceptionalism. We see, then, that this possessive individual is imbricated with the U.S. liberal humanist project of erasing the hierarchies of power on which it depends. In this articulation of American exceptionalism, Europe is tainted by the residues of its feudal structures of inequity, while the United States is composed of individuals who make their own fortunes in a society structured by horizontality and equivalence in a gesture that erases the United States' history of colonial and racialized violence.

This historical narrative of American individualism materialized through the novel form. The nation-state's uneven incorporation of heterogeneous populations and regions produced contradictions that emerged and were only partially resolved through the category of the "literary." Cathy Davidson notes that the novel constitutes "a genre emerging within a culture precisely as that culture attempts to define itself," and argues that the novel allowed for complex contestations over the definition of America (1986, viii). Looking at archival evidence of readers' reception of novels and their interaction with novels as texts, Davidson emphasizes the novel's accessibility for new readerships, in particular the sentimental novel's readership of middle-class women, to argue that the novel's influence was not monolithic or prescribed. Richard Brodhead insightfully argues that crises in U.S. national identity in the nineteenth century were negotiated through the formation of an East Coast–based elite U.S. literary canon. Attempting to counter conventional wisdom, which claimed that the United States had no great literature or high culture like that of Europe and thus no substantive basis for a national identity, East Coast literary elites such as James

T. Fields, the publisher of the *Atlantic Monthly*, contributed to the construction of a national identity ostensibly defined through elevated, "quality" works of art. The invention of a high literary canon, of course, created the terrain for a series of contestations that reverberated throughout the twentieth century. As Lisa Lowe argues, contradictory subjectivities are formed through the novel's dissemination in colonized sites. As Lowe demonstrates through readings of Asian American "novels," these sites include racialized populations within the geographical confines of the United States. Lowe writes:

> Just as the English novel was a central cultural institution in British colonial education and contributed to the formation of subjects in the British colonies of India, Nigeria, and Jamaica, so we can observe this legacy of cultural authority in the relationship between the American novel from *The Scarlet Letter* to *The Sound and the Fury* and the literary and cultural traditions of African Americans, Native Americans, Chicanos/Latinos, and Asian Americans in the United States. (1996, 100)

What we see is not that the novel works evenly and monolithically, but that it produces a variety of discrepant subjectivities. Yet this process of differentiation is occluded by the novel's claim to universality and equivalence. That the novel functions both as a means of differentiation and as a means for the erasure of this process is best exemplified by its role in the production of propertied subjects.

By "propertied subjects," I refer to the ways that the literary canon and the U.S. novel in particular define subjectivity through the ability to own, a definition that replicates the narrative of citizenship under U.S. liberal democracy. The U.S. nation-state is based on a liberal political theory that posits the protection of private property as the only justification for the formation of the state. Locke begins his *Second Treatise of Government* by defining the state as such: "*Political power*, then, I take to be a *right* of making laws with penalties of death, and consequently all less penalties, for the regulating and preserving of property" (1980, 8).[3] Thus, the liberal-democratic state does not merely allow for capitalism to exist; rather, capitalism is the justification for the liberal-democratic state's existence. Capitalism's dependence on the contract form necessitates this propertied citizen. Property thus does not only mean the actual objects or consumer goods that are owned, but a complex social network that relates each subject to the state and to each other.

The concept of property defines the subject and also constructs the subject's relationship to the state—the state is narrativized as guaranteeing the citizen's right to property. Locke's famous declaration, "every man has *property* in his own *person*" (1962, 19) is extremely revealing in this regard. Often read as Locke's definition of property, it is also obviously Locke's definition of personhood. The subject is defined by his ability to own, and indeed, the first and foremost thing he owns is himself. Subjectivity, then, is a possession. This subject's relationship to others is also defined through ownership of property. In Locke's conception, civil society forms out of the desire to protect one's property interests. This civil society agrees on a form of government that will establish and protect property rights, and the state is created. In theory, each person's property rights are equally guaranteed by the state, thus creating "abstract" citizens equivalent to each other. The community thus formed between these members of this civil society, these abstract citizens, is the nation. Thus "property" does not refer only to the actual objects that are owned, but describes a complex set of social relations.

Karl Marx's critique of this modern liberal capitalist state as the protector of property rights reminds us that this process attempts to resolve a fundamentally unresolvable contradiction. In his essay, "On the Jewish Question," Marx notes that membership in the political sphere requires the shedding of individual particularity for the "unreal universality" of the abstract citizen (1978, 34). However, representation through abstract citizenship does not mean that men in this society somehow relinquish their self-interestedness; rather, the state becomes the guarantor of those interests through being the guarantor of private property. Marx argues this by examining the Declaration of the Rights of Man, which defines the right to property as "that which belongs to every citizen of enjoying and disposing *as he will* of his goods and revenues, of the fruits of his work and industry" (42). Thus, Marx notes, the right to property is "the right to enjoy one's fortune and to dispose of it as one will; without regard for other men and independently of society. It is the right to self-interest" (42). The state thus protects capitalist enterprise and accumulation through the protection of private property. Because the abstract citizen is the propertied subject, the state must profess equality while actually functioning as the guarantor of unequal property relations and capitalist modes of production. Extending

Marx's argument, I will argue in the readings below that the uneven material histories of racialization and gendering likewise cannot be resolved to the universal. Rather than being the guarantor of property relations, the U.S. state is the very agent of dispossession for people of color.

We can see through an examination of U.S. narratives of development the ways that their function is to interpellate the propertied subject as the citizen of the nation. Yet we can also read for the ways this process reveals its own contradictions and instabilities, precipitated by the crises around national identity, by no means a stable concept at the time.

Twain's novel, from which Ernest Hemingway proclaimed, "all modern American literatures comes," has been discussed as mediating a variety of historical crises at the time of its writing and construction, from the anxiety over juvenile delinquency to concerns over the apparent failure of Reconstruction.[4] I would argue that this text registers the importance of the possessive individual in the nineteenth century as the site on which these anxieties were negotiated. *Huck Finn*'s centrality to the American literary canon to this day demonstrates the ways that the propertied subject is a central object of both validation and contestation. *Huck Finn* validates a liberal white masculine possessive individualism, demonstrated through benevolence toward racialized subjects. While a critique of the often violent version of conservative whiteness that devalued black lives, this very liberalism is itself a version of the possessive individual that necessarily casts racialized others as devoid of will, or in other words, devoid of subjectivity.

Huck Finn is perhaps the most famous example of white liberal possessive individualism. Literary scholar James Cox (1995) has noted that the critique of slavery could hardly have been this text's primary purpose, as it was published over twenty years after the end of the Civil War. Rather than a heroic critique of a morally corrupt institution, *The Adventures of Huckleberry Finn* can be read, in part, as legitimating the liberal white masculine subject who makes this critique. In other words, this text renders heroic the possessive individual whose act of will consists of choosing to identify with the racialized other over the constraints of "society," coded as domestic and feminizing. In so doing, Twain's novel negotiates the crises attendant upon the end of official Reconstruction in 1877. *The Adventures of Huckleberry Finn* in part responds to the general sense of the failure of the Reconstruction project by rendering heroic Huck's decision to abet Jim's escape, thus legitimating the ostensible purpose and outcome of the Civil War at a moment when it had became apparent that the ensuing sectionalism was not to be easily resolved. We can also see the ways that this valorization of liberal whiteness, marked by benevolence toward racialized subjects, resonates with the racial politics that became dominant in the post–*Brown vs. Board of Education* era—one reason, certainly, why *The Adventures of Huckleberry Finn* has remained an enduring classic into the twenty-first century. Yet the text also incorporates a variety of elements that have made this book the center of considerable controversy. The slapstick and buffoonery of the last eleven chapters, in which Huck recedes and Tom Sawyer steps in to play a variety of pranks on the imprisoned Jim, have been the object of a variety of critiques, both aesthetic and critical.[5] I would situate these controversies as grappling with contradictions within the narrative, which are not, as many scholars have posited, a sign of the failure or success of Twain's authorial discretion, but rather a result of the fact that the possessive individual's ability to exercise will must be established at the expense of another's subjection to that will.

We see such a contradiction in Jim's important status as the crux of Huck's moral transformation, which requires that he function both as the instigator and the object of Huck's subjectivity as possessive individual. *Huck Finn*'s interpellative mechanism is the narrative of Huck's moral development as he transitions from amoral immaturity to moral maturity; this is the narrative of Huck's development into the possessive individual. Huck begins as a boy who wonders "[W]hat's the use of learning to do right, when it's troublesome to do right and ain't no trouble to do wrong, and the wages is just the same?" and decides that he won't "bother no more about it, but after this always do whichever came handiest at the time" (Twain 1990, 307). By the novel's end, Huck has cast off this unsophisticated definition of "right" and "wrong" instilled in him by the Widow Douglas. Instead, in an oft-quoted passage, Huck makes the decision to put the runaway slave Jim's welfare before his own. Instead of turning Jim in, which he has been taught is the Christian thing to do, Huck decides, "All right, then, I'll *go* to hell" (Twain 1990, 381).

Henry James's *Daisy Miller: A Study* constitutes possessive individualism in a different valance: by addressing nineteenth-century crises in gender and sexuality by creating an analogy between American individualism and masculinity, and between European tradition, society, and femininity. James's text encourages the reader to identify with a central hero confronted with a choice, or an opportunity, to exercise his will. James begins by immediately situating the reader within the moral economy of the propertied, elite leisure class about which he writes. James uses a third-person limited omniscient narration that follows the main character, a young man originally from the United States named Winterbourne. The novel's opening, however, is unlike the rest of the book in that it does not begin by immediately following Winterbourne's movements. Rather, it begins with a description of the small Swiss resort town and the lovely and comfortable hotel where we first meet Winterbourne. The narration does not start with Winterbourne, of course, because at that point, the reader has not been properly introduced to him. The text follows the pattern one might imagine that introductions would take among the mannered leisure class of James's novel. The reader does not immediately "meet" Winterbourne, but is told gossipy details of his life, the kinds of minor scandals that would certainly circulate within the exclusive society of wealthy American travelers. We are told that Winterbourne is from the United States, but that he resides in Geneva and purports to be "studying," which everyone understands to mean that he is conducting an affair with an older foreign woman. He is "vouched" for by the fact that he is visiting his aunt, a woman whose sensibilities are so rarified that she suffers chronically from headaches and so confines herself to her hotel room most of the time. It is only after this elaborate introduction that the reader actually "meets" Winterbourne, and becomes privy to his thoughts and feelings.

In this way, James's text assumes that the reader understands the moral and mannered sensibilities of the leisure class that populates his study. The text carefully observes all proper form lest we, the readers, take offense at an inappropriately abrupt introduction to its main character. Thus structured, the text presumes that both Winterbourne's concerns and epiphanies about Daisy Miller's behavior only reinforce this sense of belonging created by the opening of the text. James's text creates a "we," a sense of imagined community fostered by a supposedly shared understanding of the niceties and manners of the nineteenth-century U.S. leisure class. Though this text is a cautionary tale about the damage done by callous snobbery, the text presumes and depends on the reader's understanding and internalizing these mores.

In many ways, *Huck Finn* is as opposite to *Daisy Miller* as a text can be.

Unlike the erudite, mannered, cosmopolitan characters of James's text, *Huck Finn*'s characters are, for the most part, poor, rural, and heavily marked as regional by their dress, speech, and customs. Yet despite their differences, *Huck Finn* and *Daisy Miller* ultimately work to consolidate the formation of a propertied subject, and to bind this subject to the nation. What links these two seemingly opposite texts is that they both assume the preexistence of a certain type of interiority in the reader, an interiority shaped by iden-tification with the central character. That is, James's text can only assume the internalization of social mores if the reader has this kind of interiority. Likewise, Huck Finn's transformation can only parallel the moral forma-tion of the reader if the reader assumes Huck's interiority.

This interiority is specifically valanced: the self is defined through its abil-ity to exercise free will. In this way, we can see a crucial difference between the U.S. novel and the European bildungsroman. In the European con-text, the form or genre of literature whose emergence parallels the rise of the modern nation-state—the novel—was historically an important site for the suturing of the subject to the state. As studies of the novel have noted, the *formal* aspects of the novel do this work through the valorization of a developmental narrative of the citizen-subject. As Benedict Anderson has argued (1991), the novel calls into being a national subject through the creation of new conceptions of time ("empty, homogeneous") and space (bounded by the borders of the nation). Anderson gives the novel a cen-tral place in the construction of an "imagined community" of citizens who will never actually meet, but who can imagine themselves as a discrete, dis-cernible group progressing simultaneously through this "empty, homoge-nous time." Franco Moretti's study (1987) of the classic bildungsroman adds to Anderson's thesis by offering a description of the interpellative mecha-nism through which the *bildung* contributes to the formation of the sub-ject of the liberal capitalist state: the narrative of moral development, the telos of which is resolution with the bourgeois institutions of the state, such as work or marriage. As Moretti has argued, the role of the bildungsroman is to negotiate the tension between individual will and resolution with cap-italist society. It does so, Moretti argues, through the "valorization of neces-sity" (69). That is, the bildungsroman is resolved when the individual has gone from immaturity, defined as the inability to resolve oneself with soci-ety, to maturity, which is often signified through the central character's will-ful acceptance of bourgeois institutions such as marriage or work. As Moretti notes, "as a 'free individual,' not as a fearful subject but as a convinced citizen, one perceives the social norms as *one's own*. One must *internalize* them and fuse external compulsion and internal impulses into a new unity until the former is no longer distinguishable from the latter" (16).

Yet for the U.S. novel, "external compulsion" is ironically the same thing as "internal impulses" because the "social norm" valorized by U.S. nationalism is exactly individualism. Narrated as unfettered by the stifling traditions associated with Europe, the United States is emblematically a nation of individuals who perform their "Americanness" exactly through breaking with social constraints, whether it be the symbolic image of the lone cowboy more at home in frontier "wilderness" than in polite company, or the national origin story of the Pilgrims braving the journey across the Atlantic to escape religious repression.

In keeping with this narrative, the effectiveness of both *Huck Finn* and *Daisy Miller* lies in the fact that rather than presenting a straightforward resolution with societal mores, they both actually critique the blind acceptance of certain societal norms. In *Huck Finn,* much of the humor and poignancy of Huck's eventual moral transformation comes from his lack of discernment about the Widow Douglas's dictates on good and evil. At the beginning of the narrative, Huck knows he must be "good," but he associates being good with wearing starched clothes and not swearing. His utter lack of moral discernment is emphasized by the blithe, guiltless enjoyment he gets from joining a band of robbers (actually a group of boys led by Tom Sawyer) who plan to rob coaches and kill people. His eventual decision to put Jim's freedom above his own well-being in the afterlife is obviously his moment of moral transformation in the narrative, but in doing this, Huck must violate the Widow Douglas's religious instruction.

Likewise, as I have noted earlier, *Daisy Miller* can be read as a cautionary tale about the negative effects of an elitist, constraining European society, which disciplines and rewards certain types of behavior. The text first invites internalization of this elitism, as I have shown, but then undermines it. Winterbourne realizes after Daisy's death that he had made a mistake in judging her by the same stifling criteria—criteria the text assumes we understand—as the other Americans abroad. But because of this mistake, he is, in a sense, punished at the end of the narrative. He is relegated to a lack of growth and his character ends where it began. The novel closes: "Nevertheless, he went back to live at Geneva, whence there continue to come the most contradictory accounts of his motives of the sojourn: a report that he is 'studying' hard—an intimation that he is much interested in 'a very clever foreign lady'" (James 1990, 590). Like Winterbourne, readers are also faced with a choice, having understood and appreciated both sets of codes.

These novels narrate a kind of individual morality that breaks with the societal values presented in the texts, but which constructs and follows another "truer" set of values with which the abstract reader is supposed to identify. Whether, like Huck, one is successful in adopting and implementing this other set of values (often amorphously defined, but with more truth value to the reader), or, like Winterbourne, one is not, the important function of both texts is to establish the choice. This is the moment when the possibility of free will is assumed, both for the character and for the reader. In other words, while the classic bildungsroman narrates a resolution with society, these texts narrate a break from society. However, in so doing, these texts encourage resolution with another set of social values: the ability to exercise free will that characterizes American individualism. In other words, if what defines the particularly American ethos is individualism, to assert one's will as an individual is to ironically become a part of a collectivity. This collectivity is made up of subjects who are bound together by their resistance to bonds.

In both *Huck Finn* and *Daisy Miller*, these "bonds" are signified as femininity. Being an "individual" means expressing one's resistance to feminization. *Huck Finn*, of course, has been read often as allegorizing the masculine will toward "freedom."[6] At the beginning of the narrative, Huck chafes under the Widow Douglas's attempts to "sivilize" him, because of how "dismal regular and decent the widow was in all her ways" (244). At the end, of course, is Huck's famous declaration of his intent to "light out for the Territory" (429), this time to escape Aunt Sally's "sivilizing" influence. Although *Huck Finn* seems to be positioned explicitly against domesticity (a particularly middle-class institution), its brand of individualism and the interiority upon which it relies depends on a particular, historically specific conception of public and private. Literary scholar Gillian Brown argues that the development of domesticity was a crucial step in the construction of American individualism, as "nineteenth-century American individualism takes on its particularly 'individualistic' properties as domesticity inflects it with values of interiority, privacy, and psychology" (1990, 1).

The characters in *Daisy Miller* also seem like they would be quite disdainful of Aunt Sally's brand of middle-class domesticity, but for quite different reasons—because the feminine ideals of the properly domestic woman were first constructed in nineteenth-century novels in opposition to the kind of aristocratic, "wasteful" woman described as the recipient of Winterbourne's desire in *Daisy Miller*. Yet there is a version of femininity in this novel that stifles masculinity and crushes Winterbourne's ability to be the master of his own fate. The public privacy of gossip, which is indulged in by both women and men but is cast as a particularly effete and effeminate activity, comprises the gilded bars of their social milieu. In effect, Daisy Miller, who remains resistant to the many nuances of manners and rules that regulate the other Americans abroad, is portrayed as too individuated and too American, and she is eventually punished for not being feminine enough. As Lynn Wardley notes, Daisy's ambiguously gendered behavior elicits anxieties about "the integrity of the 'American Man'" (1991, 233). As Winterbourne himself observes, Daisy behaves in both feminine and masculine ways, and her actions highlight Winterbourne's choice between American masculinity and European effeteness. Winterbourne's failure is that, unlike Huck, he chooses the comforts of society, narrated as European decadence, rather than affirming his own sense of right and wrong, as the headstrong and therefore distinctly American Daisy does. In this way, the white masculinity described by the U.S. novel as distinctly American is created through a strategic performance of distance from femininity, a positioning that must be constantly repeated. In so doing, these texts reproduce the idea of American individualism as dependent on the iconoclastic frontier mentality. We can see the ways that Huck's desire to "light out for the Territory" only makes sense within the context of the many discourses that posited the frontier as the site for unfettered masculine freedom. Likewise, although *Daisy Miller* doesn't explicitly reference the frontier, it sets up an opposition between European traditionalism and American individualism that references the various articulations of American identity through an exceptionalism from the European model.

The contradictions we see in these texts' expression of the propertied subject can be understood by examining the material and ideological dependence of this subject on native dispossession, African enslavement, and the recruitment of Asian and Latino immigrant labor, as well as the ways this dependence is exactly that which the propertied citizen-subject—and the narrative of development that articulates this subject—must erase. Rather than narrating a trajectory of the self-made man that universally applies to all, the narrative of development operates differentially. Basic to this process is the assumption that certain subjects exist who lack the ability to exercise will, epitomized in the antithetical relationship between freedom and enslavement.

Freedom, defined in liberal democracy as the ability to exercise one's will without influence from others, needs an antithetical analogue: enslavement. Orlando Patterson's term, "social death," aptly names this relationship. We might understand social death as the defining antithetical condition to the possessive individual. In *Slavery and Social Death,* a study that ranges from tribal societies to classical antiquity to the modern world, Patterson argues that social death is fundamental to all forms of slavery. "Social death" describes the condition in which the slave's entrance into social relations happens entirely through his master. Although Patterson argues that this condition is inherent to slavery in all contexts, he differentiates societies based on what he calls the "personalistic" versus the "materialistic" idioms of power. I take his descriptions to be models or explanatory narratives, rather than transparent descriptions of actual modes of social organization. Societies with a "personalistic" idiom of power, which Patterson states are nonmodern and tribally organized, openly accede to the power hierarchies inherent in social relationships. In such societies, no one is free from hierarchical power relations, and no one would desire such an alienated state of being. Embeddedness in social relations is not articulated as enslavement, but as a web of protections. In this context, "[T[he most unslavelike person was the one in whom a small number of claims, powers, and privileges were spread over a large number of persons; the slave, on the other hand, was someone in whom a large number of claims, privileges, and powers were concentrated in a single person" (1982, 28). As such, the difference between a slave and a free man was not a difference of kind, but degree.

In contrast, the "materialistic" idiom of power, which Patterson ascribes to Western, modern, and capitalist societies, completely denies the existence of the coercive aspect of power relations. Patterson argues that enslavement is ideologically, as well as materially, fundamental to modern modes of rule, because in this "materialistic" idiom of power, freedom is articulable only as the opposite of enslavement, its absolute antithesis. Yet because in the "materialistic" idiom, there is no vocabulary for power or force, the coercive or unequal aspects of social relations must be disavowed. In other words, because modern, liberal humanist societies are based on conceptions of equivalence and horizontal comradeship, these societies' material and ideological dependence on inequality and hierarchy must be erased. In this narrative of social organization, enslavement is distinctly aberrant and pathological to the normative condition of freedom, rather than a generalizable condition in which everyone is constrained, albeit to greater or lesser degrees, by their embeddedness within hierarchies of power. Enslavement, as an undeniably unequal condition, must be disavowed as freedom's antithesis. In such a case, freedom has no meaning without the opposite meaning of enslavement, but this fact must always be occluded or erased. We can thus see that this narrative of social organization is fundamentally contradictory.

In the context of the nineteenth-century United States, the terms of this freedom and enslavement were articulated through will. Freedom is, in Patterson's words, "the modern Western 'bourgeois' sense of isolation from the influence of others" (1982, 28). The free self is the self-possessed self who can determine his own fate through the exercise of his will, free from the "influence of others." The concept of possessive individualism thus sutures together the condition of freedom and the condition of being propertied. Enslavement, on the other hand, is the condition of being subjected to the will of others, a condition that led to slaves being the figure for what Patricia Williams terms "pure antiwill" (1991a, 219). This particular version of social death, the condition of "antiwill," means, in a liberal humanist context where will is the basis for subjectivity and the precondition for personhood, that slaves were precluded from subject status. If property refers not only to the actual things that are owned but to the entire social system that bases one's entrance into civil society and one's relationship to the state on the ability to own, slaves are the "object of property" rather than the subject. The narrative of the propertied subject as the individual, the self-made and self-determining man, is fundamentally contradicted by its dependence on the enslaved, as the free, propertied subject does not exist without its antithesis.

Even after the formal abolition of enslavement in the United States, the legacy of possessive individualism and its necessary but erased corollary, social death, continues to perform powerfully epistemological erasures of alternative notions of subject and community, and to structure material conditions for racialized populations. Patricia Williams's essay "On Being the Object of Property" links *contemporary* modes of dispossession to a long history of foreclosure of propertied subjectivity for racialized and gendered subjects. After discussing the forced sterilization of African American, Latino, and Native American women in the twentieth century, Williams writes, "As I reflected on all this, I realized that one of the things passed on from slavery, which continues in the oppression of people of color, is a belief structure rooted in a concept of black (or brown or red) antiwill, the antithetical embodiment of pure will" (1991b, 219). Contract law presumes an individuated subject who can freely enter into contract relations, which then extends the state's protection of that subject's property, including the self. Given this situation, the process of racialization is to have a distanced, contradictory relationship to the state and to nationalist notions of subjectivity. In such a system, "to be perceived as unremittingly without will is to be imbued with an almost lethal trait" (219). In other words, even to this day, to be without will—to be foreclosed from the subject position of the possessive individual—is to approximate the condition of social death. Williams thus explains how such violations as forced sterilizations are possible within a society that purports to provide the greatest protections to self-determination and to one's right over one's self. Cast as inhabiting the state of "antiwill" and thus not capable of inhabiting the subjectivity of the possessive individual, African American, Latino, and Native American women have no self that the state is duty-bound to protect, and thus the state acts as the very agent of violation and dispossession.

As such, we can read for the compelling power of the possessive individual in cultural texts written after formal emancipation. We can also read for the contradictions of the propertied subject even, or perhaps especially, when racialized subjects attempt to use the form of the novel to resolve and displace the contradictions produced when subjecthood is based on notions of property. In other words, in *Huck Finn* we saw the ways that will or choice demands its unfree analogue in the form of the slave, over whom will is enforced. Being the object of someone else's will is the condition of "social death" in a social structure in which subjectivity is the ability to exercise will and thus be propertied in one's own person. This narrative of freedom through maturity and resolution with the social order, however, resolved these fundamental contradictions, albeit inadequately and incompletely.

These resolutions break down and are exposed as incoherent in African American thought, which grappled with the complex legacies of "object" status, or "social death." As such, in this next part of my discussion, I examine Booker T. Washington's *Up from Slavery* to argue that this text must centrally address the problem of writing from the point of view of those who were never supposed to have a point of view, of the contradictory subjectivity wrested from writing out of the situation of "being the object of property." These texts demonstrate the contradiction inherent in the possessive individual that comes to light when put to the project of narrating racialized subjects.

Indeed, nothing more effectively demonstrates the allure of the narrative of development than Booker T. Washington's *Up from Slavery*. Writing in the era that historian Rayford Logan called "the nadir of African American history," Booker T. Washington advanced a program for African American self-improvement that promised to address the crushing problems of impoverishment, racist violence, and labor exploitation that characterized African American life after the failures of Reconstruction. Narrating his life as an against-all-odds trajectory from abject slave to self-made man, educator, and leader, Washington advocates hard work, humility, frugality, temperance, moderation, and to an almost obsessive degree, cleanliness. Yet Washington's story is not only his own, of course; the entire "Negro Problem" (and, ostensibly, its solution) gets mapped onto this narrative. Washington's contribution to the debate over how to incorporate the supposedly backward, primitive former slaves, presumably unfit for self-governance or citizenship, into the national citizenry was to offer himself as an example and a template. In *Up from Slavery*, Washington attempts to narrate the conditions of propertylessness and property through linearity, along a model of temporal progress. Propertylessness did not fundamentally enable the existence of the propertied subject, but was something that could be transcended and left behind in African Americans' journey to modernity. In other words, *Up from Slavery*'s promise that African Americans could transcend their differentiation erased the ways that the entire economy of the United States was dependent on the processes of differentiation that made African American labor exploitable. Saidiya Hartmann (1997), for example, writes of the ways the transition from enslavement to "free" status was marked by a shift in the modes of discipline that conditioned African Americans to labor. In the post-Emancipation era, African Americans in the

South lived under a system of debt peonage that in many respects was not unlike the conditions of work and life under slavery. Yet unlike slavery, African Americans were bound to sharecropping through the structure of debt, a structure that depended on a conception of African Americans as *individuals* who were supposed to internalize a sense of responsibility for their own economic well-being. After all, the formal abolishment of slavery ostensibly made African Americans citizens, equal under the law, and thus equally responsible for their own condition. In such an arrangement, which Hartmann calls the "burdened individuality of freedom," those who could not work off their debt were not trapped in a fundamentally exploitative labor system, but were merely not hardworking or responsible enough.

Washington's autobiography reproduces this narrative of individual responsibility, with himself as its exemplar. Yet as confident as Washington seemed in the saving powers of modernity and progress to address African American woes, *Up from Slavery* contains contradictions that mark the impossibility of this narrative of development. The two functions most readily associated with *Up from Slavery* end up undermining each other. On the one hand, *Up from Slavery*'s adherence to the developmental form is certainly prescriptive; this text was intended to have a quite explicit pedagogical function for African Americans. On the other hand, *Up from Slavery* was also quite deliberately written as a missive to whites, reassuring them that they had nothing to fear from the African American self-determination he outlines in his text.[7] As we well know, Washington has gone down in history as the Great Compromiser, as most scholars, both supporters and detractors, have interpreted his entire career as informed by his conciliatory attitude to Southern whites. The most quoted moments and most well-known aspects of Washington's text are exactly those where he attempts to resolve two competing aims or goals: articulating African American self-determination and assuaging white fear. His famous declaration in the Atlanta Exposition Address, ostensibly an appeal for whites to accept limited African American progress, reassures everyone that "in all things that are purely social we can be as separate as the fingers, yet one as the hand in all things essential to mutual progress" (Washington 1996, 100). In other words, unlike the unfettered self-determination that marks maturity and ethical formation in a text like *Huck Finn,* in *Up from Slavery* progress and development for African Americans are qualified by the need to address the historical particularities of white resentment, as well as the violence that this resentment bred. By the time of *Up from Slavery*'s publication, this era saw over ten thousand lynchings, couched in terms of the need to protect white femininity, but testifying to white anxiety over African American financial prosperity and political enfranchisement. In this context, the stakes for Washington's ability to mollify white resentment were high indeed.

As such, ironically, *Up from Slavery* narrativizes Washington's coming into being as a self-made man through representations of his grateful submission to whites, both men and women. Unlike Huck Finn, Washington does not narrate himself against domesticity, which at the time became coded as internalizing standards of bodily cleanliness and developing consumerist discernments.[8] Rather, he is completely submissive to it. Washington recounts his first contact with disciplining femininity not as a narrative of rebellion against it, but as docile submission to it. Describing his first job, as the house boy of a white woman, Washington writes,

> I had heard so much about Mrs. Ruffner's severity that I was almost afraid to see her, and trembled when I went into her presence. I had not lived with her many weeks, however, before I began to understand her. I soon began to learn that, first of all, she wanted everything kept clean about her, that she wanted things done promptly and systematically, and that at the bottom of everything she wanted absolute honesty and frankness. Nothing must be sloven or slipshod; every door, every fence, must be kept in repair. . . . At any rate, I here repeat what I have said more than once before, that the lessons that I learned in the home of Mrs. Ruffner were as valuable to me as as any education I have ever gotten anywhere since. (25)

Indeed, rather than marking his masculinity by fleeing feminizing domesticity, Washington becomes the disciplinary figure, enforcing domesticity on others. Remembering his first teaching job at the "coloured school" in his hometown as "one of the happiest periods" in his life because he "had the opportunity to help the people . . . to a higher life," Washington recounts what he taught the students there: "In addition to the usual routine of teaching, I taught the pupils to comb their hair, and to keep their hands and faces clean, as well as their clothing. I gave special attention to teaching them the proper use of the tooth-brush and the bath. In all my teaching I have watched carefully the influence of the tooth-brush, and I am convinced that there are few single agencies of civilization that are more far-reaching" (38). In *Up from Slavery*, resistance to domesticity for African Americans is the sign of the savage, which must be firmly repudiated to share in American modernity.

This contradiction registers how one of the most important forms of dispossession and exploitation at the time was the denial of a protected domesticity for African Americans, and, correspondingly, that the concept of domesticity was itself defined over and against racialized households. The enslaved state of "antiwill" was particularly expressed through a differential, distanced relationship to the institutions of the "private." If, as Gillian Brown argues, possessive individualism was based on the notion of domesticity, the opposite condition of antiwill was exactly conveyed through the utter lack of a protected "private" sphere for slaves, a condition that reproduced itself beyond the era of legal slavery. In liberal ideology, the private sphere is ostensibly where one's own individual will is law. In other words, a notion of the "private" developed in which domesticity became the "haven in a heartless world," to reference Christopher Lasch, a counterpart to both the capitalist discipline of work and the state's control of the public sphere.[9] Gillian Brown argues, "Domestic ideology with its discourse of personal life proliferates alongside this economic development which removed women from the public realm of production and redirected men to work arenas increasingly subject to market contingencies. . . . Maintaining a site of permanent value, the domestic cult of true womanhood facilitated the transition to a life increasingly subject to the caprices of the market" (1990, 3). The private became defined, however erroneously, as the site where one was unencumbered by the will of others. The definition of the "private" was one's ability to exercise one's will particularly in relation to self and family. Yet while this may have been accurate for white, middle-class men and women, this transition from a stable work space to an unstable one never happened for people of color in nineteenth-century America, simply because the site of work for people of color was never stable, but was always hyperexploitative, dangerous, and insecure. Correspondingly, for people of color, the "private" space of domesticity was never an option; rather, the protection of normative white domesticity was predicated on the pathologized, racialized status of what Nayan Shah has termed "queer" domesticities.

Thus, while Huck can gleefully embrace savagery and, presumably, severe tooth decay to escape what he might call "sivilization," and thus ironically mark himself as the apotheosis of the propertied individual, Washington must choose between two markers of civilization. Because the narrative of the propertied subject cannot frame nonnormative forms of domesticity inhabited by African Americans as anything other than deviant and in need of correction, Washington must be either individuated or domesticated. In the end, *Up from Slavery* does not so much describe an individual born in the moment of rebellion against society, as *Huck Finn* does, but narrates the African American subject's submission to the social order as the proof of his readiness for modernity. *Up from Slavery* believes in African Americans' ability to exercise will—to be rational, self-determining subjects—but narrates this as a willingness to submit to the will of others. In its own way, *Up from Slavery* inadvertently narrates a kind of simultaneous object-subject position. *Up from Slavery* marks the impossibility of "modernization" for African Americans because this demands that a narrative of propertyless-ness, defined as object status or "social death," be expressed as a narrative of property.

Up from Slavery contends that the object status of slavery, and the impoverishment, disenfranchisement, and dispossession this status implies for African Americans, can be transcended through compliance with the program of moral improvement, hard work, and physical discipline that Washington champions. While this seemingly airtight plan for African American self-improvement springs more than a few leaks, as we have seen, *Up from Slavery*'s stated purpose is to be a disciplinary text, and it explicitly puts the responsibility of addressing the failures of Reconstruction and the resulting conditions of impoverishment squarely on the shoulders of individual African Americans. If lack of opportunity for advancement persists, Washington's text implies, it is due to the inability of African Americans to be self-disciplined, willful, propertied subjects, rather than the historical situation wherein African Americans are fundamentally foreclosed from the subject position of being propertied. In so doing, Washington's narrative articulates the "burdened individuality of freedom."

In their contestations around possessive individualism, texts such as *The Adventures of Huckleberry Finn*, *Daisy Miller*, and *Up from Slavery* register the ways that this nationalist developmental narration of subjectivity is fundamentally contradictory. As I argued in my introduction, women of color feminism likewise articulated this contradiction. Women of color feminism suggested that claiming a propertied subjecthood for a racialized self was not the only way to challenge the histories of dispossession. Indeed, women of color feminism argued that these projects, which attempted to secure possessive individualism for racialized subjects, were inherently contradictory. Patricia Williams articulates the contradiction in a particularly elegant manner: "Reclaiming that from which one has been disinherited is a good thing. Self-possession in the full sense of that expression is the companion to self-knowledge. Yet claiming for myself a heritage the weft of whose genesis is my own disinheritance is a profoundly troubling paradox" (1991a, 217). To claim the version of subjectivity that is narrated as "self-possession"—to claim the status of possessive individualism, in other words—is to claim a structure that depends on the dispossession of racialized subjects. This "profoundly troubling paradox" underscores the need to imagine subjectivity differently, a project we can see in one incarnation as women of color feminism.

As I have demonstrated in the above readings, possessive individualism and social death constituted racialized difference as simultaneously a gendered formation, carved out of contradictory relationships to domesticity. As such, the texts discussed above demonstrate the fundamental interdependence of the possessive individual on modern conceptions of the public/private split. In other words, as we have seen throughout, the U.S. possessive individual's ability to be a self-made man is dependent on a sense of independence from the constraints of society, embodied by domesticity and femininity. The possessive individual is hewn in the public sphere. The notion of social death, as described by Patterson, likewise presumes the public sphere as the proper site of contestation over freedom and agency. Patterson's notion of social death assumes that the social death of the slave happens because the slave's entrance into a public sphere is entirely mediated through the master. The incursions into the slave's private life are enabled by the slave's lack of access to social/public institutions, because the slave's familial relations—as father, as husband—are not protected by the institutions of the state. When women of color feminists addressed the condition of social death for enslaved peoples, they underscored the ways in which dispossession was fundamentally enacted through the "private," and as such, women of color feminist critiques of the possessive individual exceed Patterson's analysis.

For example, Angela Davis links the lynching of black men to the erasure of the rape of black women in "Rape, Racism, and the Myth of the Black Rapist" (1981), arguing,

> Slavery relied as much on routine sexual abuse as it relied on the whip and the lash. Excessive sex urges, whether they existed among individual white men or not, had nothing to do with this virtual institutionalization of rape. Sexual coercion was, rather, an essential dimension of the social relations between slave master and slave. In other words, the right claimed by slave-owners and their agents over the bodies of female slaves was a direct expression of their presumed property rights over Black people as a whole. The license to rape emanated from and facilitated the ruthless economic determination that was the gruesome hallmark of slavery. (175)

Davis implicitly critiques the masculinism of narratives of slavery that articulated slavery as primarily about the lack of a public selfhood for slaves. Davis's argument that the condition of social death experienced by slaves had its exemplary expression in the rape of enslaved women gives us insight into the ways that Patterson's narrative itself participates in the production of public and private spheres by imagining the public sphere as separate and coherent and by narrating "life" and "death" as entirely determined by access, or lack thereof, to the public sphere. Patterson's understanding of social death privileges the public sphere and makes the violence of the private sphere its corollary. In so doing, he subordinates the "private" component of social ("public") death, and implicitly ascribes a normative masculinity to the slave who is the subject of his study. Davis revises Patterson's notion in arguing that the license to rape was the primary means of rendering slaves the property of the owners, as well as being the means for capital accumulation and reproduction.

Intersectional analyses of enslavement are particularly helpful in understanding the gendered investments implied by Patterson's notion of social death. Patterson's conception of "natal alienation" is a case in point. Fundamental to Patterson's definition of the social death of slavery is the concept of natal alienation: a "genealogical isolate," the slave was "denied all claims on, and obligations to, his parents and living blood relations" and "by extension, all such claims and obligations on his more remote ancestors and descendents" (1982, 5). This condition of natal alienation was crucial to the reproduction of enslaved populations because it guaranteed that children born of slaves were themselves enslaved: "The hereditary factor [justifying the enslavement of the children of slaves] only entered when the servant lost his natal claims to his own parents and community. Having no natal claims and powers of his own, he had none to pass on to his own children. And because no one had any claim or interest on these children, the master could claim them as his own" (9). Patterson narrates the reproduction of slavery as occurring through the denial of the masculine slave's right of patrilineage. Yet as we know from Hazel Carby's work, this was not the case: the black woman's "reproductive destiny was bound to capital accumulation; black women gave birth to property and, directly, to capital itself, in the form of slaves, and all slaves inherited their status from their mothers" (1987, 24–25). The *female* slave's condition *was* inheritable, in other words; the child took on the status of the mother, not the father, who was often the white planter. The white father's lack of right of patrilineage—the fact that he did not confer his free status to his children—is actually what reproduces capital accumulation through rape. Patterson's valuable concept of social death still shares with its implicit object of critique, the possessive individual, an uninterrogated investment in masculinist notions of subjectivity that women of color feminism displaces.

Because the ideal of a privatized domesticity is so important to the ideological constitution of the possessive individual, as well as to the racialized property relations that this subject position protects, texts by women of color writers must center the complex interdependence of domesticity and dispossession. In the next chapter, I will turn to the ways in which women of color writers Hisaye Yamamoto and Toni Morrison interrogate the legacy of this interdependency through two of its most important manifestations in the twentieth century: segregation and internment.

chapter 2

HISTORIES OF THE DISPOSSESSED: PROPERTY AND DOMESTICITY, SEGREGATION AND INTERNMENT

If something is to stay in the memory it must be burned in.

—FRIEDRICH NIETZSCHE, *On the Genealogy of Morals*

Bourgeois ideology—and particularly its racist ingredients—must really possess the power of dissolving real images of terror into obscurity and insignificance, and of fading horrible cries of suffering human beings into barely audible murmurings and then silence.

—ANGELA DAVIS, *Women, Race, and Class*

One of Japanese American short story writer Hisaye Yamamoto's most acclaimed stories, "Yoneko's Earthquake," offers this seemingly extraneous bit of information about the rural California community in which the protagonist, ten-year-old Yoneko, lives:

> Yoneko, her father, her mother, and her little brother Seigo were the only Japanese thereabouts. They were the only ones, too, whose agriculture was so diverse as to include blackberries, cabbages, rhubarb, potatoes, cucumbers, onions, and cantaloupes. The rest of the countryside there was like one vast orange grove. (46)

The connection between Yoneko's family's racial exceptionality in the farming region of California in the early 1930s and their agricultural exceptionality is not as offhand as the narrator, limited to Yoneko's naive viewpoint, makes it seem. In California, the Alien Land law of 1913 and subsequent amendments in 1920 reserved all rights to the ownership of agricultural land for citizens and aliens eligible for citizenship. Although these laws were written without the mention of race, they were written to specifically target Japanese American farm owners, since the only aliens *ineligible* for citizenship were Asian immigrants, and these laws were mainly enforced against Japanese immigrants. These land laws, which were not completely repealed until 1952, profoundly affected the livelihood of many Japanese Americans, the majority of whom were farmers (Chan 1991, 142). Given this precarious and arbitrary status of Japanese Americans in relation to land ownership, it is not surprising that Yoneko's family, the Hosoumes, are the only family in the area unwilling to invest in orange trees in favor of short-term crops. This story, written in 1950 and published in 1951, shows that even Yamamoto's early writings reveal an understanding of how fragile the claim to property was for Japanese Americans. In this chapter, I will elaborate on this understanding by focusing on a later work by Yamamoto, her 1988 memoir, "A Fire in Fontana."

Toni Morrison's first novel, *The Bluest Eye,* even more overtly thematizes the uneasy and anxious relationship between African Americans and property ownership. Morrison first describes being "put outdoor," or being homeless, as the omnipresent fear in the lives of African Americans in Lorraine, Ohio, in 1941:

> Knowing that there was such a thing as outdoors bred in us a hunger for property, for ownership. The firm possession of a yard, a porch, a grape arbor. Propertied black people spent all their energies, all their love, on their nests. Like frenzied, desperate birds, they overdecorated everything. . . . Renting blacks cast furtive glances at these owned yards and porches, and made firmer commitments to buy themselves "some nice little old place." In the meantime, they saved, and scratched, and piled away what they could in the rented hovels, looking forward to the day of property. (18)

Morrison makes clear the tenuous nature of property ownership for even the African Americans who own homes, as well as the burden of being a "renting black." Unlike Japanese Americans, whose distance from property was most overtly signified by the lack of access to agricultural property, African American dispossession from ownership from the 1930s to the 1960s

took the form of the lack of access to what sociologists Melvin Oliver and
Thomas Shapiro call "one of the most successful generators of wealth in
American history—the suburban tract home" (1995, 13). Oliver and Shapiro
note that the single most accessible form of wealth for the middle class is
the ownership of a home. They argue that this form of wealth was structurally and systematically denied to African Americans, to the benefit of
whites. Suburbanization was supported by state policies that gave businesses
tax incentives to relocate, built freeways and subsidized fuel and automobile
production, and spurred the development and financing of the tract home
(16).[1] These incentives for accumulating wealth through property ownership, however, were structurally inaccessible to African Americans, who were
prevented from buying homes in these areas by racist government loan policies, restrictive covenants, and overt violence.

Thus, Morrison, writing in the late 1960s about the early 1940s, stresses
the importance of home ownership and the impoverished state that comes
with renting. However, in doing so, she emphasizes the ways that home
ownership is never a sign of stable wealth accumulation for African Americans, but is always marked by the fear of dispossession. Morrison implies
that even those who own their homes know the "hunger for property,
ownership" indicated by "firm possession." This "firm possession," she implies, is always outside the reach of African Americans, whether propertied
or renting. Rather than contrasting propertied and renting African Americans as categorically different, she depicts them as expressing two different
reactions to the same instability of ownership.

This chapter focuses on texts by these two women of color writers,
Hisaye Yamamoto and Toni Morrison, to argue that their writings register
the differential processes of racialization for African Americans and Asian
Americans through private property relations. These two authors constantly
thematize the impossibility of ownership for Japanese Americans and African Americans. Rather than placing faith in the propertied subject or even
working to expose it as contradictory, the authors of these texts must necessarily articulate the possibility of alternative subjects, who are not modeled on the free-willed, possessive individual. Instead, these texts articulate
subjects that are not constituted as whole by property as much as they are
split and contested by it. From this distanced relationship to property come
alternative imaginings of self and community. These texts demonstrate that
such subjects form communities and coalitions in ways unimagined by the

nation, which, as I argued in chapter 1, normatively imagines collectivity as individuals who agree to a relationship of equivalence and uniformity administered by the state to protect their property. As I noted in the previous chapter, this propertied citizen-subject of the U.S. nation-state is simultaneously constituted and contested through the U.S narratives of development, in particular the novel.

I further argued that the women of color feminism that emerged in the 1970s, 1980s, and 1990s wrote an alternative narrative of dispossession that likewise exposed the contradictions of the possessive individual, but through the centering of the "private" sphere, in the form of a protected domesticity, as the site where the possessive individual is created and contested. This is the context for Morrison and Yamamoto, who articulate community through difference rather than through similarity and identification. Unlike nationalist understandings of the possessive individualist self, which must elide difference, Yamamoto's and Morrison's texts imagine the subject and her community as not predicated on the enforcement of formal equivalence, the erasure of difference, and the privileging of the discrete, individuated, willful subject. Rather, both Yamamoto and Morrison imagine coalition and community formation as dependent on the recognition of difference. As such, these texts are aligned with the women of color feminism that I discussed in the introduction.

In articulating the importance of the process of property dispossession as a mode of racialization and gendering, these texts reveal that lack of access to private property does not work monolithically. Rather, the U.S. state reproduces itself through the *differential* racializations of people of color through the lack of access to private property. Lisa Lowe argues in *Immigrant Acts* that the U.S. state tries to resolve the competing and conflicting demands of the nation-state and capital through the racialization of Asian immigrants. Lowe demonstrates that in the period between 1850 and World War II, the contradiction between the demands of the national economy (which needed a large influx of cheap, vulnerable, and *differentiated* labor) and those of the nation-state (which needed to constitute itself through a *homogeneous* citizenry) were "sublated" by the racialization of Asian immigrants through a series of exclusion acts, bars to citizenship, and other disenfranchisements (1996, 13). The period from World War II forward, on the other hand, saw Asian racialization as the locus of contradictions between global capital (which needs an economic internationalism that undermines the power of the nation-state) and the U.S. nation-state (which needs to consolidate a strong, hegemonic state to dictate the terms of the global restructuring of capital for its own benefit). In the United States these processes have created a demand for low-wage labor in the service sector (as production moves overseas), which is filled by new waves of Asian and Latin American immigration. Yet the contradictions of the earlier period that were repressed—sublated through the racialization of Asian immigrant labor—return in the form of these new immigrants, who, coming as they do from societies ravaged by U.S. imperialist wars and neo-colonial regimes, "retain precisely the memories of imperialism that the U.S. nation seeks to forget" (Lowe 1996, 17). Lowe's analysis enables my own discussion of differential racialization and alternative modes of community. Lowe's discussion of the immigrant as the figure for the "return of the repressed" of the U.S. nation-state allows her to suggest new forms of affiliation and affinity: "One of the important *acts* that the immigrant performs is breaking the dyadic, vertical determination that situates the subject in relation to the state, building instead horizontal community with and between others who are in different locations subject to and subject of the state" (36). Because Lowe focuses on the importance of Asian American racialization for the sublimation of these contradictions, she necessarily centers categories of citizenship and immigration (citizen and alien). This project prioritizes a different but related category—property—in order to elaborate upon Lowe's notion of "horizontal community" by examining the forms of community that materialize from the differential racializations of people of color. The contradictions inherent in the private property system manifested in multiple ways, each of which were temporarily sublated through the specific historical processes of racialization, which posited racial groupings in order to subordinate them to whiteness.

In "A Fire in Fontana," Yamamoto highlights the contradictions inherent in her location within a middle-class domesticity based on property ownership and the sanctity of the private sphere. Japanese immigrants and Japanese Americans were dispossessed of property, beginning with the Alien Land laws and extending to internment, through both their legal classification as aliens ineligible for citizenship and through racist characterizations that posited Japanese Americans as the other to "whites" and "Americans" (virtually synonymous in these characterizations). As I argue below, both of these justifications for property dispossession required conceptions of the separation of private and public, and the gendering of these spheres. Although Yamamoto's memoir is clear that her access to the suburban home makes her relationship to suburbanization and segregation different from that of African Americans, Yamamoto's foregrounding of her uneasy lack of resolution to her role as middle-class, property-owning housewife excavates the history of Japanese American racialization through property dispossession. This critical perspective enables Yamamoto to link the histories of African Americans and Asian Americans. Yet rather than connecting these histories through a logic of commonality or similarity, which can elide differences, Yamamoto's story points to the possibility of cross-racial solidarity by showing that the connection between Japanese Americans and African Americans is relational, based on differential access to property rights. Cross-racial solidarity is based on a common critique of the U.S. state, structured by a property system that privileges white property interests. Such a critique can only be articulated and understood when it is not based on attempts to find superficial similarities between Japanese American and African American histories. Rather, this critique must be based on a recognition of the differences in these very uneven and discrepant histories.

Yamamoto herself makes these connections explicit by beginning her memoir with an anecdote from early in her life. She describes an incident in which a young blonde seatmate on a bus trip during World War II is "filled with glee" at the sight of an African American man being forced to drink from a water faucet outside a restaurant after being refused service within (2001, 151). The narrator recalls, "Here I was on a bus going back to camp in Arizona where my father still lived, and I knew there was a connection between my seatmate's joy and our having been put in that hot and windblown place of barracks" (151). What is the connection to be made between internment and segregation, between Japanese Americans and African Americans? Rarely juxtaposed, these two processes are certainly quite different. And indeed, this passage stages those very differences by contrasting this African American man, relegated to an outdoor tap, and Yamamoto herself, who is allowed to sit in the same section of the bus as the white woman. Yamamoto's memoir centers entirely around this theme of difference—the difference between herself, a journalist in the 1940s, and the African American man who comes to the newspaper for help. Yet she just as constantly insists on the possibility of solidarity. Although she says,

"I wouldn't go so far as to say that I, a Japanese American, became Black, because that's a pretty melodramatic statement," she names the transformation she went through as a result of her journalism experiences as her "inward self being burnt black in a certain fire" (2001, 150, 151). What fuels this contradiction she inhabits, the constant foregrounding of difference paired with the equally insistent assertion of the possibility of solidarity? Excavating the privileging of white property rights that underlies the racialized history of the United States allows us to understand this connection that Yamamoto makes.

The focus of *The Bluest Eye,* in contrast, is not explicitly on cross-racial solidarity. The text, however, presents instances of what Angela Davis has termed "unlikely coalitions" across a variety of differentiated histories (1997, 322). *The Bluest Eye* shows that communities are not just created through property, predicated on the separation of private and public and the sanctity of the middle-class domestic home. Rather, the text emphasizes the ways that communities are formed through such vehicles as gossip (which circulates privately through the public and publicly through the private) and stitched together by prostitution (a form of sexuality at the margins of normative domesticity). These communities are constituted by, and provide the formation for, subjects who are racialized through property dispossession, for those who are formed in contradiction to the property-owning subject. *The Bluest Eye* demonstrates the ways that African Americans are characterized through "excess." The behavior and appearance of African Americans are rendered excessive, deviant, and subject to eradication, a disciplining process that posits African Americans against a normative subject. I argue that Morrison's text shows this normative subject to be white, male, and property owning. As such, Morrison's text constantly thematizes the impossibility of ownership—of inhabiting the free-willed, individuated subject of property who does with his person and his property as he wishes—for African Americans. Yamamoto's depiction of her access to the suburban home (as conflicted as this access is) clearly demonstrates a different kind of relationship to private property and the possibility of home from that depicted in Morrison's text. But these different histories of property dispossession allow different, but allied, forms of critique. They also allow for different forms of alternative imagining, collectivity, and subjectivity through memory.

My readings of these texts depart from the ways they have usually been

discussed. Yamamoto's stories have been anthologized widely and acclaimed
in a variety of contexts for several decades. She received mainstream attention at a time when anti-Japanese sentiment was still rampant; "Yoneko's
Earthquake" was included in *Best American Short Stories: 1952,* and several of
her stories appeared on Martha Foley's lists of "Distinctive Short Stories" in
1948, 1951, and 1960 (Cheung 1994a, 7). She was also identified as an Asian
American writer as soon as that designation began to be used. The editors
of *Aiiieeeee!,* the first anthology to self-consciously define "Asian American"
literature, considered Yamamoto to be "Asian America's most accomplished
short story writer, as of this writing" (Chin et al. 1974, 20).

Because of this acclaim, a substantial body of critical work has been written on Yamamoto's more well-known stories, including "Seventeen Syllables" and "Yoneko's Earthquake." Some of this critical work is summative,
intended to introduce readers to Yamamoto's writing.[2] Perhaps because of
the carefully crafted, technically sophisticated nature of Yamamoto's plots,
most critics tend to produce formalist readings of her stories.[3] Certain liberal feminist scholars have also focused solely on the critique of gender
relations in Yamamoto's stories, which examine the lives of immigrant and
second-generation women and girls, as well as mother-daughter relationships; they have lauded these stories as proto-feminist.[4]

Yamamoto's stories, as I have mentioned earlier, have also been incorporated into an Asian American canon. Within an Asian American critical
tradition, there was also a summative, introductory moment, which sought
to gain recognition for Asian American literature.[5] Later critics working
within the Asian American tradition also often provided a formal reading,
but one that contextualized Yamamoto's texts within the racialization of
the United States. For example, literary scholar King-kok Cheung notes
the ways that her stories register the racism facing Japanese Americans,
both by subtly presenting the racism experienced by the characters in her
stories and by mediating the racism of the moment of their production.[6]
She notes that the formal style of "Yoneko's Earthquake" and "Seventeen
Syllables" involves muted plots, where the naive narrator's point of view
only implies certain feminist and antiracist plot lines. She attributes this to
the sexism and racism that Yamamoto faced in the 1950s, which prompted
her to submerge her subversive tendencies. This formalist reading is important because it highlights the complexity of Yamamoto's texts, and in so
doing, implies that her texts have a nonmimetic relationship to context.

My reading of Yamamoto's work elaborates on this implicit argument by considering specifically the ways these texts mediate the historical and material pressures of their context. My argument also departs from formalist readings by focusing on the ways these texts register the material histories of property dispossession and serve as sites for the production of alternative subject formations, thus refusing to see literature as transcending material and social forces.

In contrast to formalist readings, Jim Lee's insightful discussion situates Yamamoto's "A Fire in Fontana" as registering the globalization of U.S. capital in the 1980s. This process, Lee argues, restructured the political economy to more greatly immiserate racialized populations in Los Angeles, while at the same time, racialized cultures were fetishized through a discourse of multiculturalism. Lee sees Yamamoto's story as reproducing such a multiculturalist discourse, which occludes the impoverishment and exploitation of racialized populations. Yet as I argue in the introduction, race and gender are constitutive contradictions to capital, and these contradictions emerge in culture. In other words, culture is not totally and unidirectionally determined by capital, but is rather a site where capital's contradictions and incoherences emerge. Rather than seeing "A Fire in Fontana" as only and entirely enabling capital's exploitation of racialized and gendered populations, I read it as an example of how capital's exploitation of racialized and gendered difference leads to alternative modes of knowing and being.

As acclaimed as Hisaye Yamamoto's works have been, she has not been as widely and highly acknowledged as Toni Morrison. Morrison's accomplishments are so well known they need no rehearsing here. As such, the literature on Morrison is extensive.[7] In the discussion that follows, I will focus mainly on the critical response to *The Bluest Eye*. Some scholars situate Morrison in relation to a literary tradition, or contextualize her work historically; but much of the response to Morrison's first novel focuses on her critique of standards of white beauty.[8] In an essay on *The Bluest Eye, Sula,* and *Song of Solomon*, Valerie Smith argues that *The Bluest Eye* "does not undertake to explain, for example, why black Americans aspire to an unattainable standard of beauty; why they displace their self-hatred onto a communal scapegoat; how Pecola's fate might have been averted" (1993b, 274). Citing a brief passage from the novel where Claudia opts to tell *how* the story happened over *why,* Smith argues, "not only Claudia, but the novel itself, avoids 'why,' taking refuge in 'how'" (275).

I believe that if we focus *only* on the text's description of the damaging effects of racialized standards of beauty, it may indeed seem as if the text eschews the "why" over the "how." However, I would argue that the novel *does* explain "why" racialized standards of beauty exist. To understand how the text explains the "why," I argue that we must focus on the text's critique of racialized and gendered private property relations. The text articulates the ways that property relations are protected through white, middle-class domesticity, a mode of organizing social relations that depends on the patriarchal and racist disciplining of black women. One of the most prevalent disciplinary measures, as Morrison powerfully demonstrates, is the construction of unattainable standards of beauty. Thus, although it is important to attend to Morrison's explicit and biting critique of racialized standards of beauty, I focus on the novel's commentary on private property relations so we can understand the structural and historical conditions that produced such standards—in other words, to explain "how" such standards come to be.

The historical and material pressures reflected in "A Fire in Fontana" and *The Bluest Eye* stem from the fact that property rights and racialization are mutually constitutive processes in U.S. history. These processes made themselves felt through the racialized and gendered history of Asian Americans, and are connected in many ways to those processes that racialized African Americans.

Internment has traditionally been understood as the denial of the rights of citizenship, with the seizure of property being only one of several violations of due process. As important as that critique is, focusing primarily on the rights due to citizens, it has had the inadvertent effect of reifying "citizen" as a privileged category. The hypocrisy of the state in denying due process to some of its citizens is surely important, but it was through the very denial of naturalization rights, the denial of access to citizenship, that Asian immigrants were rendered an exploitable source of labor. Even a brief survey of citizenship legislation reveals the racialized and racializing nature of naturalization rights in the United States. In 1790, federal legislation was passed granting naturalization rights only to "free white persons." In 1870, Congress passed legislation granting naturalization rights to "persons of African nativity or descent" as part of Reconstruction reforms. In 1922, the U.S. Supreme Court ruled in *Ozawa v. United States* that Japanese immigrants, or *issei,* were not allowed to naturalize (Chan 1991, 47). The issei were not given naturalization rights until the efforts of the Japanese American Citizens League led to the inclusion of a clause in the 1952 McCarran-Walter Act granting rights to naturalization (Chan 1991, 142). This lack of access to citizenship, of course, did not prevent Asian Americans from bringing cases to court, from trying to attain citizenship, or from claiming their rights.[9] However, the lack of access to citizenship, combined with racist immigration exclusion legislation, kept Asian immigrants an exploited, vulnerable source of labor.[10] Thus, a critique of the denial of *substantive* rights of citizenship to the second-generation children of Japanese immigrants, or *nisei,* must always be made in conjunction with the critique of the denial of *formal* rights of citizenship to the issei.[11] The situation of the issei and nisei demonstrates how the access to property is structured by both formal and substantive rights of citizenship.

In examining the legal history of Japanese Americans, we can see how the lack of access to citizenship itself, for the issei in particular, became intimately tied to the eligibility to own property. The lack of access to naturalized citizenship for Japanese (and other Asian) immigrants was the chief legal mechanism by which property was denied. The Alien Land laws passed by the state of California in the first part of the twentieth century made eligibility for citizenship a requirement for owning agricultural property, a move calculated to dispossess Japanese immigrant farmers. The original 1913 Alien Land law and subsequent amendments eventually prohibited Japanese immigrants from owning or leasing agricultural land or stock in corporations that owned agricultural land, from bequeathing or selling agricultural land to other Japanese immigrants, and from acting as guardians of minor children who owned agricultural land, effectively barring Japanese Americans from accumulating the form of property that would have best enabled them to accrue assets.[12] The 1920 amendment to the 1913 law was designed to close loopholes and had a particularly deleterious effect on Japanese immigrant land ownership. The total agricultural land owned in 1920 by Japanese immigrants was 458,056 acres; by 1925, after the enforcement of the 1920 amendment, the total acreage had shrunk to 307,966 (Ichioka 1984, 241). The effect of the land laws was to force many Japanese immigrants back into the vulnerable and low-wage labor sector.

The Alien Land laws, ideologically as well as materially, denied property rights to Japanese immigrants and citizens alike, while further articulating and reinforcing the property rights of whites, whether citizen or alien, in the United States. Although most historians note that the phrase "aliens ineligible to citizenship" was used to target Japanese immigrant farmers, the laws as they were written in the books never actually used that phrase. Rather, the first section of the 1913 law and the 1920 amendment elaborates on *white* property rights, asserting that "all aliens *eligible* to citizenship under the laws of the United States may acquire, possess, enjoy, transmit, and inherit real property, or any interest therein, in this state, in the same manner and to the same extent as citizens of the United States except as otherwise provided by the laws of this state" (emphasis added). The second section states that "all aliens other than those mentioned in section one" have property rights as stated in treaties between the U.S. and the country to which the alien is a subject or citizen, "and not otherwise." The United States had ratified a treaty with Japan in 1911 that stated that the citizens of either nation could own commercial or residential property in the other nation. However, through an oversight, this treaty did not guarantee the ownership of agricultural land (Coletta 1967, 155). Thus, the Alien Land laws could follow the letter, if not the spirit, of the treaty, while targeting the Japanese immigrants.

The reasons for not actually using the phrase "alien ineligible for citizenship" are not clear. There was certainly much controversy over the land laws, which the Japanese government decried as discriminatory. Diplomatic tensions between the two governments ran so high during this episode that the Wilson administration, which was entertaining fears of a war between Japan and the United States (Coletta 1967, 157), dispatched then Secretary of State William Jennings Bryan to California to try to convince the California legislature to make it apply to all aliens, rather than singling out Japanese immigrants (Ferguson 1947, 182). Yet the Japanese government was not at all placated by the absence of the phrase "ineligible to citizenship," if that was why it wasn't included in the actual statute text. In practical application, the wording did not change the laws' intended effect—to single out Japanese immigrant farmers and protect white farming interests. Rather, the wording of the laws increased this effect by further articulating and reinforcing the property rights of whites over and against the people of color. That is, the Alien Land laws demonstrate how rights for whites are based on the denial of rights to people of color.

Citizenship, whiteness, and property are thus woven together, each fundamentally structuring and supporting the other. The denial of access to citizenship is an important way that whiteness and property are sutured together in U.S. law. In "Whiteness as Property" (1993), legal scholar Cheryl I. Harris describes the process by which this suturing happened. She finds that in the history of U.S. law, the concept of property is mutually constitutive of the concept of whiteness. Harris argues that through the historical processes by which African Americans were turned into property via slavery and by which Native Americans were divested of their property, "courts established whiteness as a prerequisite to the exercise of enforceable property rights." Thus "it was solely through being white that property could be acquired and secured under law" (1724). However, the law not only established whiteness as a prerequisite to owning property; it also established whiteness itself as property that white people own. Citing precedents in which law has "protected even the expectation of rights as actual legal property," Harris contends that in a racist society, white privilege becomes an expectation that is then reified as property by law (1729).[13] In this way, property is a category that cannot be divorced from whiteness in the U.S. context. Extending Harris's argument, I would contend that the experiences of Asian Americans, specifically the issei in this case, as mediated by the denial of formal citizenship and the consequent denial of access to property, must be seen as a fundamentally structuring facet of the creation and maintenance of whiteness as property.

We can thus see internment within a larger context of a series of legislative manifestations of the state's protection of white property interests through the lever of citizenship. The links between the Alien Land laws of 1913 and 1920, the 1924 Immigration Act (which barred all Asian immigration, also through the convenient mechanism of eligibility to citizenship), and internment are clear. One by-product, for example, of internment-era hysteria was a 1943 amendment to the 1920 Alien Land law enacting stricter reporting requirements for Japanese guardians of minors; another was a renewed enforcement program (E. Ferguson 1947, 188). We can thus trace the long prehistory of the internment through the Alien Land laws.

The collusion of the state and white economic interests was a foundational principle structuring internment. Japanese Americans on the West Coast during World War II had their assets frozen and were given only one week to dispose of their property. Internment of the Japanese Americans was thus obviously not a military necessity, but was instead economically advantageous. For example, during the post–Pearl Harbor anti-Japanese hysteria, the white agricultural associations in California agitated for Japanese evacuation and internment using the same rhetoric used in earlier decades to justify the Alien Land laws. The economic ulterior motive was clearly demonstrated a few months after the passage of Executive Order 9066, when the managing secretary of the Grower-Shippers Vegetable Association was quoted in the *Saturday Evening Post:*

> We're charged with wanting to get rid of the Japs for selfish reasons. We might as well be honest. We do. It's a question of whether the white man lives on the Pacific Coast or the brown men. They came into this valley to work, and they stayed to take over. . . . They undersell the white man in the markets. . . . They work their women and children while the white farmer has to pay wages for his help. If all the Japs were removed tomorrow, we'd never miss them in two weeks, because the white farmers can take over and produce everything the Jap grows. (tenBroek, Barnhart, and Matson 1954, 80)

Internment is thus arguably the most blatant example of how one must be white to have rights to property that are maintained and supported by the state. Indeed, the state was the very agency through which Japanese Americans were divested of their property.

This statement also demonstrates how the protection of private property and the maintenance of the white nuclear family are closely imbricated. Chandan Reddy (1998) notes that the discourses of the "family wage" or the "American Standard of Living" developed in opposition to the "Oriental Standard of Living"; while the wages of the white male worker were purportedly being raised so he could support his family, women's wages were simultaneously depressed, and the differential wage scale between white men and nonwhite laborers was justified. The rationale contending that Chinese laborers, for example, could be paid less because they did not have to support wives and children erased the material realities of immigration and antimiscegenation laws, which had effectively prevented the formation of Chinese American families. Reddy notes that these discourses attempted to transform individuals into "subjects as equivalent units of abstract labor" (360), ignoring the historical differences that enabled the white male worker to form a family while preventing the Asian immigrant male worker from doing so. This imposed a narrative of development and progress—from the "backward" Asian laborer without a family to the more "progressive" white family norm—onto what was intrinsically an uneven process dependent on the creation and maintenance of informal and vulnerable racialized and gendered labor forces. From the perspective of people of color, then, the supposed universality of the "family wage" or "American Standard of Living," as well as the concept of the "home" it raises, is impossible to attain, simply because it is defined against them.

Though specifically centering on discourses around Chinese immigrant labor at the beginning of the twentieth century, Reddy's analysis is also useful for examining the statement made by the Grower-Shippers managing secretary in 1942. Claiming that the labor of Japanese American women and children put white farmers at a competitive disadvantage, which the state could then remedy through internment, he simultaneously defended the white farmers' need for a "family wage" while erasing the effects of racist policies and exclusionist legislation (such as the Alien Land laws), which made Japanese-run farms require full-family participation, including the labor of children and women. The limits of citizenship, then, are delineated via the laboring bodies of women of color, by defining "American" families, whose children and women do not labor, against "non-American" families, which are defined by fact that the women and children do perform labor. Simultaneously, this statement erases the domestic labor done by women *within the home,* as it is not really labor, while also making perfectly clear *which* homes and *which* families must be protected by the state, and indeed, which homes and families can even be defined as such. Thus, "private sphere" and "private property" are inextricably linked and mutually constitutive.

The property dispossession that Japanese Americans experienced through the struggles over who was a "citizen" and who was an "alien" was experienced by African Americans as bars to the suburban home, the late twentieth-century embodiment of domesticity, which was the foundation for the racialized access to education, medical care, and stable employment—all the structures that guarantee life chances.[14] As corporations relocated their manufacturing operations overseas, devastating the urban industrial bases, suburbanization became the new form of segregation. However, the literature on African American property dispossession makes abundantly clear that suburbanization is a part of a longer history, in which the denial of property rights to African Americans was orchestrated through denial to middle-class domesticity, and which created domesticity as white.

When the abolishment of de jure segregation did not bring about integration, many whites found comfort in believing that the continuation of segregation was a matter of choice—black people preferred to live among other blacks, and whites preferred to live with whites.[15] In reality, de facto segregation was as purposeful and state-backed as the de jure segregation of previous eras. As sociologists Douglas Massey and Nancy Ann Denton note, "This extreme racial isolation did not just happen; it was manufactured by whites through a series of self-conscious actions and purposeful institutional arrangements" (1993, 2). Along these lines, historian George Lipsitz details the consolidation of white privilege based on de facto segregation, the foundations of which were laid during the New Deal era with the passage of the Federal Housing Act of 1934. Lipsitz notes that "by channeling loans away from older inner-city neighborhoods and toward white home buyers moving into segregated suburbs, the FHA and private lenders after World War II aided and abetted the growth and development of increased segregation in U.S. residential neighborhoods" (1995, 373). Segregation is thus a means of concentrating poverty in certain racialized communities; it results in an inability to accumulate wealth through property while impacting incomes through a lack of access or reduced access to education and jobs. Even African Americans with enough income to buy housing could only buy in certain segregated neighborhoods, where property values tended to drop rather than rise. This made the accumulation of wealth for African Americans incommensurate with their incomes when compared to whites.

In recent decades, however, segregation has increasingly meant suburbanization. This has not a little to do with the devastation of the urban centers that came with the global restructuring of production. The urban centers, long the sites of industrial production, were hit the hardest when corporations began to move their production facilities overseas. With the lack of commercial tax revenues and high-wage, protected employment, the urban centers became increasingly less appealing to potential home owners. Those who could afford to leave—mainly whites, due to racist lending policies by private institutions, in conjunction with racist federal legislation—fled to the suburbs.

The impact of the combined implication of private property, suburbanization, and racialization can be seen in Yamamoto's "A Fire in Fontana." In the story, suburbanization becomes a locus of contradiction for Yamamoto, who describes herself as a middle-class housewife watching the urban unrest in Watts in 1965 on television: "So it was that, in between putting another load of clothes into the automatic washer, ironing, maybe whipping up some tacos for supper, I watched the Watts riots on television. Back then, I was still middle-aged, sitting safely in a house which was located on a street where panic would be the order of the day if a Black family should happen to move in" (2001, 157). In her descriptions of the "burning and looting" of the Watts riots, Yamamoto could have very well excised the rather inconvenient details of her comfortable life in a middle-class white suburban house, complete with all the amenities available to a consuming public (automatic washer, iron, television set). Instead, she foregrounds these details, thematizing her complex and conflicted location through a description of her reaction: "Appalled, inwardly cowering, I watched the burning and looting on the screen and heard the reports of the dead and wounded. But beneath all my distress, I felt something else, a tiny trickle of warmth which I finally recognized as an undercurrent of exultation" (157).

The televised image of urban uprising in Watts was a profoundly formative national moment that served to interpellate the citizen of a nation undergoing the "new segregation" structured around the racialized separation of inner city and suburb. Televised images serve as complex mediators of memory. Although usually represented from a journalistic, omniscient viewpoint and taken as "objective" proof of an event, televised images actually enable narrative closure and facilitate forgetting by imposing a narrative. The image of the African American violence serves as an interpellating mechanism for the citizen. Cultural critic Marita Sturken notes, "When Americans watch events of 'national' importance . . . on television, they perceive themselves to be part of a national audience. . . . Citizenship can thus be enacted through live television" (1997, 13–14). Not surprisingly, the subject interpellated by the coverage of the Watts riot is the citizen of liberal democracy, that is, a property-owning, white, middle-class, male. For rather than communicating that the destruction of property during the uprising is a material trace of the long history of denying property rights to people of color, the brief televised image inverts causality. The lack of respect for property explains the denial of property rights, and not the other way around. It rationalizes racially stratified segregation and suburbanization through the specter of black criminality. It makes white flight right by showing the need to defend the sanctity of the domestic, supposedly "private," sphere of the suburban home—embodied in the figure of the stay-at-home wife—from the ravages of the animalistic brutality of blacks. However, we can see how this criminalization of black communities results from liberal democracy's privileging of the sanctity of private property. If the purpose of the state is to protect property relations, criminality then becomes defined as the threat to private property.

The narrator's conflicted reaction reflects her contradictory location. Because she is materially benefiting from suburbanization, as thematized by her location as the viewer, she is interpellated. She is "appalled, inwardly cowering." However, because of her memory of how citizenship and property rights were denied to Japanese Americans, and indeed, how citizenship and property in the United States had been defined by this very denial, she cannot completely participate. She cannot completely be interpellated as citizen, as property owner, though she is officially both of these things. Her contestatory location does not allow this image to resolve for her the fundamental contradictions of citizenship in a liberal democracy.

Her contradictory reaction also signals her ambivalent position vis à vis the suburban, nuclear home. The protection of her safety and virtue from the ravages of the black criminality represented on television is ostensibly that which justifies segregation and suburbanization. Yet the middle-class, nuclear family can only exist when nonwhite and immigrant labor is rendered into vulnerable, informal, unregulated labor forces (against which the "American Standard of Living" or the "family wage" can be instituted), when the labor of women in the home is devalued as "not really work," and when the labor of women of color is erased. As a housewife in an affluent suburb, she repeats the devaluation of women's work: she sees herself "whipping up some tacos for dinner," negating the labor-intensive and time-consuming nature of cooking. Yet her litany of the multiple tasks of her day, from laundry to ironing to cooking, reveals the impossibility of envisioning herself apart from the work she performs. Of course, the mere representation of the devaluation of women's work in the home may not in itself challenge the valorization of the white, middle-class heterosexual home. Sociologist Evelyn Nakano Glenn notes that the focus of Marxist feminists on unwaged domestic labor in the home reifies white, middle-class heterosexual domesticity by ignoring how the very construction of that home depends on the *waged* domestic labor of women of color. However, Yamamoto's experience as a housewife does not transcend her racialization.

We have seen earlier that the American family (supported by the "American Standard of Living" or the "family wage") exists only as it excludes non-whites, and this exclusion is rationalized by the fact that women and children of color labor, while the women and children of "proper," "American" families do not. In addition, the defense of the chastity of women from the supposed threat posed by men of color has only been to "protect" white women. Women of color have never been the benefactors of state-enforced protection. Rather, as Angela Davis has noted, the punishment inflicted on the black rapist for the supposed violation of white women has been predicated on erasing the threat to black women from white men (1981, 201). This history of racialized and gendered dispossession thus plays an integral part in the narrator's contradictory response to the events before her, making her unable to fully accept the dominant interpretation.

Yamamoto must instead offer a counter-image of a fire in Fontana, a family dying in flames, which again reverses causality from that offered by the televised image of the Watts uprising. She writes:

> To me, the tumult in the city was the long awaited, gratifying next chapter of an old movie that had flickered about in the back of my mind for years. In the film, shot in the dark of about three o'clock in the morning, there was this modest house in the country. Suddenly, the house was in flames and there were the sound effects of the fire roaring and leaping skyward. Then there could be heard the voices of a man and a woman screaming, and the voices of two small children as well. (2001, 157)

She offers a moment that does not serve as a defining national moment, one that does not and cannot interpellate the citizen because it does not allow for resolution, but instead reveals the contradictions of a liberal democratic state that promises equality while foreclosing its very possibility. She offers an image of an event not captured by cameras, one that "objective" journalism did not cover, in a move that displaces the hegemonic interpretation of the televised image of the Watts riots. In referencing the fire in Fontana, she calls into memory the history of violence underlying residential segregation.

The narrator's experience with the contradictions revealed by her forays into journalism also contribute to both her participation in, and skepticism about the events presented through televised media. During the narrator's stint at the *Los Angeles Tribune,* shortly after World War II, an African American man, Mr. Short, came to the paper to try to publicize his story. His purchase of a home in the segregated city of Fontana had been met with "threats of 'get-out-or-else' and his family was living in fear" (2001, 153).

Given the story by a busy editor, she writes, as an "unbiased" journalist, "a calm, impartial story about the threats Short described, using 'alleged' and 'claimed,' and other cautious journalese" (2001, 154). She critiques this response retrospectively. Although Short came to the *Tribune* in an attempt to mobilize the African American community, the manner in which the narrator actually wrote the story would have ensured that "[a]nyone noticing the story about the unwanted family in Fontana would have taken it with a grain of salt" (2001, 154). Because she had written this story before the firebombing happened, she had had the opportunity to save the Short family. If she had written a story that conveyed the Shorts' urgency, instead of placing their desperation in doubt, she implies, the story might have generated enough reaction in the African American community to prevent the Short family's deaths. By critiquing her actions, which were, after all, what she as a reporter was supposed to do, she implicitly critiques the very notion of "journalistic objectivity," which supported dominant ideologies by failing to expose or refute them.

Journalistic objectivity mandates the disappearance of the subject in the writing of the text. In this way, the language of journalism approximates the language of the state, which similarly attempts to erase the particularities of subjects by maintaining the concept of the abstract citizen. Journalistic objectivity thus supports the processes through which the state is able to maintain its pretense of disinterested equality for all citizens while hypocritically denying property rights to all but the most privileged few. Because the narrator, as a journalist, was once complicit with the state's attempts to naturalize its own ideology, she demonstrates that failing to resist this attempt can undermine the possibility of a basis for solidarity among people of color. Ironically, at the moment when, as the only Japanese American at an African American newspaper, she was expected to bridge the two communities, she finds herself supporting the very ideologies that make coalition impossible.

To avoid complying with racism, objectivity must be refused for an antiracist stance. The memoir, in eschewing journalistic neutrality for subjective autobiographical writing, the generic conventions of which require the specification of the author's fixed social location, allows for a different kind of intervention, one that critiques, rather than supports, the maintenance of the racist state. She ends the memoir with the image of the dying family, prompted by her viewing of the Watts riots from the safety of her home.

By ending the memoir with this graphic description, quite unlike the staid prose of "objective" journalism, the narrator attempts to communicate the urgency that her earlier journalistic writing had failed to do. The memoir is posited as a site of personal memory that counters the ways that official histories, here represented by journalism, erase the histories of people of color. The article she wrote some forty years earlier in "cautious journalese" is first mentioned as the last anecdote in a series of stories about the attempt of state apparatuses to facilitate forgetting, demonstrating how ideological and repressive state apparatuses work together to do so: the police deem the fire a suicide and close the case, and a priest who writes a play about the event is "suddenly transferred to a parish somewhere in the boondocks of Arizona" (154). The only way to counter this erasure is through the narrator's memory, recalled through the act of writing the memoir; after she gets the news of the death of the family in Fontana, she remembers feeling as if there were "something forgotten which should have been remembered" (154). Forty years later, this memoir remembers what had previously been forgotten.

This act of willful remembering is, on one level, the narrator's solution to her own personal dilemma. After her reportage on the family in Fontana, the narrator finds unbearable the helplessness she feels in the face of unavoidable and recurring reminders of the racializing property system. Hospitalized for an undisclosed illness, she lies next to a woman whose brother confides to her that "he kn[ows] it's wrong, but he didn't want Blacks moving into his neighborhood in Alhambra—no Moors in Alhambra?—because of the drop in property values that would ensue" (373). With her ironic question—"no Moors in Alhambra?"—which bursts through and interrupts her summary of the man's statement, she notes the hypocrisy of naming an all-white town after the famed city in Spain built by African invaders. This seemingly flippant and sarcastic question also disinters the buried legacies of Spanish colonialism, as well as the acquisition of wealth and property, including what is now Los Angeles, through the expansionism of the U.S.–Mexican War. Like the names of streets and towns, and the "Spanish-style" architecture so common in California, the name of the incorporated municipality of "Alhambra" is a facile, sanitized signifier that references the history of Los Angeles—a history of violent conflicts over property—in a palatable manner.

Other contradictions over property add to her growing sense of helplessness and anger:

> An attractive Korean lady friend and real estate agent put her children into Catholic schools because, as her daughter explained it, the public schools hereabouts were "integrated," while on the other hand she winsomely urged local real estate onto Black clients because, as she explained to me, "it's the coming thing," and her considerable profits ("It's been very good to me") made possible her upward mobility into less integrated areas. (373)

Although the narrator details other critical conversations she's had with friends, she does not report her response to this hypocritical friend. Rather, this is the point at which she notes her response to the Watts riots, and then concludes the story with her act of remembering. Her response—at long last discovered—to the contradictions embodied in herself, the Korean real estate agent, and the property system, is the act of remembering.

Personal memory, however, also becomes a collective memory in the form of this memoir, which can be read not only as the narrator's personal response, but as a device to mobilize people to form cross-race alliances. The family in Fontana, however, has already perished and this sense of urgency comes too late to protect them. Also, she seems to imply, the unrest symbolized by the uprising in Watts provides, if not necessarily "justice," then a reciprocal violence for the firebombing in Fontana and, by extension, the state-sponsored violence of segregation, internment, and the denial of the rights of citizenship to people of color. The uprising in Watts demonstrates the disregard for the sanctity of private property by a collectivity of people—people of color—to whom private property has always been denied. If this is indeed the case, what alarm can this story spread and what good can it still do? What is the intended effect of this memoir?

One way to get at the answer is to consider the moment of production. This memoir about Los Angeles in the 1940s and 1960s was written in 1985, during the height of the movement for redress and reparations for the internment of Japanese Americans during World War II. The redress movement was one that mobilized many Japanese Americans of all generations, many of whom spoke about internment for the first time since World War II. Many interpreted the aim of redress, however, as correcting an anomalous injustice that had occurred in the operation of a Constitution that was structurally egalitarian. One text on redress entitled *Repairing America* (a title suggestive in itself) states, "[W]e believe that a little group, with little more than its remembered pain and desire to have its grievances redressed, can act to repair a breach in our democratic society. . . . Our movement has become our legacy to America, our contribution to American democracy" (Hohri 1988, 225). Yamamoto's story emerges at a moment when hope that the rights of citizenship could be gained through the American democratic process fueled a major movement within the Japanese American community. Her cautionary tale recalls the impossibility of equality in American democracy. The very "remembered pain" that Hohri names as the driving force of the redress movement gives rise to Yamamoto's story. It reminds us of the unresolvable contradiction inherent in demanding equal rights for people of color from a system created to protect white property rights.

Another clue to the intended effect of this memoir is its nonresolution. The story ends with the image of the family in flames, included to imply that there is still, to this day, no resolution to the events that precipitated this violence. If the newspaper article can contribute to the maintenance of the state-sponsored racism of segregation, this memoir can likewise critique it. Yet even at this moment, where the memoir suggests a basis for cross-race solidarity through the creation of an alternative collective memory, it thematizes difference. While Yamamoto "remembers" something she did not witness—the fire in Fontana—and in so doing proposes the possibility of cross-race identifications, she foregrounds the mediated and distanced nature of any such activity by using the language of film. Describing the scene as the "next chapter of an old movie that had flickered about in the back of my mind for years," she stages her distance and difference at the very moment that she bridges this difference. This memoir thus maintains to the very end its strategy of keeping identification and disidentification, similarity and difference, constantly in balance.

"A Fire in Fontana" undermines an aesthetic of resolution in a way that resists incorporation into a narrative of development. Though the form of the autobiographical memoir conventionally demands a narrative of development that constitutes a mature, coherent subject looking back on a linear history, the telos of which is this subject, this memoir refuses such a linearity through its nonchronological narrative. Situating the fire in Fontana chronologically at the middle of the narrative would constitute it as the crisis or climax of the story, which then would be resolved later through the narrator's incorporation into the marriage plot; the loss of property for the African American family is unfortunate, but ultimately negated by the narrator's gaining property through marriage. Such a resolution would enable the erasure of material histories and would level the historical differences between this African American family and Yamamoto's Japanese American narrator. Instead, the placement of the death of the family at the end of the memoir locates this event as resistant to resolution, as the violence that splits the property-less subject and denies this subject wholeness. As such, we can see why this text looks to the future for new forms of community that allow for cross-race coalitions, rather than finding them in the present. In "A Fire in Fontana," the racialized and gendered subject cannot form communities based on the erasure of difference and the insistence on equivalence. But what such a community may look like, the text can only imagine as a creation of the future, not of the present.

The Bluest Eye also thematizes the impossibility of domesticity as a narrative of resolution for African Americans, but it registers a longing for such a resolution. Partially narrated by a preadolescent girl and focusing on the experiences of this girl, Claudia, and her friend Pecola, Morrison's text has many of the elements of a narrative of a girl's journey into mature womanhood: the first menstrual flow, socialization experienced as racialized, classed, and gendered disciplining in the family and at school, the first glimpses of adult sexual life. The differences in Claudia's formation and Pecola's lie in their different distance from domesticity. For Morrison, normative domesticity is the mechanism for the racialization and dispossession of African Americans through the construction and eradication of difference, coded as "excess." Thus, African Americans are held at a distance from domesticity. In the character of Claudia, who experiences racialization as being terrorized by the threat of dispossession and the loss of the domestic home, the text creates an unfulfilled longing for a particular kind of privatized domesticity to resolve racialized, gendered, and classed contradictions. Claudia experiences property as tenuous and not guaranteed; in effect, not property, which means control and security. Pecola's only experience is of actual dispossession (rather than the threat of it); she has never had a domestic, privatized home to begin with. Yet this completely alternative subject is rendered illegible and untenable as she descends into madness. The impossibility of developmental formation is underscored again and again in this novel through the character of Pecola, who is even described as a seed that never came to flower. Through this character, the text demonstrates the impossibility of a whole, propertied subject.

The Bluest Eye opens with a critique of white, middle-class domesticity, a critique that underscores the impossibility of this narrative for African Americans. The oft-analyzed opening of the novel is a version of the "Dick and Jane" primers used to teach children to read. This story, which involves Dick, Jane, their "nice" mother, their "big and strong" father, their "pretty green-and-white house," and assorted pets, establishes an idealized version of the white, middle-class, modern nuclear family (Morrison 1970, 4). In this idealized story, childhood is protected and innocent, and gender roles are clearly defined. The relationship between normative gendering, nuclear family relations, and property is drawn immediately. The first line of the "Dick and Jane" story (which is also the first line of the novel itself) is "Here is the house." From the house derives the family, and the text proceeds from there: "It is green and white. It has a red door. It is very pretty. Mother, Father, Dick, and Jane live in the green-and-white house. They are very happy" (4). Yet this impossibly idealized version of wholesome domestic relations begins to break down immediately. Morrison repeats the entire text of this Dick and Jane story two more times, one right after the other, first with no punctuation and capital letters, and then enjambed, with no spaces. Each subsequent chapter that is not narrated in the first person by Claudia McTeer begins with a brief section of this story, enjambed, fragmented, and thus rendered nonsensical and confusing. The section of the "Dick and Jane" story that introduces these chapters roughly corresponds to the subject of the chapter as its idealized opposite. For example, the first chapter not narrated by Claudia McTeer is introduced with this section of the story:

HEREISTHEHOUSEIT IS GREENANDWH
ITEITHASAREDDOORITISVERYPRETT
YITISVERYPRETTYPRETTYPRETTYP (33)

The chapter following this epigraph of sorts describes the Breedloves' house, which is as unlike the norm as it possibly could be. When juxtaposed with the material circumstances of African Americans, Morrison demonstrates, it is the ideal—and not the lived experiences of African Americans—that breaks down, makes no sense, and loses its explanatory potential. This theme gets elaborated further throughout the novel, as Morrison details the destructive consequences of valuing the nuclear family norm and the structures of private property that give it material and ideological weight.

The beginning of the first chapter after this "Dick and Jane" preface immediately intervenes in this story's articulation of the mutual dependence of middle-class domesticity, whiteness, and property. Claudia McTeer's story emphasizes what the "Dick and Jane" story leaves out. For Claudia, a nine-year-old African American girl growing up in a working-class family, the intersection of race and gender is experienced as the profound impossibility of ownership. Even Claudia's description of her and her sister Frieda's quotidian existence underscores this impossibility:

> Rosemary Villanucci, our next-door friend who lives above her father's cafe, sits in a 1939 Buick eating bread and butter. . . . We stare at her, wanting her bread, but more than that wanting to poke the arrogance out of her eyes and smash the pride of ownership that curls her chewing mouth. When she comes out of the car, we will beat her up, make red marks on her white skin, and she will cry and ask us do we want to pull her pants down. We will say no. We don't know what we should feel or do if she does, but whenever she asks us, we know she is offering us something precious and that our own pride must be asserted by refusing to accept. (9)

Rosemary Villanucci is herself obviously of a different class than the children of the "Dick and Jane" story. Her father most likely derives his income from the local industry—Zick's Coal Mine—whose workers compose his clientele. Although the Villanuccis are *working-class* whites, whiteness connotes ownership. Rosemary Villanucci "owns" more than the bread and butter or the 1939 Buick, however, as this passage deftly demonstrates. Her white femininity is ascribed value through its vulnerability. Claudia and Frieda are positioned as estranged from this particular form of vulnerable white femininity, so much so that they are positioned as threats to Rosemary Villanucci's "virtue" in her muddled yet somehow compelling logic (compelling because it reiterates the underlying structures of racialization that structure Claudia and Frieda's lives). This scene underscores the ways that white femininity, because it can be understood as vulnerable, is protectable (though often not protected in practice). Black women's and girls' bodies, however, are not even valued, and thus are not constructed as something to protect. This renders black women and girls even more vulnerable, as we see later in Cholly Breedlove's rape of his daughter Pecola, and Mr. Henry's molestation of Frieda. Given that these are the conditions that structure Claudia and Frieda's lives, their anger at Rosemary's "pride of ownership" reflects more than petty childish jealousy. Their reaction to Rosemary's act of offering to them the most valuable of all of her possessions—more precious than bread and butter or a seat in the Buick—is their refusal to acknowledge its value, and to establish centrally their own worth, to preserve their "own pride."

This struggle to resist the valuation of white femininity at the expense of black femininity is, of course, a preoccupation of the text. Claudia's "unsullied hatred" for Shirley Temple and her white baby doll (and, by extension, all white girls) gives way grudgingly, "from pristine sadism, to fabricated hatred, to fraudulent love" once she realizes that "adults, older girls, shops, magazines, newspapers, window signs—all the world agreed" (20–23) that white beauty was the standard. Family and community ("adults, older girls"), the ideological apparatuses of the state ("magazines, newspapers"), and market forces ("window signs") working in concert are too much for a young African American girl to resist. Other little girls, like Pecola Breedlove, do not even try to offer any kind of resistance to this value system.

This scene thus describes at the very beginning of the novel the processes that the text takes up. The novel demonstrates the link between white, middle-class domesticity and property and then shows how racialized and gendered subjects are formed differentially through the disciplinary mechanism of the dispossession of property and the lack of property rights. In the following reading, I focus particularly on the production of African American *femininities* in relation to different kinds of domestic spaces.

Morrison's novel highlights the ways that "proper" domestic arrangements are those that produce, and are produced by, "properly" gendered subjects. But these gendered subjects are racialized. That is, to be "properly" a white woman is not the same formation to be "properly" a black woman. This is particularly emphasized in Morrison's description of Geraldine, who is not important as an individual, but as the embodiment of a certain class of women, these "girls" who are "properly" formed African American women.

These light-skinned "sugar-brown girls" are the models of good behavior, "not fretful, nervous, or shrill," and "as sweet and as plain as buttercake" (82). These women "learn how to do the white man's work with refinement" and keep their own houses orderly, mannered, and clean (83).

There is, however, a destructive consequence of privileging and assimilating to middle-class domesticity. These women have so completely internalized the standards of proper femininity that they take upon themselves the task of disciplining others.[16] This conception of women as moral arbiters is fundamentally necessary to the form of domesticity to which Geraldine ascribes. This role stems from the nineteenth-century "cult of true womanhood," which narrated the emerging form of modern domestic relations through the separation of spheres. That is, women were the guardians of morality, since they, unlike their male counterparts—their husbands—were supposedly protected from the immorality of the "public" sphere of work in a competitive and savage economic market. Thus rendered the paragons of morality, women were charged with the duty of raising their children to be proper, ethical subjects. We can see Geraldine carrying out this duty scrupulously. The kind of domestic space produced and inhabited by women like Geraldine is inviting in its security, its efficiency. But the men who marry these women, and the children they produce, are domesticated by them: "[T]his plain brown girl will build her nest stick by stick, make it her own inviolable world, and stand guard over its every plant, weed, and doily, even against him" (84).

The attempt to assimilate to middle-class domesticity does not only involve the relentless regulation of Geraldine's own family in an effort to reproduce appropriate subjects, but also manifests itself as brutal anger against those "improper" subjects against whom she is defined. For the Geraldines of the world, Pecola represents the exact opposite of proper domesticity, rather than the product of it. When Geraldine finds Pecola in her house, she sees only that Pecola is poor, unkempt, and uncared-for. In Pecola, Geraldine sees an entire class of people who live "like flies," the girls who "grew up knowing nothing of girdles" and the boys who "announced their manhood by turning the bills of their caps backward" (92). Geraldine's response to Pecola, whom Geraldine mistakenly thinks has killed her cat, is: "You nasty little black bitch. Get out of my house" (92). The very expressions of Geraldine's hatred for Pecola offer insight into the shape and form of her character. She despises these people for whom development into adulthood does not mean the internalization of discipline: either the bodily discipline of the girdle for women or the disciplining mechanisms of work and responsibility for men. She is confronted with a mode of development that is outside her influence, her role: to ensure the formation of proper, responsible subjects. Thus confronted, she can only understand it as deviant, worthy of hate, and needing discipline. Her articulation of distaste at Pecola's "blackness" collapses the categories of dirt, skin color, and morality.

The disciplining of others is articulated as the fight to eradicate "eruptions of funk," or in other words, any form of excess: "Wherever it erupts, this Funk, they wipe it away. . . . The laugh that is a little too loud; the enunciation a little too round; the gesture a little too generous. They hold their behind in for fear of a sway too free; when they wear lipstick, they never cover the entire mouth for fear of lips too thick, and they worry, worry, worry about the edges of their hair" (83). They are the most vigilant enforcers of moderate behavior. They attempt to conform to the standards of beauty that demand the effacement of any trace of physical specificity. These women attempt to replicate the ideal of privatized, middle-class domesticity by erasing any trace of difference, which is articulated and experienced by them as excess.

The consequences of "excess" are clearly delineated for African Americans in Lorraine, Ohio, in 1941, so clearly that even a nine-year-old knows them intimately. Claudia lives in mortal fear of being "put outdoors," of becoming homeless (a state that Pecola actually experiences). This state, in which a lack of privacy, of domesticity, means lack of property, is the "real terror of life" (17). The fear of this property-less, privacy-less existence regulates behavior: "the threat of being outdoors surfaced frequently in those days. Every possibility of excess was curtailed with it. If somebody ate too much, he could end up outdoors. If somebody used too much coal, he could end up outdoors. People could gamble themselves outdoors, drink themselves outdoors" (17). This excessive behavior echoes precisely the "eruptions of funk" that Geraldine has dedicated her life to eradicating. This relationship between "proper" and "property" demonstrates that gendered and racialized subjects are always formed through the threat of dispossession and the lack of rights to property.

The concept of "excess" itself implies a normative subject. To ascribe to this subject position, African American "excess" must be curtailed. This normative subject is obviously a white subject whose physical attributes would never make them worry about "a sway too free"; a male subject whose sexuality wouldn't need to be protected, but who would instead be the protector; and such a subject would never be threatened by the possibility of dispossession, because they would have no excess that would need to be punished through being "put outdoors." This normative, excess-less subject is white, male, and propertied. However, this subject is defined only negatively, against the "deviant" African American subjects. We can see, then, why the idealized "Dick and Jane" domesticity, predicated on such a negatively defined subject, breaks down when held against the material conditions of African American lives. However, the violence of such an ideal and the structures that support it are the mechanisms of African American racialization.

These "proper" subjects are formed by internalizing such threats of dispossession to such an extent that this fear guides all behavior. In this way, Claudia, who internalizes this fear, is in some ways a "proper" subject. Yet *The Bluest Eye* also describes other kinds of subjects, excessive subjects. These "properly" formed subjects have their "improper" opposites, who have not internalized such standards and thus behave in ways that fall under state regulation. For example, the state intervenes in the Breedloves' destructive family, jailing Cholly for burning down his house and temporarily putting Pecola in the McTeers' custody.

The Breedloves epitomize the "improper" subject in this novel. They cannot even attempt to reproduce protected, middle-class domesticity like Geraldine, whose domestic arrangements are the opposite of the Breedloves'. Instead, their lives demonstrate the ways that the private is not possible. In this light, we can revisit the chapter in which we are first introduced to the Breedloves. Morrison immediately contextualizes the Breedloves by emphasizing that the Breedloves do not constitute a "family" in the usual sense. She begins by describing their house, which is not a house like the "green-and-white" house, but an abandoned storefront. Instead of then introducing the history of the family, its lineage, and its history, Morrison can only situate the Breedloves in relation to the history of the storefront, a backward chronology that begins after the Breedloves move out. A pizza parlor, a baker, a real estate office, and a gypsy family occupy this building after the Breedloves, pointing to both the periods of boom and bust in Lorraine and the interchangeability of "public" businesses and "private" residences. The arrangement of the Breedloves' living space also demonstrates the impossibility of "privacy" in a home where parents and children sleep together, eat together, and exist together in the bedroom "where all the living was done" (35). The toilet bowl is "inaccessible to the eye, if not the ear," and thus only semiprivate. Pecola and Sammy, eleven and thirteen years old, respectively, sleep (or try to sleep) in the same space in which their parents have sex. Their living situation is the epitome of "excess," of immoderate and unregulated behavior. Their domestic space is thus unprotected from violent incursions by the state and by poverty; indeed, it is marked by its constant vulnerability.

In such a context, ownership is also impossible. As I have argued, the negative consequence of excessive behavior—denoted by the inability to conform to middle-class, privatized domesticity—is the threat of the dispossession of property and the lack of property rights. The Breedloves' relationships to the objects they supposedly "own" do not produce the "pride of ownership" of Rosemary Villanucci, but rather a sense of hopelessness and futility. The objects provide "no memories to be cherished" (36). Morrison illustrates this with the example of the Breedloves' sofa, which was bought new but damaged by time of delivery, leaving them to pay "$4.80 a month for a sofa that started off split, no good, and humiliating," and creating a situation where "you couldn't take any joy in owning it" (36). For the Breedloves, who do not even own the sofa outright but must pay for it in installments, "ownership" does not mean that one has control over one's property and one's person to do what one wills; instead, "ownership" is yet another reminder of their utter vulnerability to poverty, to a complete lack of control that structures their lives. In this way, the history that is written into property relations, and the property relations that are written into history, are inaccessible for African Americans. Morrison writes, "The furniture had aged without ever having become familiar. . . . There were no memories among those pieces. Certainly no memories to be cherished" (35, 36). As subjects for whom "choice" or the exercise of will is thus rendered impossible, the Breedloves are forever immature. Cholly and Mrs. Breedlove's parental authority over their children is taken away by the state, for example, while Mrs. Breedlove is infantilized by her employers, who call her "Polly."

The Breedloves are destroyed by the confluence of these forces. In this novel, the lack of access to the propertied category of domesticity and privacy result in utter chaos and violence: rape and incest. But the text can also imagine other ways of structuring social relations that do not try to either replicate white middle-class domesticity or crumble under the weight of failure to conform to this domesticity. The three prostitutes who live and work above the Breedloves' storefront home, for example, maintain a "domestic" space that does not attempt to reconstruct the separation of public and private. Yet this version of the home is capable of nurturing and caring for Pecola, unlike the Breedloves' home. The prostitutes' home, however, is one that fills Claudia with unspeakable terror and is utterly inaccessible to her.

Claudia does eschew ownership for memory and community. Although Claudia describes the ways in which "knowing that there was such a thing as outdoors bred in us a hunger for property, for ownership" (18), her own desires speak to quite different possibilities. Claudia rejects the white baby doll she's given at Christmas and says:

> I did not know why I destroyed those dolls. But I did know that nobody ever asked me what I wanted for Christmas. . . . The real question would have been, "Dear Claudia, what experience would you like on Christmas?" I could have spoken up, "I want to sit on the low stool in Big Mama's kitchen with my lap full of lilacs and listen to Big Papa play his violin for me alone." (21)

Memory, as we saw in the case of the Breedloves' couch, does not inhere in relationships of ownership for African Americans in Morrison's novel. Property ownership does not narrate the history of a subject formed through the *dispossession* of property. For such subjects, histories must be sought elsewhere, in memories of social relations that are not predicated on the protection of property relations. Yet we can also see that Claudia longs for a version of domesticity that may not be structured around the desire to "possess any object," but which is privatized and protected. Claudia's nostalgic longing for such forms of domesticity make her unable to recognize the community formed by the prostitutes as anything other than a monstrosity. Claudia's longing also underscores the unattainability of such a version of domesticity for proletarianized African American women. Yet in this novel, the alternative to such a subject formed through desire for domesticity is Pecola, who is unable to form community with anyone except the imaginary friend who shares only her desperate valorization of white ideals of beauty.

Morrison's and Yamamoto's texts thus underscore the importance of subjects forming collectively that—unlike the collectivity of citizens called the
nation-state—do not have as their purpose the protection of property. These
texts demonstrate that if the nation-state formally requires all citizens to be
homogeneous and equivalent in their property-owning status, these alternative communities formed by subjects through the lack of property ownership need to forge solidarities across difference. Morrison's and Yamamoto's
texts remind us of the impossibility of resolution, identification, and equivalence, and delineate an imperative to find ways to form collectivities based
on difference. Their disruption of the narrative of development allows them
to articulate the material histories of segregation, racialized and gendered
labor exploitation, and dispossession through the valance of citizenship.
As such, they lay the groundwork for the articulation of alternative forms
of community.

PART II

chapter 3

BAD WORKERS, WORSE CONSUMERS:
U.S. IMPERIALISM AND THE TROUBLE
WITH INDUSTRIAL LABOR

Dick Savage, one of the many characters in John Dos Passos's trilogy *U.S.A.,* exclaims, "We've got to break the whole idea . . . into its component parts" (1171). Savage, a dissipated and weak-willed public relations flack, seems hardly the type to come up with a description of what could arguably be called the dominant episteme of his era. Indeed, Savage, a would-be writer turned PR executive, comes up with this strategy for marketing "Doc" Bingham's dubiously effective medicinal remedies almost accidentally while attempting to hide a hangover from his boss, J. Ward Moorehouse. Yet this irresponsible and obsequious yes-man's suggestion not only accurately describes the formal character of *U.S.A.,* an extremely compartmentalized text in which the component parts are indeed broken apart in a highly controlled feat of formal experimentation, but also sums up the cultural logic of the bureaucratized, rationalized modes of production associated with the Fordist economy of that moment.

    U.S.A. takes up the logic of rational categorization to identify the ways that logic is at the service of something much greater than the individual human subjects who deploy it. In *U.S.A.,* the logic of rationalized categorization, measurement, and classification is that of Fordist capital, which is portrayed as having its own self-perpetuating existence. Rather than validating the human will, it subsumes the human as merely another component of the factory. Human agency is pointless and nonexistent, and instead, what we see in *U.S.A.* are the ways that the forces of capitalism produce their own contradictions and are themselves the cause of their own demise.

U.S.A. thus ironically describes capitalism as that much more totalizing, because it produces even its own failure. Yet *U.S.A.* also serves as an archive that describes subjects who find it structurally impossible to become "good" workers and "good" consumers. As such, this text hints at the myriad alternative epistemologies and lifeworlds that may have existed in the shadow of Fordist capitalism. Ever fragmented, rendered deviant, and hard to grasp, these alternatives surface in *U.S.A.*

In this chapter, I examine a variety of manifestations of the cultural logic of modernist bureaucracy, including Dos Passos's *U.S.A.,* the documents of U.S. imperialism, and modern modes of industrial management and regulation. I read these texts for a new dominant episteme that became the site for negotiation and contestation in the early twentieth century. These texts articulate the new set of conditions that produced both imperialist capitalist modernism and the contradictions within and challenges to that formation. These conditions, which emerged in the early twentieth century, displaced the earlier nationalist formation of the possessive individual, a subject based on the valorization of human will and agency.

In chapter 2, I argued that Yamamoto's "A Fire in Fontana" and Morrison's *The Bluest Eye* displace the developmental temporality that constitutes this subject as willful and thus self-possessed. They do so through alternative, nondevelopmental modes of temporality, signified by their use of memory as a literary form. This alternative temporality displaces a developmental temporality—located in empty, homogeneous time—that constitutes the subject of the U.S. novel, a genre that attempts to homogenize what is an uneven and contested process: the incorporation of propertied subjects to the nation-state. In chapter 1, I showed how *Daisy Miller, Huckleberry Finn,* and *Up from Slavery* illustrate the historical moment that saw the volatile intersection of property, citizenship, and developmental subjectivity in the form of the possessive individual, a subject that Yamamoto and Morrison's texts critically dismantle through the use of different temporalities. Yamamoto's and Morrison's displacements of the homogenizing tendencies of possessive individualism are quite different from the critique of the possessive individual we see in modernist bureaucracy. Yet because Yamamoto's and Morrison's formal strategies of differentiation and nonlinear temporality emerge out of the same conditions of possibility as the possessive individual, these strategies meet their limit when confronted with a different genealogy of the U.S. as empire. In this chapter and the next, I situate the conditions of emergence for U.S. imperialism, and posit racialized immigrant women's culture as emerging as a contradiction to this genealogy.

In the late nineteenth and early twentieth centuries, as William Pomeroy recounts, U.S. capital faced a crisis as surpluses of capital and manufactured goods lacked outlets for reinvestment. The response to this crisis was twofold. On the one hand, new markets were established domestically, through the creation of new forms of consumerism as the privatized counterpart to an increasingly rationalized and bureaucratized division of labor under Fordist capital. On the other hand, U.S. capitalists eyed overseas markets, in particular China, which meant, as Pomeroy notes, "obtain[ing] Pacific military bases to protect trade routes," foremost of which was the Philippines (1970, 13). In reading these processes, Fordism and imperialism, as epistemologically and culturally manifested in modernism, I resist a determinist reading that would make culture a simple reflection or function of economic processes. Rather, in understanding the dominant episteme of modernist bureaucracy as that which legitimated and naturalized relations of rule, I argue that culture was fundamental to capital's reproduction—and thus to its crisis—in this era.

In this chapter, I examine the emergence of bureaucracy, a mode of organization that emphasizes simultaneous compartmentalization and categorization over the linearity of a developmental narrative intrinsic to the possessive individual. Bureaucracy was the preeminent form of surveillance in the Fordist era. Rationality became mobile through bureaucracy, controlling and categorizing space. In other words, in this era, the normative and disciplining function was displaced from the individuated citizen-subject of the nineteenth-century U.S. novel and was instead bestowed upon this new modernist, imperialist logic, constituted through a spatialized bureaucracy rather than a developmentalist narrative. Because this modernist bureaucracy is not coincident with the individual or the human, the narrative of development operational in this era is not that of the individual subject in society, but of development in a historical sense. This specialized bureaucratic modernity was ostensibly to replace "primitive," "nonrational" modes of labor and social organization all over the world, thus contributing to the story of empire as the triumphant forward march of progress. So while this new bureaucratic mode assumed its superiority within the historical narrative of progress, its own internal logic privileged space. This bureaucratic mode thus became a new site of contestation and contradiction, displacing the possessive individual of the nineteenth century.

While modernist bureaucracy rendered the human will and agency of the possessive individual irrelevant, it replaced that particular mechanism of abstraction with another. This new bureaucratic mode was marked by what Henri Lefebvre calls "abstract space," an epistemological concept that is the spatial equivalent to Walter Benjamin's "empty, homogeneous time." I derive the term "abstract space" from Henri Lefebvre's elaboration of the concept in *The Production of Space* (1991). Lefebvre notes that capitalism depends on its tendency to turn differentiated and varied spaces into abstract space. This has its very specific and practical implications—the homogeneous ubiquity of the tract home in suburban developments, for example. Yet what underlies this is a question of epistemology. "Abstract space" as a concept refers more to a way of imagining space than to any particular space or even kind of space. Abstract space is an episteme, a conception of space in which all spaces are interchangeable and empty of historical or material significance, or, as Michel Foucault describes, "a void, inside of which we could place individuals and things" (1986, 23). As such, abstract space suppresses all other ways of knowing or understanding space. Analogous to the way that subjects not narrated through developmental temporality are rendered "immature" or incomprehensible within a developmental narrative, alternative spaces are read as lacking the coherence and stability of abstract space; under this episteme, spaces that are not empty, homogeneous, and interchangeable are read as deviant or transgressive. More to the point, these alternative ways of knowing and imagining space are violently suppressed: "Though seemingly secured against any violence, abstract space is in fact inherently violent" (Lefebvre 1991, 387).

Yet, as Foucault notes, "we do not live in a homogeneous and empty space" (1986, 23). Foucault argues that "heterotopias" exist in every culture, spaces where the contradictions of abstract space allow alternative epistemes of space to exist. Likewise, Lefebvre maintains that alternative spatial practices and epistemes are never completely suppressed or eradicated, but actually emerge through the process by which they are violently suppressed. Indeed, Lefebvre, quoting Marx, concludes that "[t]he categories (concepts) which express social relationships in the most advanced society, namely bourgeois society . . . also allow 'insights into the structure and the relations of production of all the vanished social formations out of whose ruins and elements [bourgeois society] built itself up, whose partly still unconquered remnants are carried along with it, whose mere nuances have developed explicit significance within it'" (1991, 66). In this chapter I examine what remains "unconquered" by this history of modernist bureaucracy.

Bureaucracy as a form of surveillance is a profoundly modernist technology. Following such scholars as Donald Lowe and David Harvey, I use the term "modernism" to describe a cultural logic, that of early twentieth-century imperialism and capitalism. Harvey describes modernism as a cultural movement that tried to come to terms with the crises in the experience of time and space engendered by changes in the world economy. As useful as Harvey's work is, I find this description of the relationship between culture and capital to be too deterministic. In other words, capital does not simply determine cultural formations, which then become a kind of secondary by-product. Rather than posit modernism as only a reaction to economic shifts, I understand modernism as the code through which abstract space was articulated and presented as ostensibly universal and monolithic, and thus it reproduced and legitimated capital in this era. Further, culture is the site where that which cannot be rendered homogeneous and uniform, as abstract space, might emerge.

Thus, while Harvey limits himself to literary, artistic, and architectural instantiations of modernism, I find Donald Lowe's more expansive understanding of the epistemological tendencies of that era to be more helpful. Lowe notes an epistemological shift in the beginning of the twentieth century, in which the linear developmental temporality of the nineteenth century was displaced in favor of what he has called multiperspectivity. This shift to the multiperspectival mode in the arts and literature is generally termed "modernism," yet as Lowe has thoroughly described, this mode has not only encompassed the visual arts (through cubism) and literature (through the high modernism of Stein or Joyce), but has even manifested itself in such seemingly nonaesthetic fields as mathematics (in the theories of relativity of Einstein). The previous mode of representation, the single-perspective, developmental narrative that characterized the nineteenth-century U.S. novel, was displaced in favor of a spatialized mode of knowing the world, one that demanded this multiperspectival model. Taking Lowe's analysis to its logical extension, I would note that alongside the aesthetic and intellectual movements that are more often associated with modernism, the spatialized regime of bureaucracy—a mode of industrial and colonial surveillance—can also be called modernist. Indeed, the totalizing, categorizing nature of bureaucracy is multiperspectivity in its most rationalized and institutionalized form.

In this way, in the early part of the twentieth century, abstract space as an episteme emerged as bureaucracy, which attempted to organize and compartmentalize varied and differentiated space under one spatialized logic, but which produced incommensurabilities. The logic of bureaucracy underwrote two interrelated and mutually dependent processes: industrial capitalism within the United States and U.S. imperialism abroad. Modernism became, in Lefebvre's terminology, the "code" through which this abstract space was comprehended in this era. Lefebvre writes that "spatial codes have existed, each characterizing a particular spatial/social practice" and that "these codifications have been *produced* along with the space corresponding to them" (1991, 17). As such, "codes shall be seen as part of a practical relationship, as part of an interaction between 'subjects' and their space and surroundings" (18). "Modernism" was the code corresponding to the spatial politics of early twentieth-century capitalism, a crucial means by which the spatial reorganization of the early twentieth century was understood, articulated, and transformed. As such, I use the term "modernism" to reference not only the formal elements of artistic, architectural, and literary movements, but a variety of cultural, epistemic, and discursive practices, including the logic of bureaucracy underlying Fordism and Taylorism, on the one hand, and U.S. imperialism on the other. Thus, in my discussion of John Dos Passos's *U.S.A.* trilogy, I demonstrate that its formal aspects embody the modernist aesthetics of rationalization, compartmentalization, subordination to production, and interchangeability that were the hallmarks of Fordism and Taylorism. I also show that Dos Passos's text constitutes an omniscient, disembodied gaze that reproduces the surveilling gaze of the imperialist subject. In other words, I submit that *U.S.A.,* Fordism and Taylorism, and the technologies of U.S. imperialism are all mediations of a modernist logic. Certainly, Fordism and Taylorism as mechanisms of capitalist reproduction belong in the sphere of the economic. However, Fordism and Taylorism, dependent as they are on bureaucratic apparatuses of surveillance, can be read as instances of modernist multiperspectivity. Likewise, while U.S. imperialism in this era encompassed a variety of political, diplomatic, militaristic, and economic practices, we can trace a logic of surveillance and bureaucracy that can be identified as a form of modernism. In this vein, I examine the ways that three sets of different yet interlinked texts address the bureaucratic logic of "modernism": John Dos Passos's *U.S.A.* trilogy, the documents of the U.S. census of the Philippines, and the writings of Fredrick Winslow Taylor and the practices of Fordism.

I first examine the U.S. census of the Philippines of 1905 as an example of imperialist governmentality, one that called into being differentiated colonial subjects as the populations to be ruled. The census is the modernist grid par excellence—a version of the panopticon. We can thus imagine the colony as a kind of factory. This "factory," however, does not produce surplus value, but racial knowledge and hierarchy. Through my reading of these texts, I support Donald Lowe's contention that the epistemic shift between the developmental narrative of the nineteenth century and the multiperspectival, spatialized forms of the "modernist" era signals the shift from "bourgeois society to the bureaucratic society of controlled consumption" (Lowe 1982, 109). And this shift, I argue, is fundamentally dependent on shifts in the organization and production of whiteness and of racialized difference.

I then turn to a discussion of the writings of Fredrick Winslow Taylor and historical accounts of labor under Fordism to examine the reorganization of industrial production around modernist principles of rationalization, surveillance, and compartmentalization. I argue that Taylor's "Scientific Management" and Henry Ford's assembly line aimed to produce an undifferentiated, homogeneous worker whose embodied, human differences and particularities are foreclosed in the workplace and relegated to the space of the home, which then was to accrue new significance as the site for consumerist individualism. In other words, Fordism and Taylorism privileged a particular kind of worker: the producer as consumer. Yet a close examination of this form of labor disciplining reveals the various recalcitrances and contradictions produced by this process. The production of a normative worker/consumer through the prescription of whiteness, Americanness, and middle-class domesticity produced new forms of incommensurability with those ideals. In other words, the principle behind these forms of industrial organization was that the worker was able to consume the products that he made. Fordism and Taylorism were thus predicated not only on the reorganization of space and time on the shop floor, but on the reorganization of factory space in relation to domestic space. Fordism and Taylorism thus tried to produce a white, male, working class that was defined against those who could not consume or who consumed improperly: racialized workers in the United States as well as colonial subjects abroad. In this way, the whiteness produced by Fordism and Taylorism and the racial hierarchy produced through U.S. imperialism had some mutually constitutive functions. Yet workers could not easily and completely relinquish the variety of material, embodied histories that had to be sloughed off to become these abstract workers. Taylorism and Fordism narrated as normative and monolithic the processes by which work shifted from an exercise of skill and craftsmanship to routinized and monotonous labor, by which ethnic immigrants were "converted" into white Americans, and by which a variety of living situations and domestic arrangements were set aside in favor of consumption-based nuclear families. The white working class found itself both complying with and contradicting these forms of discipline.

Though I focus much of my discussion of Fordist and Taylorist modes of production on the making of a white working class, this is not to imply that racialized workers were not incorporated into Fordism. As William Harris documents, African American workers, relocating in the Great Migration from the South to industrial centers like Detroit, were increasingly finding jobs in manufacturing: "As a government report put it in 1924, newer black arrivals became industrial laborers, finding jobs in mills, stockyards, and factories rather than in hotels, restaurants, and domestic kitchens" (Harris 1982, 59). Henry Ford recruited African American workers for his Detroit plant, mainly through association with African American ministers and civic leaders, and the Ford Motor Company was the only place where African Americans could become apprentices for more skilled jobs, rather than being permanently relegated to unskilled positions (Harris 1982, 62). In looking at Fordism and Taylorism as mechanisms for the production of whiteness, I do not mean to imply that this mode of capitalist production did not also depend on racialized U.S. labor. Rather, I trace how the Fordist era was characterized by a dominant, bureaucratic mode for producing whiteness that created a variety of subaltern positions. While racialized U.S. workers certainly make up one of these subaltern formations, in this chapter I look mainly at colonized subjects abroad, as well as those ethnic European immigrant or rural white working-class subjects who were not so evenly or completely interpellated as a part of the white working class. I focus on these subaltern formations in order to trace a genealogy for the interventions into neocolonial consumerism that I discuss through readings of racialized immigrant women's culture in chapter 4. These uneven integrations of ethnic European immigrant and rural white working-class subjects demonstrated the crises of U.S. capitalism, which, while different from those critiques produced in colonized sites and by racialized populations, can be read as allied with them.

These crises are made legible through John Dos Passos's *U.S.A.* trilogy, which I read as a critical examination of Fordist and Taylorist modes of industrial production. Attempting to fight fire with fire, Dos Passos produced a text organized by the very bureaucratic, modernist logic of U.S. capitalism that it decries. In this way, *U.S.A.* also replicates the mastery of modernist imperialism over space and time. Unlike the developmental realism of *Daisy Miller* or *Huck Finn,* Dos Passos's trilogy does not privilege narrative; rather, it makes central another kind of expression that privileges space. I argue that Dos Passos's particular blend of formal strategies reproduces "abstract space," a new logic of time and space that was both reorganizing U.S. industrial capitalism and producing an imperialist ordering of the world. Yet while Dos Passos's formal strategies emphasize the crushing, totalizing nature of bureaucratic multiperspectivity, the text does not represent this process as monolithic or even particularly effective. Instead, the text demonstrates time and again the ways that workers are rendered contradictory, recalcitrant, and unresolvable to the capitalist machinery by their very incorporation within it. These excesses, which could not be resolved to modernist capitalism, emerge in *U.S.A.*

A rationalized, bureaucratic logic was pervasive in the early twentieth century, providing the epistemic framework for capitalist and imperialist ventures. In 1903, the United States began conducting the first U.S. Census of the Philippine Islands, an ambitious effort that was finally concluded and published in 1905. Coordinated by American officials, with the actual data collected by 7,502 Filipino census officials, the census aimed to undertake the monumental task of classifying and collecting statistical data for an incredibly large and diverse population. In the same year that the United States began its Philippines census project, Fredrick Winslow Taylor delivered a speech, entitled "Shop Management," to the American Society of Mechanical Engineers (ASME). The fruit of years of work and study, this speech was a practical, technical description of his now-famous method of "Scientific Management," or "The Taylor Plan," as it has also been called.

It was later published along with Taylor's better-known text, "The Principles of Scientific Management," originally written in 1911. Although Taylor's two presentations to the ASME failed to stimulate widespread interest in Scientific Management, the Eastern Rate Case of 1910–11, in which the International Commerce Commission advocated the use of Scientific Management in the public administration of the national rail to keep rail rates low, made Taylor a national icon (Hooker 1997, 20). Henry Ford and his managers implemented Taylor's ideas in the Ford Motor Company plants and began a new era in industrial production: Fordism was inaugurated.

Instrumental to the undertaking of both the Taylor Plan and the census was the form: a blank spatialized grid, mapped on two axes, into which the particularities and differences of a worker or colonized subject, as the case may be, could be noted. These two mechanisms of Fordist bureaucracy, the Taylor Plan and the census, operated through remarkably similar logics and formal strategies. In particular, these processes depended on the practice of surveillance, a practice that constituted both a disciplining subject and a desiring subject. This subject was mapped out on a form—either the schedules that recorded the populations for the census or the Time Study Note Sheets in the Taylor Plan—on a spatialized grid, rather than on a linear trajectory of time. Yet rather than being analogous or parallel formations, the census and the Taylor Plan are mutually determining. They need their differences and similarities from each other to exist. In other words, as imperialist governmentality in the form of the U.S. census of the Philippines was producing a racially differentiated, particularized, and embodied subject, corporate governmentality was attempting to produce a homogeneous white working class through both labor discipline and the production of a consumerist domesticity as the private compensation for the public life of work.

Under Taylorism, the goal and effect were to unmark subjects, to turn them into abstract labor. In practice, Taylorism attempted to create uniform, regular, and indistinguishable workers, characterized by their supposedly unmarked status, out of a variety of differentiated workers. As compensation for their brutal incorporation into this highly regulated form of work, Taylorism and Fordism offered their workers an ostensibly protected and comfortable domesticity, at this time increasingly defined through consumerism. This combination of alienated work and compensatory domesticity produces the particular formation that is the white working class.

Imperialism's goal, on the other hand, is to register and codify difference and diversity in order to constitute subjects marked by their difference from a universal imperialist subject. Like the U.S. workers incorporated into Taylorist and Fordist modes of production, the colonized populations counted, categorized, and compartmentalized by the U.S. census of the Philippines were subjected to (and thus produced by) bureaucratic surveillance. Yet the colonized relationship to colonialism was complex, and different from that which constituted the U.S. white working class. As I will argue in a reading of Jessica Hagedorn's *Dogeaters* in chapter 4, the colonial condition can be described as consumerism without means; in other words, feeling as if one should consume, but not being able to. The white working class produced through an exchange of control over labor for privatized domesticity is implicated in the imperialist project insofar as it validated consumerism. Yet as I will argue, this process produced a variety of recalcitrances. To the extent that some European immigrant and rural populations could not be incorporated into this normative white working-class model, they are aligned with colonial populations.

Theorists have long argued that surveillance, and the corresponding production of a seeing subject and a seen object, is a hallmark of imperialism.[1] The tendency of U.S. imperialism to rely less on the establishment of a colonial government and more on cultural and economic control makes surveillance even more necessary; indeed, theorists have argued that surveillance is the primary mechanism of U.S. imperialism and neocolonialism.[2] Although the United States did establish a colonial government in the Philippines in its period of official imperialism (1898–1945), Pomeroy has noted that this period demonstrated the inefficacy of the technologies of an older European imperialism, and was more useful to the United States as a nascent version of neocolonialism. If neocolonialism is less about overt and direct modes of coercive power and more about the production of neocolonial self-discipline through surveillance, then surveillance and the corresponding construction of an imperialist seeing subject is not a by-product, but the central process of U.S. imperialism.

Modes of surveillance produce and regulate racial, gendered, and sexual difference. By the same token, these mechanisms of surveillance implicitly valorize whiteness, masculinity, and heteronormativity, and ascribe these categories to the imperialist subject. This imperialist subject, I will argue, is disembodied, rendered objective and omniscient, and presented as devoid of materiality. Yet this very condition of immateriality marks this subject as raced (white), gendered (male), and heteronormative (patriarchal). Surveillance depends on abstract space to produce racial, gender, and sexual difference. Institutions of imperialist surveillance are ways of ordering and imagining space; in other words, they are ways to impose abstract space over a variety of differentiated spatial epistemes. The different ways that space is imagined, produced, and inhabited are forcibly subsumed into an imperialist episteme of space, in which all spaces can be conquered and assimilated.

The idea of surveillance and modern subject formation is important to this discussion because it allows me to note that capitalism fundamentally reproduces itself through epistemological and cultural formations. Foucault has named the process by which power shifts from governing from without to governing from within. "Governmentality" describes the process in which self-regulating and self-disciplined subjects are produced through the constitution of a particular version of the "self." In particular, Foucault traces the creation of a *population* over which this new form of government has jurisdiction. Population is a concept that, as Foucault notes, is not limited to a concept of "territory," nor is it "a matter of opposing things to men . . . but rather a sort of complex composed of men and things" (1991, 93). Intrinsic to the process of producing a population in this era is the bureaucratic apparatus, which systematizes and catalogs the relationship of men and things. Foucault's notion of governmentality stresses the importance of knowledge production and subject formation to the relations of rule. In other words, contestations and crises in these relations of rule emerge around epistemology and subjectivity. Implicit in Foucault's concept is the notion that at the exact moment these modes of governmentality are reproducing the relations of rule, they are also providing the vocabulary for contestations to those relations of rule. In other words, the process by which modern subjects are formed produces those subjects as contradictory. In this discussion I trace the development of populations of governance in early twentieth-century United States through two different forms of governmentality: corporate governmentality within industrial production and imperialist governmentality abroad. These modes of governmentality demonstrate that in this era, the relations of rule were established and contested through bureaucracy.

Foucault notes that modern governmentality depends on the production of a population, and on the corresponding science of statistics to define

and measure this population: "[Statistics] now gradually reveals that population has its own regularities, its own rate of deaths and diseases, its cycles
of scarcity, etc.; statistics shows also that the domain of population involves
a range of intrinsic, aggregate effects, phenomena that are irreducible to
those of the family, such as epidemics, endemic levels of mortality, ascend-
ing spirals of labour and wealth" (1991, 99). In other words, to create a
population requires an apparatus that produces certain categories of statistical knowledge about that population, what Foucault calls "a whole complex of *savoirs*" (1991, 103). A population thus cannot exist without some
form of a census. The primary *savoir* produced by the U.S. census of the
Philippines is racial differentiation.

Compiled into four enormous volumes, cataloging geography, history,
population, mortality, education, agriculture, and the like, the U.S. census of the Philippines was an extraordinary feat of colonial surveillance.
Vicente Rafael notes that the census produced both a white surveilling gaze
and a racial hierarchy that ascribed racialized difference onto colonized subjects. Extending Rafael's argument, I add that the mechanisms of the census organize and produce racialized difference as simultaneously gendered
and sexual difference. Rafael describes the ways the census was conducted
via a form on which people of a given area were counted and classified.
There were two versions of this form, one for more "civilized" populations
and the other for "non-Christian tribes." What becomes immediately apparent when examining these forms is the ways that "civilized" and "savage"
are differentiated in sexual and gender-based terms. The forms for the
"civilized" populations are organized first and foremost via an imagined
privatized domesticity, as each person is listed as part of a nuclear family
arrangement, and their status is marked based on their relationship to the
patriarchal designation of "head of the family." In contrast, the form for
"non-Christian peoples" lists each individual by their residence within a
town and their affiliation with their tribe. The mark of "civilization" here
is the adaptation of nuclear family models and gendered hierarchies. The
inclusion of some Filipinos in the category of "civilized" by virtue of their
family formation marks the difference of the "uncivilized."

Likewise, the embodied particulars of each individual are registered in
categories that read "Color," "Sex," "Age at the last birthday," "Whether
married, single, widowed, or divorced," and "Insane, deaf, dumb, blind."
Colonial categorization and disciplining are felt first and foremost at the

level of embodied difference. To be "colonized" is to be subjected to modern regimes of measurement and surveillance at the level of the body, which is subject to notice at the moment of its difference (insane, deaf, dumb, blind) from a whole and well body. In other words, the whole and well body is not materialized or documented; this body is, in a perverse way, disembodied. As I will argue later, this subject is reminiscent of the disembodied, omniscient imperialist subject of *U.S.A.*

In contrast to the exceedingly material and embodied status of the colonized subject, the imperialist subject is marked by the lack of marking; it is disembodied, seemingly objective, and omniscient. Rafael notes that "census reports are curious texts," arguing that the "bureaucratic nature of its writing renders its authorship and authority dispersed and anonymous. Consequently, while the workings and the results of census reports are never completely visible to an individual, censuses can claim to see everything that can be individuated, that is, counted, tabulated, and classified" (Rafael 1993, 188). The census thus constructs a disembodied, omniscient, imperialist subject that sees but cannot itself be seen, that categorizes and comprehends but cannot itself be categorized or comprehended. In a description of the U.S. census of the Philippines that applies to *U.S.A.* to an uncanny degree, Rafael notes the census's "remarkable ability to picture in unambiguous, quantitative terms the totality of the world's multiplicity" (188). In other words, the very quality of disembodiment, of omniscient viewership, is what marks this subject as imperialist.

The census produces abstract space through the regularization of difference. Lefebvre's differentiation between what he calls "induced difference" and "produced difference" is instructive here. Lefebvre writes,

> An *induced* difference remains within a set or a system generated according to a particular law. It is in fact constitutive of that set or system. . . . Similarly: the diversity between villas in a suburb filled with villas; or between different 'community facilities'; or again, variations within a particular fashion in a dress, as stipulated by that fashion itself. By contrast, a *produced* difference presupposes the shattering of a system; it is born of an explosion; it emerges from the chasm opened up when a closed universe ruptures. (1991, 372)

We can see that the census's creation, categorization, and arrangement of differences ("civilized" versus "savage," "married versus single," and so forth) is its way of producing *induced* differences. This imperialist mechanism of surveillance suppresses *produced* differences inherent within the colony that threaten to displace the imperialist episteme through the creation of *induced* differences that only reinforce it. For example, the induced difference between "civilized" and "savage" reinforces a hierarchical and developmental narrative that legitimates colonial control by characterizing colonialism as a benevolent and civilizing mission. In seeing, mapping, and categorizing the world, the imperalist gaze reinvents the world. It turns the varied, heterogeneous, and differentiated spatial epistemes into abstract space. In other words, imperialist surveillance obfuscates all other ways of knowing or imagining space, and imposes abstract space as the only way of knowing space. Yet race is a dialectic, an induced difference but also a produced one. Race is both capitalism's effect and its excess.

Fordism and Taylorism were themselves forms of governmentality. As such, I call this "corporate governmentality" and argue that, like imperialist governmentality, it also produced racialized ways of knowing. Under these forms of imperialist and corporate governmentality—the U.S. census, Fordism, and Taylorism—the production of self-regulating subjects was both an explicitly stated and implicitly implemented goal. Both modes of corporate governmentality—Scientific Management and welfare work—aimed to produce self-disciplined workers who would internalize values of thrift, diligence, cleanliness, and sobriety. As Rafael notes, the census was simultaneously an official U.S. assertion of the cessation of war with the Filipino insurrectionists and a condition "for holding elections within two years of the census's publication for Filipino representatives to the colonial legislature, to be known as the Philippine Assembly" (1993, 188). The successful completion of the census was to prove that the Philippine people were capable of self-administration and rule. This was only possible, however, after the Philippine people had demonstrated their ability to be rational, disciplined subjects. Despite these similarities, however, the fundamental difference between colonial and corporate governmentalities was the way that corporate governmentality centered whiteness rather than racialized difference by attempting to produce a white working class that accepted protected consumerist domesticity as compensation for the alienation of labor in the workplace.

As a mode of corporate governmentality, the Taylor Plan depended as much on the mechanism of surveillance as the census did. Arising in the context of the increased specialization and segmentation of professionalized industries in the advent of the industrial boom of the post–Civil War period, Taylorism was the most widely implemented and influential of the slew of management theories arising at the time.[3] In this context, the focus of management shifted from "material, structure, or machine processes" to "efficiency," that is, worker efficiency (Hooker 1997, 18). Taylor's professed goal was to resolve the historical antagonism between labor and capital by increasing worker efficiency to such a level that these workers could be paid more while the company gained more in surplus value. As a means to heighten worker efficiency, he proposed his method of time management, in which even the most menial and simple of tasks could be broken down into its most minute components. These components of work were then measured with a stop watch, a chart, and sometimes a slide rule, and the most efficient means of doing the work and scheduling rest breaks were ascertained. The worker was then trained to do the work in exactly this most efficient way. For his trouble, the worker was paid "30 per cent. [*sic*] to 100 per cent. more than the average of his trade" (Taylor 1947, 25). With this method, Taylor claimed, a company could triple or quadruple their workers' productivity and simultaneously maintain a happy and compliant workforce. Vital to the proper execution of the Taylor Plan was the internalization of work discipline. The goal and effect of this reorganization of work was to hierarchize workers; Taylor repeatedly remarks that the accurate categorization of workers is vital to the success of Scientific Management, noting that he "would not for an instant advocate the use of a high-priced tradesman to do the work which could be done by a trained laborer or a lower-priced man" (1947, 27). Likewise, the Taylor Plan deskilled the work, stripping the worker of any opportunity to make decisions or develop an expertise.

Yet unlike the census, which was designed to categorize racialized, gendered, and sexual difference, the Taylor Plan attempted to eradicate difference and impose uniformity. The census produces its two subjects—the imperialist, disembodied subject and the colonized, embodied subject—by mapping the difference between the two on the census population schedule. Through surveillance the census constitutes the colonized subject as lacking, inadequate. The colonized subject is marked by his inability to become civilized. The census establishes the colonial subject as a subject whose desires for civilization cannot be fulfilled. In contrast, the Time Study

Note Sheet of the Taylor Plan uses surveillance to describe a subject—the worker—in the process of becoming unmarked. Ideally, his differences are sloughed away as he better approximates abstract labor. In a telling anecdote, Taylor describes a conversation with a laborer, a Pennsylvania Dutch workman named Schmidt, in which Taylor tries to convince Schmidt to submit himself to the discipline of Scientific Management. Schmidt's initial response to Taylor is, "'Vell, I don't know vat you mean'" (Taylor 1947, 44). Yet over the course of the conversation, Schmidt becomes convinced to work for Taylor under Scientific Management. The anecdote ends with Taylor happily reporting, "He worked when he was told to work, and rested when he was told to rest, and at half-past five in the afternoon had his 47½ tons loaded on the car. And he practically never failed to work at this pace and do the task that was set him during the three years that the writer was at Bethlehem [Steel Company]" (47). All of Schmidt's particularities—from the accent marking him as an immigrant to his propensity to be "mentally sluggish" as Taylor describes him (46)—are ostensibly rendered inconsequential once he is incorporated as labor by the Taylor Plan.

The anecdote, describing the process by which Schmidt became abstract labor, can be mapped out continuously on Taylor's Time Study Note Sheets. This is particularly visible on the Note Sheet entitled "Observations of Hand Work on Machine Tools," included in "Shop Management." In this huge Note Sheet, measuring seventeen inches by seventeen inches, each column denoting a worker's time for each component of labor has next to it a column entitled "Time Should Have Taken." When the figures for the first column—denoting the individual and particular worker—match exactly the figures for the second column—denoting the abstract, unmarked worker—the Taylor Plan has fulfilled its purpose: it has succeeded. Certainly, there exists much evidence that workers resisted the bodily discipline of Taylorism, and that the constitution of a uniform working class was contentious and uneven. Taylor himself admitted later in life that his optimistic view of the possibility of worker/management cooperation was more imagined than real, reminiscing, "I was a young man in years, but I give you my word that I was a great deal older than I am now with worry, meanness, and contemptibleness of the whole damn thing. It's a horrid life . . . not to be able to look at any workman in the face all day long without seeing hostility" (quoted in Kanigel 1997, 18). Rather than claiming that this process happened evenly and monolithically, I argue that, by examining the documents of industrial reorganization, we can see the ways that the Taylor Time Study Note grid mapped out and thus produced a conception of abstract labor.

By breaking down labor into its most minute component parts and imposing repetition, the most complicated tasks become deskilled and the workers—now lacking in specialization and expertise—ostensibly become interchangeable. The worker's trajectory under Taylorism is to become more and more unmarked, undifferentiated, and disembodied. Abhorring all forms of differentiation, Taylor noted that one of the initial challenges of installing the Scientific Management plan was that "each man must learn how to give up his own particular way of doing things" (Taylor 1947, 133). Instead, he argued, "A man with only the intelligence of an average laborer can be taught to do the most difficult and delicate work if it is repeated enough times" (28). Rendering differentiated bodies into an abstract worker means that rationalization must come to constitute the worker's understanding of his body. Alienation from one's body is the hallmark of Taylorism and of the modern working subject it produces. Taylor himself confirms the disciplining involved in conforming to his system, noting the "monotony of repetition" (28) that characterizes the work under Scientific Management, and precisely assigning wage increases in proportion to the toll that various types of work take on the worker's mind and body. Thus, to submit to the discipline of Taylorism is to inhabit a disembodied, abstract, and undifferentiated subject formation.

Fordism was likewise developed as a mechanism for the extraction of abstract labor. This was accomplished through technologies of social control—in particular surveillance—that uncannily resonate with those of Taylorism and U.S. imperialism. Fordism—based on the factory organized around the assembly line—was only possible after the complicated manufacturing process was broken down into its many component parts. The technological innovation in which machine tools became sophisticated enough to produce identical interchangeable parts was mirrored by the management revolution that also treated workers as identical and interchangeable. Each task could be laid out along the assembly line and each worker assigned to this particular task to perform repetitively. As historian Clarence Hooker notes, "[T]he revolution was much more than machine tools and automated assembly systems. It also involved the standardization of management, marketing, and distribution; and it resulted in the creation

of a new occupational hierarchy" (1997, 67). Although Taylor was the recognized articulator of this system of compartmentalized labor, and though
Ford managers implemented Taylor's principles widely, in fact many aspects
of Taylorism were developed independently by Ford and his managers, who
divided the labor process into semiskilled tasks as early as 1904–1905 (Hooker
1997, 21). In whatever way these principles were implemented, the underlying principles of Taylorism were instrumental to Fordist production.

Under Ford, the skilled craftsmen of an earlier era of production were
replaced with managed, deskilled workers. With deskilled work came new
technologies of surveillance and management. Historian Stephen Meyer
notes, "The design of machines, the arrangement of men and machines, the
new forms of record keeping and inspection, and the new means of mechanical conveyance all controlled the pace, the intensity, and the quality of
production" (1981, 37–38). The shop floor became increasingly alienating,
producing new subjects: "The world of work would never be the same
again. . . . [T]he worker's daily routine became more monotonous and
more repetitive. It dramatically altered the social structure of the shop, the
factory, and in fact, modern industrial society. . . . Indeed the new industrial technology had a profound impact on modern social existence" (Meyer
1981, 35–36).

Yet, as Harvey notes, "[W]hat was special about Ford . . . was his vision,
his explicit recognition that mass production meant mass consumption"
(1990, 125–26). These Fordist and Taylorist regimes out of which abstract
labor was forged did not go uncontested. In compensation, both Taylor
and Ford offered the bourgeois domestic home—and all of the objects of
consumerism associated therewith—as compensation for one's alienation at
work, and privileged corresponding values of property ownership, sobriety,
and middle-class morality. Ironically, at the very moment that "American"
became an imperialist disciplinary category to which colonized subjects in
the Philippines were supposed to aspire, the definition of "American" was
undergoing tremendous change. Fordism and Taylorism attempted to constitute a white working class that was a consumerist class, enjoying the
privileges of domesticity and stability. Fundamental to Taylor's system was
the premise that workers who submitted to the rigors of Scientific Management would be paid substantially more for their trouble. This higher
rate of pay supposedly lifted formerly shiftless and irresponsible men into a
more respectable class marked by stability and responsibility. Taylor argued

that "most men tend to become more instead of less thrifty when they receive the proper increase for an extra hard day's work. . . . They live rather better, begin to save money, become more sober, and work more steadily" (1947, 27). In theory, Taylorism thus constituted new working subjects through stability and responsibility, and simultaneously protected this stable existence.

Fordism built upon Taylorism to produce domestic, consumerist whiteness based on the protection of the private sphere of the home as the affective, reproductive side meant to compensate for the alienation of the worker in the workplace. Accordingly, the narrativization of whiteness through the consumerist model of middle-class domesticity was even more pronounced under Fordism. "Scientific Management" composed only one-half of the management strategy under Fordism. The other half was a form of welfare capitalism called "welfare work," which emerged in the period between 1886 and 1889, when the labor and reform movements of the Progressive era prompted many companies to start profit-sharing plans and provide amenities for their laborers (Jacoby 1985, 49). Welfare work arose to mitigate the effects of Scientific Management, or in other words, to contain and manage worker dissatisfaction with and recalcitrance in response to the increasingly alienated nature of the workplace under Scientific Management. The period that saw the implementation of bureaucratized and deskilled labor also saw the highest turnover in labor in the Ford plant; in 1913, the Ford Motor company had to hire 52,445 workers to maintain a workforce of 14,000 (Hooker 1997, 110), demonstrating the difficulty of reconciling labor to the demanding and relentless nature of the new work conditions. Although a survey taken by Ford management reported that worker dissatisfaction lay largely in the harsh conditions of the workplace, the Ford Motor Company's subsequent reforms centered around rehabilitating the home. These reforms promoted consumption-based domesticity as the antidote to the demands of the workplace; correspondingly, the stability of "good home conditions" was to produce a reliable and compliant worker.

The reforms were based on a profit-sharing plan that would result in shorter shifts and higher wages (the "Five Dollar Day") for the workers. Ford is, of course, famously known for his idea of workers as consumers. As many historians have documented, Ford argued that high wages and leisure-time consumption were necessary to absorb the higher output enabled by these new, more efficient modes of production. Ford's reasoning was simple: when the Ford Motor Company introduced the forty-hour workweek in 1926, he explained the principle behind this decision thusly: "The more well paid leisure workmen get, the greater become their wants. These wants soon become needs" (quoted in Crowther 1926, 614). As these needs grow, he said, the demand for consumer commodities "will lead to more work. And this to more profits. And this to more wages" (616). Indeed, Ford described consumerism as the basis for a healthy economy, declaring, "the industry of this country could not long exist if factories generally went back to the 10 hour day, because the people would not have time to consume the goods produced" (614). The fact that workers could buy the products they made precipitated what historians of consumption call the "consumer durables revolution of the 1920s," with the primary durable good being automobiles (Olney 1991, 56).[4] Yet this democratization of the capitalist process through the extension of consumerism simultaneously sutured together whiteness, domesticity, and morality. Not only was this form of consumerist domesticity defined against those who could not consume or who consumed improperly, it also demanded that workers live in approximation of middle-class, nuclear family models by pathologizing and punishing, both materially and ideologically, alternative living arrangements and modes of domestic organization.

Like Scientific Management under Taylor, "welfare work" or welfare capitalism under Ford produced whiteness through the securing of privatized domesticity. Not everyone immediately qualified for the profit-sharing plan and the "Five Dollar Day." The qualifications for eligibility were "thriftiness, good habits, good home conditions" (Hooker 1997, 112). To determine which workers would or would not qualify, and to usher those who didn't qualify toward eventual eligibility, the Ford Motor Company established the Sociological Department, which, along with the English School, undertook to "Americanize" and domesticate the mostly ethnic European immigrant workers and thus to turn them into "good Ford men." At one point the Sociological Department housed two hundred investigators, including two medical doctors, who visited each worker in his home, interviewing the worker, his family, friends, and neighbors, and examining bank documents and other official papers to determine whether they were living correctly; they helped workers to change their living conditions if they were living incorrectly, according to Ford's standards. The powerful incentive to internalize these values of thriftiness, cleanliness, sobriety, and moral living was the potential to double one's daily wage. The surveillance did not end once a worker was determined to be morally sound and fiscally responsible; the investigators kept tabs on each worker to ensure that the increase in wages did not lead to profligate spending and other forms of dissipated living.

Ultimately, the Five Dollar Plan attempted to homogenize the labor force, blurring differences of ethnicity, class, and region, and forming the white working class. The plan's purpose was also to "modernize" European ethnic immigrants and other heterogeneous workers, including rural whites who flocked to the factories during the labor shortages of World War I. Many of the accounts of the Sociological Department's reform projects narrated the pitiful, slovenly, poverty-stricken European immigrant's transformation into a property-owning, responsible head of a household (Meyer 1981, 132–35 passim). This household's sound constitution was inevitably demonstrated by the presence of consumerist items such as new furniture and clothing, and by the internalization of bourgeois values, which prompted these workers to take care of their newly acquired goods. Indeed, the Ford Motor Company undertook to assimilate the immigrant explicitly, establishing as a part of these series of reforms an "Americanization" program, a key component of which was the Ford English School, which taught European immigrants English, as well as American customs and culture. Henry Ford described the purpose of the Sociological Department as to "explain opportunity, teach American ways and customs, English language, duties of citizenship" (quoted in Meyer 1981, 126).

According to the work of Stuart Ewen, Lizabeth Cohen, and other historians of consumerism, this conflation of consumerism and citizenship created the "consumer" identity as a means for incorporating the working class and dissipating labor mobilization. In Stuart Ewen's pioneering work on the rise of consumerism in the early twentieth century, he argues that advertising and consumerism came about as "American industry began to produce a cultural apparatus aimed at defusing and neutralizing potential unrest" (1976, 12). Along these lines, Lizabeth Cohen argues that "consumer" as a class category and a mode of political participation was cemented in the New Deal era as the U.S. state attempted to mend a "severely damaged economy without jettisoning the basic tenets of capitalism" (1992, 115). Positing that prior to the Great Depression, consumers were rarely thought of as a class with protectable interests, Cohen meticulously documents how a concept of "consumer interest" was invented and instituted into state policy. During the New Deal era, state economic policy shifted to a Keynesian model that posited that deficit spending on the part of the state would fuel job growth and consumer spending, which would in turn spur economic growth. Within this model, "consumers became responsible for high productivity and full employment whereas a decade earlier, that role had belonged to producers" (Cohen 1992, 123). Cohen argues, in other words, that "consumer" as a class emerges to displace "producer" as a class at a moment when the promises of capitalism are compromised by economic depression and questioned by radical labor movements. Consumers as a class emerged to dispel the specter of socialist revolution and to reconsolidate the free enterprise system. By extending an ideal of what historian Charles McGovern describes as "an organic classless society" (1998, 47) in which all consumers were created equal, "consumer" as a class displaced identification with labor movements and their emphasis on a "producer" class.

Yet this shift in identification cannot be dismissed as merely a form of false consciousness that allowed managers to manipulate unwitting workers. In this era, consumerist domesticity became an important site for agency and struggle as it became conflated with citizenship, Americanization, and whiteness. As McGovern notes, while "the vast social inequities of American capitalism" cannot be addressed by the policy of "more things for more people," the appeal of consumerism was powerful and compelling for those who had access to this and perhaps no other form of personal and political agency (1998, 58). Consumerism became a form of agency, albeit a limited one, in an era when Taylorized modes of industrial production were systematically stripping agency in the workplace by deskilling labor. As several historians of U.S. consumerism have argued, consumerism in the pre–World War II era became coded as a form of citizenship that resolved ethnic particularities into an American identity. In his study of two new groups of professionals that arose at this time—advertising agents and product testers—McGovern notes that in an era when personal agency was being eroded in other political, social, and economic fronts, consumerism was understood as an avenue of participatory democracy. Indeed, this notion of the consumer voting with his (or rather, her) dollars created a utopian ideal of mass-based democracy.[5] Simultaneously, echoing Ford ideologies, advertising campaigns presented the use of consumer goods as quintessentially "American," and constructed a specifically American lifestyle that was attainable only through consumerism.[6]

Yet the irony of offering consumerism as the compensation for an alienating workplace and restricted political access is that often the reward required as much discipline and alienation as the working conditions themselves. While consumerism may have offered a sense of personal agency, for the ethnic immigrant and white rural workers incorporated into Fordism, consumerist domesticity often meant having to relinquish any alternative relationships to embodiment and modes of social, familial, or domestic organization. The many (presumably cautionary) examples from the Ford documents of drunkenness, immorality, slovenliness, and nonnuclear households in various states of disarray show that the workers didn't give up without a fight. We might understand this inability to follow the norms imposed by Ford's welfare capitalism policies as due to the fact that the material conditions that were supposed to enable these norms were fundamentally inaccessible to many workers. As Lizabeth Cohen notes about factory workers in Chicago, the rising wages that were supposed to support bourgeois domesticity were more industrial self-promotion than actual fact. Cohen notes that "the uncertainty of work and the inadequacy of wages meant that more than half of the 467 families interviewed were forced to send mother or children to work, some even to take in boarders, just to live slightly above the minimum standard of living set for dependent families by the Chicago Council of Social Agencies" (1992, 102). In other words, while the nuclear family household with the father as the primary wage earner was the normative ideal, the actual conditions of factory life required many workers to live in nonnormative domestic arrangements. We can understand this more generally as an example of the ways that capital's very need to recruit heterogeneous labor forces—European immigrants, rural workers, racialized workers, women—undermined its efforts to create a homogeneous workforce.

As such, the centering of a "private" sphere enabled contestations around this category. Workers did resist and criticize these welfare work programs, at the Ford Motor Company and elsewhere, as intrusions into their personal lives. As Jacoby documents, "At a Maine textile mill, a group of angry young women told the firm's welfare secretary, whom they called 'Sanitary Jane,' that they were just as clean as she was and would not submit to further hygenic examinations" (1985, 55). Yet we can see that these categories were reified in turn through worker resistance to these invasive corporate programs. The very possibility of having a "private life" did not have a prior

existence, but was only established through the invasion of it by these welfare work programs. In the above example, the workers' internalization of
cleanliness as a virtue replaces "Sanitary Jane" and her much less efficient
modes of external coercion.

If being given the chance to relinquish the ostensibly bad habits of nonnuclear family formation and nonnormative embodiment was the process
through which the white working class was formed, racialized subjects were
constituted as the "other" to this process. As capital demanded labor differentiation and depended on the creation of a norm, racialized workers were
recruited as labor at the same time that they were pathologized as improperly gendered and sexualized subjects who did not conform to bourgeois,
consumerist domesticity. As we have seen, despite the democratic and universal promises of consumerist citizenship, U.S. consumerism was always
a differentiating enterprise. The shift in working-class identity from producer to consumer was based on conceptions of the "Living Wage" or the
"American Standard of Living," which constructed proper consumerism
as American, masculine, white, and free, simultaneously constituting such
opposing categories as alien, feminine, nonwhite, and enslaved. As Lawrence
B. Glickman argues, in the agrarian period the concept of wage labor was
considered antithetical to freedom, "based on the view that wage labor
placed the labor of white working men on an unnatural continuum of the
most dependent strata of blacks and women" (1997, 15). Yet with the advent
of mass industrialization, the difference between free workers and enslaved
(racialized) workers became not a difference in how they produced, but in
how they consumed. Eventually what defined "American" was not produc-
tiveness, as in an earlier era, but the ability to "purchase properly."

In the beginning of the twentieth century, consumerism became sutured
to whiteness, masculinity, and citizenship. In particular, the white working (and consuming) class was defined in opposition to Chinese "coolie"
labor. As Glickman notes, "White workers routinely conceded that the Chinese worked hard and competently; it was in the area of leisure where they
found them deficient" (1997, 86–87). The racist rhetoric of anti-Chinese
sentiment at the beginning of the twentieth century was as virulent as in
the era of the Chinese Exclusion Act. During the debate over the annexation of Hawaii, the AFL, led by Samuel Gompers (who served as an hon-
orary vice-president of the Anti-Imperialism League), fiercely opposed
annexation on the grounds that Chinese laborers from Hawaii could freely

enter the mainland United States, negating the effects of the Chinese Exclusion Act. Sympathetic Senator William Allen of Nebraska exclaimed in an unintentionally hilarious quote, "I am not prepared to put the American father and son, in the field or shop, in deadly competition with Chinese, who live on a bowl of rice and a rat a day" (quoted in Thompkins 1970, 109). Such rhetoric constituted the Chinese as having lower standards, which, in an interesting switch of causality, meant that they were willing to work for lower wages, live without what seemed to be the minimum of necessities ("a bowl of rice and a rat a day"), forego familial, domestic relationships (as opposed to the "American father and son"), and generally lower the standard of living for other workers (making them "deadly competition"). While Chinese "coolie" labor was the most vilified target of working-class consumerist identity, black workers did not escape unscathed. If the Chinese were faulted for not consuming enough, African Americans were deficient because they spent too much, too excessively, and without control. For while the American Standard of Living emphasized the importance of cultivating desires, only certain desires—in other words, "'civilized' needs often defined by a gender-conscious vision of domesticity" (Glickman 1997, 88)—were appropriate. In this era of U.S. imperialism, "consumer" and "American" became firmly sutured together, over and against a variety of racialized, gendered, and national identities. Glickman writes, "Whereas previously, labor leaders had distinguished the United States from other countries by the sovereignty of its large class of producers, in the late nineteenth century, they began to maintain that America's high standards set it apart. . . . American republican institutions rested on a broad bed of affluence and taste and those with lower standards of living, claimed [labor leader] Ira Steward, were 'eminently unAmerican'" (1997, 84). Thus, for the white working class to become a legible and coherent category, it had to be defined through the pathologization and exclusion of a variety of nonnormative formations: racialized, gendered, immigrant, rural, and colonized. As such, those ethnic immigrant and rural white workers who were not completely interpellated as the normative white working class were aligned, though differently formed, with those explicitly defined against it.

Where can we read for the traces of these nonnormative subjects, those whose entrance into the white working class was both compelled and barred by capital's contradictory need to both differentiate and homogenize? As I noted earlier, some of these subjects emerge through the documents of the

Sociological Department itself, yet these subjects are rendered pathological and deviant. But we might read Dos Passos's *U.S.A.* as an archive itself, one that expresses the enormity of bureaucratic modernity, but also articulates its failures and crises by bringing these nonnormative subjects to life.

U.S.A. trenchantly critiques Fordist and Taylorist logics as inhumane and alienating, and excoriates U.S. capital for failing to make good on its promises. This text stages the struggle between socialist utopic ideals and the consumerist inducements that corporate capitalism holds out to the working class. This text's lacunae around the ways in which consumerism becomes a mode of enfranchisement and property acquisition for white ethnics over and against racialized subjects within the United States and colonial subjects abroad make it a document of U.S. whiteness and imperialism. As such, *U.S.A.* constitutes an omniscient, imperialist subject, expressed through its formal characteristics. However, while *U.S.A.* replicates the crushing enormity of bureaucratic capitalism, it is far from portraying this machinery as particularly effective. Rather, *U.S.A.* demonstrates the ways that material differences and histories prevent subjects from becoming interchangeable cogs in the machine. While portraying the efficiency of modernist bureaucracy, *U.S.A.* is also ironically peopled with bad workers and bad consumers.

Many have declared Dos Passos's *U.S.A.* to be the modernist literary text par excellence. I would argue that what makes Dos Passos's text modernist is its formal expression of bureaucratic governmentality: *U.S.A.* is an example of bureaucracy as aesthetic. Perhaps the paradigmatic example of such an aesthetic—the rationalization of the shop floor—is referenced in *U.S.A.* through the subjects of two of Dos Passos's many biographical excerpts: Henry Ford and Frederick Winslow Taylor. The highly regulated forms of production introduced to the world by these men redefined the worker's relation to space and time: time was controlled through the reorganization of space, where the work flowed to a stationary laborer, and not vice versa. These processes in concert broke the production process down into infinitely reducible parts, separating production, management, and design, deskilling the work, and hierarchizing the social relations within the factory:

> The great automotive boom was on. At Ford's production was improving all the time; less waste, more spotters, strawbosses, stoolpigeons (fifteen minutes for lunch, three minutes to go to the toilet, the Taylorized speedup

everywhere, reach under, adjust washer, screw down bolt, shove in cotterpin, reachunder adjustwasher, screwdown bolt, reachunderadjustscrewdownreach- underadjust until every ounce of life was sucked off into production and at night the workmen went home grey, shaking husks). (Dos Passos 1996, 813)

In the above passage, we see how this text denaturalizes the restructuring of time and space under early twentieth-century capitalism, thus exposing this new experience of time and space to diagnosis and critique. *U.S.A.* is scathingly condemnatory of the reorganization of the workspace that pri- oritizes efficiency in production over the bodily needs, if not the very lives, of the workers. In this passage, *U.S.A.* precisely and explicitly demonstrates the dehumanizing and crippling effects of the production process. Though specifically referencing only Ford, this passage targets the aspects of Ford- ism that owe a debt to Taylor's innovations: the breaking down of labor into its component parts that is the hallmark of Taylorism. This passage marks through both content and form the repetitive, monotonous, crush- ing nature of work under Taylorist and Fordist modes of production, which blur together without a break: "reachunderadjustscrewdownreachunder- adjust." Likewise, it forcefully critiques the dehumanizing and alienating conditions that turn men into "grey, shaking husks" as "every ounce of life was sucked off into production." In so doing, this passage references the process by which workers are denied the fulfillment and replenishment to reproduce "life" in the workplace, and are thus conditioned to look to the private sphere of the home as the site for the reproduction of the "life" of the human. The home is the site where the "husks" are turned back into men, only to be reduced to husks once more, presumably the next day. This passage alludes to the ways that the "home" to which these "grey shaking husks" return at the end of the draining workday becomes the repository of the affective and the emotional, and thus becomes the site that com- pensates for the alienation experienced in the public space of work.

This passage, and indeed, the trilogy as a whole, reproduces the logics of Fordism and Taylorism to expose the process of rationalization and alienation that is intrinsic to modern industrial production. As many schol- ars have argued, *U.S.A.* is a scathing critique of twentieth-century moder- nity as structured by U.S. capitalism. Barbara Foley notes, "The sketches appearing in the opening section of the novel [*The Big Money*], those of Fredrick Winslow Taylor and Henry Ford, depict the villains of Dos Passos's epic—the industrialists and engineers who have reduced human labor to a precisely quantifiable commodity and produced the full-fledged alienation of the working class under monopoly capitalism" (1980–81, 452). As a critical response to this process of alienation, Dos Passos crafted this epic narrative of the promise and betrayal of U.S. capitalism. A trilogy made up of three books, *The 42nd Parallel, 1919,* and *The Big Money, U.S.A.* begins with the optimism accompanying the dawn of the new century ("NATION GREETS CENTURY'S DAWN," 12) and ends with the dual betrayals of the execution of Sacco and Vanzetti in 1927 and the stock market crash of 1929.

Yet this critique of industrialization's dehumanization of workers is evident not only in passages that explicitly describe industrialization, but in the very structure and form of the text. *U.S.A.*'s formal structure mimics that of industrial capitalism, in particular the bureaucratic nature of Fordist and Taylorist modes of production. Spatially rather than temporally organized, compartmentalized, nondevelopmental, and anti-bildung, *U.S.A.*'s formal composition produces the subject of industrial capitalism to expose its dehumanizing effects. In so doing, *U.S.A.*'s strategy departs from an earlier, nineteenth-century reaction against industrial capitalism. Raymond Williams explains that in the eighteenth and nineteenth centuries, the definition of "literature" changed from the earlier meaning of all printed matter to a more specialized term that referenced only creative, imaginative works. Williams notes:

> The process of the specialization of "literature" to "creative" or "imaginative" works is very much more complicated. It is in part a major affirmative response, in the name of an essentially general human "creativity," to the socially repressive and intellectually mechanical forms of a new social order: that of capitalism and especially industrial capitalism. The practical specialization of work to the wage-labour production of commodities; of "being" to "work" in these terms; of language to the passing of "rational" or "informative" messages; of social relations to functions within a systematic economic and political order: all these pressures and limits were challenged in the name of a full and liberating "imagination" or "creativity." (1977, 49–50)

While similarly critical of industrialization, Dos Passos rejected the strategy of the fetishization of imagination, refusing the aestheticizing turn. Instead, *U.S.A.* reproduces the bureaucratized modes of industrial capitalism, producing such subjects through its formal composition to demonstrate the inhumanity of such a process.

As such, this text's formal strategies depart in a variety of ways from the "imaginative" mode. Instead, *U.S.A.*'s formal composition renders the developmental formation of a coherent individual subject impossible, and instead produces a nonhuman, bureaucratic subject. *U.S.A.*'s formal composition is not primarily organized by temporal development. *U.S.A.*'s formal coherence can be accurately described by Foucault's characterization of modern subjectivity: "[O]ur experience of the world is less that of a long life developing through time than that of a network that connects points and intersects with its own skein" (1986, 22). Unlike the developmental trajectory of the bildungsroman ("a long life developing through time"), *U.S.A.*'s structure is more akin to a map ("a network that connects points and intersects with its own skein"). One effect of *U.S.A.*'s cartographic, spatialized nature is that it can be entered and exited at any point. That is, unlike the traditional novel, *U.S.A.* does not require the reader to begin at the beginning and end at the end. Its various sections are thematically but not narratively related; one does not have to read the Newsreels or the Camera Eyes or the biographical sections to follow what happens in the fictional narratives, for example. None of the sections truly needs to be read in the order they are presented, though they generally proceed chronologically. As Barbara Foley argues, the rough chronology of the text emphasizes "sequential linkage over causal explanation" (1979, 359). Even the fictional narratives centered around the major characters do not truly demand linearity, for reading them in order does not guarantee narrative consistency. Minor characters are sometimes presented abruptly with no introduction, for example, as a narrative takes up after a prolonged gap (as in the narrative of Charley Anderson, a fictionalized Henry Ford doppelgänger). Indeed, *U.S.A.* subverts or punishes developmental reading strategies. Rather than progressing in a linear trajectory, *U.S.A.* maps out a series of relationships and events that intersect with each other in myriad ways. In its formal characteristics, *U.S.A.* both registers and reproduces this new relationship between space and capital that arose in the early twentieth century. As a spatialized cartography, its organizational logic is, Michael Denning argues, "an aesthetic Taylorism, a divided and rationalized labor" (1996, 170). *U.S.A.* formally reproduces the spatial logic of this new stage of capital, which demands a different aesthetic from that of nineteenth-century realism. Dos

Passos himself made the link; Denning hypothesizes, "Perhaps Dos Passos's self-mocking reference to the trilogy's structure as his 'four-way conveyor belt' was an acknowledgment that he may have built an assembly line" (170). For while the assembly line may seem to demand causality, it also subverts it. In other words, an assembly line does require a chronological sequence: certain parts must be worked on before others can be. Yet Fordism allows for the spatialization of that process, which has the effect of breaking down chronological sequence. One hundred or one thousand or ten thousand engines can be built at once and only then attached to the chassis, or vice versa, to use an automotive analogy. While each section must be built sequentially (as each chapter of *U.S.A.* is told sequentially), the relationship between sections need not be a causal one; there only needs to be a general overarching chronology. Dos Passos's strategy thus was to critique the Fordist bureaucracy by reproducing it.

U.S.A. is compartmentalized into four distinct and juxtaposed types of writing, paralleling the compartmentalizing, rationalizing logic of Fordism and Taylorism: the Newsreels, which excerpt newspaper headlines and articles, as well as popular songs; the semiautobiographical Camera Eye sections, written in stream-of-consciousness style; the biographical sketches of real historical figures, written almost as prose poems; and the fictional narratives organized around the major characters. In other words, *U.S.A.* is organized bureaucratically. The books are spatially divided by function, as in Fordism. Extending Denning's analogy, the reader is the *object* of production, rather than a worker. Like the automobile that travels through the factory, which is spatially divided to produce that automobile, the reader travels through the book, and is the object and result of the books' four genres, which, like the various mechanical and technological processes of the factory shop floor, are applied at various times and at various levels of intensity.

U.S.A.'s similarities with Taylorism may seem more of a stretch. Although it may seem odd to suggest that a text of over 1,200 pages approximates the logic of Taylorism, with its fanatical devotion to efficiency, Dos Passos's faith in form is, like Taylorism, an extremely instrumental logic: it implies that every section of *U.S.A.* has a purpose and is included to produce an effect, that it is antagonistic to an imagining of literature as ornamental, frivolous, or romantic. Form, for Dos Passos, is the technology of literature; each genre is a tool with which to produce readers as properly formed subjects. As Harvey notes, "One wing of modernism appealed to the image of rationality incorporated in the machine, the factory, the power of contemporary technology. . . . Ezra Pound had already advanced the thesis that language should conform to machine efficiency and . . . modernist writers as diverse as Dos Passos, Hemingway, and William Carlos Williams modeled their writing on exactly that proposition" (1990, 31).

Likewise, because it excoriates the nonhuman center of industrial capital exactly by reproducing that nonhuman subject, *U.S.A.* is an imperialist text. To read this text as a document of empire requires a spatialized mode of reading, rather than one that privileges temporality. Most scholars of *U.S.A.* read for narrative, a practice that above all stresses temporality and the cause-effect dynamic. What they often find is a narrative of the "decline and fall," whether it is of "American democracy" (Foley 1979, 359) or the "Lincoln Republic" (Denning 1996). Indeed, *U.S.A.* is an epitaph for the nation-state, as well as an epitaph for that which makes the nation-state: the novel form. Yet scholars also admit to *U.S.A.*'s "non-teleological" nature (Foley 1979, 364) and its inability to narrate a national myth of origins (Denning 1996, 199). Charles Marz accurately describes *U.S.A.*'s lack of "traditional unities of character and action," its formal characteristics of "little progress, little growth, little development of character," and its "no real concern with representation, illusion or empathy" (1980–81, 399). I argue that *U.S.A.* can be read as narrative, but must also be understood as cartography. As Marz notes, "The trilogy is not held together by any chain of events or 'storyline'; it must be apprehended spatially and not sequentially" (399).[7] Each reading practice (sequential or spatial) yields different, but interrelated results. Denning argues that *U.S.A.* has lost relevance in recent years because "it is an epitaph for an America that no longer exists" (1996, 199). While I agree with Denning's assessment that *U.S.A.* fails to narrate a heroic *national* myth, that it does not provide "stories of origin . . . the birth of nations" (199), I argue that this very "failure" can rather be seen as achievement, the achievement of another purpose. *U.S.A.* as a developmental *narrative* is, indeed, a lament for the decline of the nation-state form (Denning's "the decline and fall of the Lincoln Republic"); yet *U.S.A.* as a spatial *cartography* embodies and enacts the simultaneous and at times contradictory status of nation and empire. In other words, *U.S.A.* is narratively mourning the demise of a way of imagining the nation-state as a pure, territorially bound entity, while at the same time formally enacting the very imperialist function that robs the nation-state of its supposed innocence. *U.S.A.*'s various structures and formal innovations constitute another kind of U.S. subject, one that is not reducible to the citizen and thus cannot be entirely narrated through a national myth that privileges the citizen-subject. This subject is not reducible to the human characters in Dos Passos's books, but is rather the omniscient, world-conquering gaze produced through his use of the ironic narrative voice coupled with modernist pastiche, a kind of modernist universalism that constructs an expansive, totalizing concept of the "world." This gaze presumes abstract space, and performatively enacts a kind of imperialist surveillance over the world it creates. Likewise, this gaze is not embodied, is not coincident with a "person," but rather refers to a position, located firmly in a U.S. nationalist context, from which to view. In this way, *U.S.A.* is a panopticon as Foucault describes it, in that there is no need for an actual person to occupy the viewing position. Rather, the surveilling function of the panopticon works precisely because it is not coincident with any particular person.

In constituting an omniscient, disembodied subject, *U.S.A.* takes on the formal characteristics of imperialist modernism. This subject position is most obviously constituted by the Newsreels, which mimic a journalistic sense of objective omniscience. By including, even within a single section, headlines, songs, and descriptions from a diverse a set of locations, such as the Philippines and New Jersey, and events as serious as war and as frivolous as a publicity photo shoot of a studio star, the Newsreels produce a sense that nothing important goes unnoticed or uncategorized. The implication in reverse, of course, is that nothing uncategorized or unnoticed is of importance. Marz notes the fragmentation of the individual self in *U.S.A.*, writing, "In [the Newsreels] the world is dematerialized; scale is destroyed as persons and events are uniformly fragmented in space and time. Those verbal fragments of the world are cataloged and displayed" (406). This effectively achieves the aims of abstract space, which Lefebvre describes as "the imposition of homogeneity and transparency everywhere within the purview of power and its established order" (1991, 338). This gaze levels all events, turning a variety of human endeavors into interchangeable units of information, and in so doing, authorizes the subject of this gaze with the power to comprehend, discern, and decide. The formal strategies of the Newsreels underscore the sense that the subject of *U.S.A.* is not human, but rather U.S. imperialism itself. The sudden truncation of news stories and headlines, the abrupt enjambment of obviously different news stories (sometimes to grotesque, horrifying, or comic effect), and the seemingly random juxtaposition of headlines that are often incomprehensible without their context demonstrate that the Newsreels are not primarily meant for human consumption. As Marz notes, "Contexts are ignored and unexplained; the most intriguing observations remain hermetically sealed. The reader is estranged from the text by the insufficiency and the incompleteness of information" (406). They are not meant to be faithful reproductions or approximations of actual newsreels or newspapers, but documentary traces of U.S. empire.

While the Newsreels most obviously constitute a U.S. imperial subject, each of the different kinds of writing reproduces the gaze of U.S. empire. Even the form of writing that seems to most closely approximate a traditional genre, the fictional narratives of the twelve major characters, helps to constitute this omniscient subject. While the books do unfold in chronological time and each of the many characters' narratives begins in childhood and progresses to adulthood, *U.S.A.*'s characters do not develop and mature, unlike those of the traditional bildungsroman, for, as Marz notes, "Dos Passos chronicles a world in which psychological space disintegrates" (412). When the characters do change, their changes are seemingly unlinked to their previous experiences. Their narratives, though full of internal monologues, are not psychologized. Neither Richard Ellsworth Savage nor Charley Anderson's narratives, for instance, situate their postwar actions and motivations as reactions to the horrors of war they witnessed during their World War I service. Indeed, the fictional narratives are characterized by repetition and redundancy rather than growth. Thus, Charley Anderson starts off as a reckless youth who crashes his brother's new car and ends up a reckless adult who dies in a car crash. We repeatedly see each character making resolutions—whether it's Fainy "Mac" Macreary's resolve to stay true to the revolutionary cause of the IWW or Joe Williams's resolve to finally settle down and have a family—but for naught. None of these characters' desires to inhabit a narrative of development come to fruition. The success or failure of these characters in their careers and relationships has less to do with their own skill, desire, or motivation than with luck, coincidence, or most important, the social forces of their times. Margo Dowling's acting career, for instance, is doomed to soon fail as we learn that her physical beauty is not matched by a similar quality in her speaking voice in an era when silent films are beginning to be rendered obsolete by sound. Yet J. Ward Moorehouse, a seemingly callow, not particularly bright man, becomes one of the most powerful and influential people in the United States when he invents the field of public relations as a corporate management strategy to contain worker unrest.

The insignificance of these characters' lives leads to a sense of their interchangeability. Not only are the events of characters' lives repetitive within their own narratives, but they start to repeat each other. Mary French, "Daughter," Helen Mauer, Mac's wife Maisie, and Charley's one-time girlfriend, Emiscah, all find themselves pregnant after premarital sex, for example. The characters' stories are also often incomplete, with many unexplained breaks in the narrative, which further underscores the fact that they exist only insofar as they help illuminate the actual subject of the book. Mac's narrative ends abruptly, abandoned in the first book at a seemingly random moment. Charley Anderson's narrative finds him going off to war at the end of the first volume, *42nd Parallel,* and returning home at the end of the war at the beginning of the third and last volume, *The Big Money.* What happened to Charley in the intervening period is never mentioned. Eleanor Stoddard's narrative leaves off with her move to New York and consequent friendship with J. Ward Moorehouse, and it is only through her occasional appearances in other characters' narratives that we find out that she becomes an established interior decorator—given to throwing cocktail parties—who eventually marries minor European nobility. The fictional characters are also distorted mirror reflections of the subjects of the historical biographies: Charley Anderson, the ingenious mechanic, is Henry Ford if Ford had been outmaneuvered by competitors; Mac the idealistic Wobbly is Big Bill Haywood diverted from the cause of the working man, and so on. Savage is a version of the unnamed protagonist of the Camera Eye sections, whose experiences incorporate elements of Dos Passos's own autobiography. Coupled with the distanced, ironic third-person narration, the repetitive, interrupted, and nondevelopmental nature of these narratives has the effect of making these characters' lives seem partial and inconsequential, and their opinions and analyses of the world in which they live untrustworthy. As such, these characters do not invite identification. *U.S.A.* demonstrates that the individuated, privatized subject can only be narrated through developmental temporality. What Marz notes about the Camera Eye sections, that they "[represent] the slow dissolution of a coherent, private individual" (401) holds true for the entirety of *U.S.A.* When space rather than time is privileged, these individuated subjects break down, and another subject comes into view. The characters of *U.S.A.* exist only insofar as they help illuminate the true subject of the text: the United States, not only as nation, but as empire.

Like the fictional narratives, the biographies of historical figures convey the futility of individual will or effort, as each biographical subject meets betrayal, death, decline, and ironic reverses. Eugene Debs, the subject of the first biography, finds his supporters scarce when he is arrested and ends up a feeble man "on his porch in a rocker" (32). Henry Ford, his name practically synonymous with modernity and progress, ends up a "passion-ate antiquarian" who "had the new highway where the newmodel cars roared and slithered and hissed oilily past (*the new noise of the automobile*),/moved away from the door,/put back the old bad road,/so that everything might be/the way it used to be/in the days of horses and buggies" (814; italics in the original). Perhaps the grimmest "biography," entitled "The Body of an American," recounts the many possible births, lives, and deaths of an un-known soldier who dies brutally in war. The posthumous celebration of his heroic death by the representatives of the nation-state is depicted as hollow and self-aggrandizing: "Where his chest ought to have been they pinned/the Congressional Medal. . . . All the Washingtonians brought flowers" (760–61). Good-hearted working men are hounded to their graves, inge-nious inventors see their work appropriated for the ends of capital, and idealistic radicals are jailed, beaten, and betrayed by their comrades. The few "success" stories (Carnegie, Hearst, Morgan) are not so much about individuals as they are about the institutions they have built, which eventu-ally dwarf them. One such "biography" is "The House of Morgan," which, true to its title, does not concern one man or even a family, but the capi-talist juggernaut the Morgan lineage helped establish: "(Wars and panics on the stock exchange,/machinegunfire and arson,/bankruptcies, warloans,/starvation, lice, cholera and typhus:/good growing weather for the House of Morgan)" (645). The biographies lament that only capitalism, with its ability to transcend the individual, the historical, even the national, wins out in the end. Yet in constituting a subject that itself transcends the indi-vidual, the historical, the national, in order to comment on it all, *U.S.A.* replicates the omniscient subject of imperialist capitalism.

This is nowhere more evident than in the final of the four modes of writing, the "Camera Eye" sections. Dos Passos scholars have established these sections, written in an unpunctuated stream-of-consciousness style, as roughly autobiographical episodes, culled from life experiences such as Dos Passos's boyhood at elite boarding schools and his experience with the ambulance corps in World War II.[8] Yet these sections, which would seem to be the most personal and specific to an individual of all of the sections of this book, are perhaps most exemplary of *U.S.A.*'s transcendent, omniscient style. As Dos Passos himself noted, his purpose in the Camera Eye was to "drain off the subjective."[9] Accordingly, in this section, the text expresses the constitution of an individuated subject as observed through and by a camera: the "Camera Eye" as opposed to the visual eye. As such, rather than a consecutive, coherent narrative, these sections present individuated experience as successive flashes of images. A concept basic to the understanding of film is that film is not a seamless flow of visual images, as it seems to the naked eye, but a series of still images passing before the viewer's vision at a fast enough rate to appear fluid and uninterrupted (Bordwell and Thompson 2001, 2). A literary approximation of this process would look not unlike Dos Passos's Camera Eye sections. Granted, a developmental narrative, such as Donald Pizer's convincing argument that the Camera Eye sections chart a male authorial subject's "maturation into literary radicalism both as a sexual development into proper masculinity and as a discovery of a literary creed which is symbolically a father and a home" (419), can be traced through the Camera Eye sections. My argument is not that the style of the Camera Eye sections are not developmental, but that this section depicts this subject as it would look to a nondevelopmental perceptual regime, through a multiperspectival regime like that of film, rather than a uniperspectival one like that of a novel.

In this way, not only do each of the separate forms of writing individually constitute this omniscient subject, but the juxtaposition and use of these four kinds of writing (arguably representative of the major genres of writing: fictional narrative, biography, autobiography, and journalism) implies a kind of completion, of *U.S.A.*'s ability to represent totality. The epistemology of the subject of *U.S.A.* is abstract space, an epistemology that imagines all space as homogenously knowable, transversable, and malleable toward the aims of production and that underwrites the imperialist inclination. Denning observes, "The heart of Dos Passos's history was the story of the 'big money,' of 'the great imperial steamroller of American finance.' . . . Dos Passos was always uncomfortable with the slogan of 'proletarian literature'; his was more a tale of capital" (172). We can see that telling the story of U.S. capital in this period is telling the story of U.S. imperialism; more to the point, it is inhabiting and reproducing the subject of U.S. imperialism. In other words, the multiperspectival emphasis of early twentieth- century modernism can be understood as the cultural logic of U.S. imperialism. *U.S.A.* thus inhabits a contradictory, dual position. The modernist sense of alienation, of not being at home, is both keenly felt and inapplicable. On the one hand, the working class is always exiled, never at home in the United States, where "deputies crane their guns they stand guard at the mines they blockade the miner's soupkitchens . . . they have made us foreigners in the land where we were born" (1209). On the other hand, the subject of *U.S.A.* is quintessentially American, or in other words, imperialist. The text's traveling, imperialist gaze ensures that there is nowhere you cannot be, no space on earth that is not subject to its scrutiny.

Yet as omniscient and omnipotent as this apparatus of modernist bureaucracy seems, in *U.S.A.* it doesn't ever seem particularly effective. In other words, if the purpose of this mode of rationalization is to produce compliant, uniform, interchangeable workers who willingly relinquish their control over the work process for the security and stability of consumerist domesticity, the effects are far from reliable. Every worker in *U.S.A.* is a bad worker in one way or another. Charley Anderson is a rash hothead who becomes increasingly unreliable at his job. Dick Savage is an alcoholic who can barely keep himself together. We see time and again in *U.S.A.* that as much as bureaucratic modernity tries to produce good workers and consumers, this process itself creates recalcitrant, contradictory subjects. These contradictory recalcitrances on the part of the workers are not about the heroic narrative of individual struggle against the impersonal forces of capitalism. In fact, as noted earlier, the characters' will and desire have nothing to do with their eventual outcomes. The characters' collective inability to become cogs in the machine is not portrayed as the individualized faults of these flawed characters. The irony of evacuating agency and will from human subjects is that their failings are not their own either. Rather, the process of being incorporated into labor discipline produces the material histories of difference at the very moment these differences are supposedly being erased. Capitalism must attempt to perform the impossible trick of using these differences in the service of uniformity and standardization.

The very qualities that make characters good workers are what ultimately make them inadequate. Charley Anderson's iconoclasm and risk-taking mentality make him an innovator who jump-starts a fledgling industry—air travel—but the same characteristics make him reckless and immature, unable to be resolved to the social order. Dick Savage's extreme anxiety and desire to please the boss enable him to produce winning PR campaigns, but also turn him into an alcoholic. Indeed, Dick Savage's dependence on alcohol demonstrates the ways that consumerism often does not lead to good, conscientious laborers, as Ford suggested, but to frivolous ones with no self-control. We see this as a theme throughout *U.S.A.*, so much so that Michael Denning has noted the importance of the cocktail party to the narrative structure of the text. Alcohol becomes a metaphor for the simultaneously creative and destructive nature of consumerist capital.

U.S.A. thus underscores the fallacy of imagining consumerism as the panacea to all of life's troubles. It also stresses the ways that consumerism is not universally accessible, but depends on the exclusion of some. Joe Williams's attempts to settle down and become a part of the respectable working class repeatedly end in failure, and Joe ends up dying in a bar brawl. Joe's narrative underscores the ways that the wheels of capitalism were lubricated not only by the white working class's attainment of respectability, but by the concomitant creation of the nonrespectable classes. Yet the existence of these unassimilable subjects hints at alternative modes of being that are not exhausted by capitalism's totalizing narrative. Joe, as well as many of the other characters, represents what must be pathologized, repressed, and sloughed off in the process of creating a coherent white working class. Consumerist domesticity often goes awry, not providing the satisfying resolution it promises, and in so doing, relegates would-be consumerists to uneven and unruly modes of life.

Consumerism thus becomes less a monolithic force than a field or terrain composed of uneven and disparate modes of interaction, incorporation, and contestation. Consumerism attempts to create an ideal of equivalence, but instead produces differentiation. In chapter 4 I trace this differentiation as it extends into the late twentieth century, when consumerism becomes the vocabulary of neocolonialism. Examining texts by Jessica Hagedorn and Helena Maria Viramontes, I argue that consumerism's importance does not preclude modes of struggle, but rather demands new ways of apprehending how contestation and contradiction emerge.

chapter 4

CONSUMERISM WITHOUT MEANS: IMMIGRANT WORKERS AND THE NEOCOLONIAL CONDITION

They went into my closets looking for skeletons, but thank God, all they found were shoes, beautiful shoes.
> —IMELDA MARCOS, on the occasion of the opening of her shoe museum, February 16, 2001

The irony of Imelda Marcos's statement is, of course, that the skeletons in her copious closet actually have very much to do with shoes. The world was scandalized when, during the 1986 coup that ousted her husband Ferdinand Marcos as military dictator of the Philippines, it emerged that she reputedly owned three thousand pairs of shoes while the majority of her country lived in crippling poverty. To be fair, Imelda has claimed that the number was exaggerated and that she owned only 1,060 pairs; still, it seems safe to say that Imelda is the consummate consumer. The woman who once reportedly proclaimed "win or lose, we go shopping after the election" is the symbol of conspicuous consumption gone to extremes, a subject who has so adeptly internalized the neocolonial injunction to consume that she embodies all of its perversities and contradictions. While Imelda is not mentioned by name in Jessica Hagedorn's *Dogeaters* (1990), an uncannily similar character, referred to only as the President's Wife, can be read as an unlikely representative. Quite unlike the anticonsumerist politics of *U.S.A.*, *Dogeaters* embraces consumerism and in so doing, exposes the many contradictions of neocolonial capitalism. *Dogeaters* demonstrates that even late twentieth-century global capital is not so much composed of an internally coherent, totalizing logic as it is productive of excessive desires that go beyond capital's ability to manage or satisfy.

I begin with this reference to Imelda Marcos to introduce my discussion of the many contradictions of late twentieth-century capital. In this chapter, I identify specific formal strategies in Jessica Hagedorn's *Dogeaters* (1990) and Helena Maria Viramontes's *The Moths and Other Stories* (1985) as examples of alternative epistemologies that register racialized immigrant women's specific relationship to late twentieth-century global capital. These alternative epistemologies, like the "postmodernism" described by Fredric Jameson or David Harvey, emerge from the conditions of "flexibility" that constitute the logic of late twentieth-century global capital. However, I do not read these texts as "postmodern" in that way, for such a reading would occlude more than it would reveal. Unlike the totalizing view of commodified culture that Jameson's or Harvey's "postmodernism" describes, I read Hagedorn's and Viramontes's texts as demonstrating the ways that late twentieth-century global capital produces differentiated, contradictory formations.

In using the term "flexibility," I reference political economic discussions that note that late twentieth-century global capital is marked by the hyperextraction of profits through the use of a variety of strategies of accumulation. Scholars have termed this accumulation strategy "flexible accumulation," wherein Fordist modes of production exist side-by-side with ostensibly "nonmodern" modes, such as patriarchal, artisanal, semilegal and illegal modes such as sweatshops and home work. In other words, in political economic analysis, the notion of "flexibility" refers to the explicit use of differentiation and diversification as an accumulation strategy. Racialized women—often very young—are the preferred workforce for transnational capital in the contemporary era, as corporations deliberately exploit and thereby reproduce racialized and gendered difference to more efficiently extract profits. Taking the idea of "flexibility" from political economic analyses of late twentieth-century capital, I extend this notion of the use of differentiation as a strategy to argue that this logic structures in general all of the practices of late twentieth-century capital, not only specifically economic accumulation strategies. Although the cultural logic of late twentieth-century capital seems to prioritize differentiation, it ultimately attempts to instantiate a new form of universality in the notions of consumerism and commodification. In this context, postmodern accounts of globalization, like those of Fredric Jameson or David Harvey, posit consumerism as a totalizing process that completely commodifies culture; this commodified culture is what they term "postmodern" culture. These descriptions of postmodernity describe culture as completely saturated by capital, and therefore preclude the possibility of culture as a site for contestation or crisis.

As categories of race and gender are mobilized to reproduce capital, however, they must also exist as capital's contradiction. While keeping in mind that no space is "untouched" by the processes of late twentieth-century global capitalism, we must also remember that capital does not operate homogeneously. As such, I read these texts by Viramontes and Hagedorn differently than Harvey or Jameson might read commodity culture insofar as I situate these cultural texts as sites of contestation, in which alternative understandings of globalization might emerge. To restate, rather than understanding culture as completely commodified and thus merely an extension of late twentieth-century global capitalism, I take up racialized immigrant women's culture to situate culture as a terrain of struggle, where the contradictions of late twentieth-century global capital materialize. Hagedorn's text does so by taking up the idea of the consumer itself. In *Dogeaters*, consumerism is the vocabulary through which different, neocolonial histories are expressed. As such, Hagedorn's text does not posit neocolonized and racialized cultures as autonomously formed or irreducibly other to the consumerist culture of late twentieth-century capitalism, but as inextricably conditioned by it. Yet *Dogeaters* demonstrates that racialized, gendered, neocolonial subjects differently experience, inhabit, and articulate even something as seemingly universalizing as consumer culture. As such, these subjects attest to the ways that capital produces excessive desires that it cannot contain or resolve. Viramontes's text attests to the fact that other forms of culture, not entirely reducible to consumerism, exist. The culture of migrant racialized and gendered labor—expressed in Viramontes's text as a kind of magical realism, the mundane fantastic—does not develop autonomously from late twentieth-century global capital, but is as much an expression of global capital as consumer culture is. Yet the cultures of racialized and gendered labor are an expression of global capital's contradictions, excesses, and ruptures.

As I have argued in the previous chapters, the "empty, homogeneous time" that was the epistemic dominant of the nineteenth century, which narrated its ventures and legitimated its rule, was replaced in the early twentieth century by its spatial equivalent: abstract space. New modes of industrial production within the United States, as well as U.S. imperialism abroad, arose in abstract space, sustaining and being sustained by it. Yet these very conditions of abstraction—the attempt to remake the world in the image of abstract space—are exactly what produce difference and unevenness, because "profit" (in the form of surplus value, as in the Fordist factory, or racialized difference, as in the colony) is derived from this unevenness. While in the early twentieth century abstract space found expression in the totalizing logic of bureaucracy, in the latter half of the twentieth century, the orderly bureaucratic apparatus of Fordism proved too unwieldy. Post-Fordist capital jettisoned the bulky bureaucratic apparatus of Fordism, but retained and, indeed, expanded on, the consumer culture initiated in the Fordist era. A seemingly totalizing culture of commodification emerged as the defining cultural form of post-Fordism. In this post-Fordist era, the logic of capitalism is explicitly differentiation or "flexibility," rather than the abstraction of "empty homogeneous time" of nineteenth-century narratives of development or the "abstract space" of early twentieth-century multiperspectival bureauracy. The fetishization of difference seen in late twentieth-century discourses is what I am calling "flexibility."

It may seem that this new logic, which explicitly utilizes differentiation, is a break from previous models, which attempted, however incompletely, to produce uniformity and abstraction, whether through the empty homogeneous time of the possessive individual or the abstract space of totalizing bureaucracy. But I argue that the explicit fetishization of difference inherent to the logic of flexibility is a mode that attempts to universally and uniformly extend a form of production and consumption, albeit a form based on differentiation. In other words, because differentiation was such a disruption to these previous dominants, flexibility makes virtue out of necessity and utilizes differentiation. But flexibility cannot account for the material histories that are in excess of even itself. In other words, while these logics of flexibility may seem to privilege historically and materially constituted particularities, they are themselves actually forms of abstraction, which, like the narrative of development of the late nineteenth century or the modernist bureaucracy of the early twentieth, occlude the material and historical conditions of their own possibility. The effect of the earlier modes of temporal or spatial abstraction was to occlude the inequities of power and the forcible relations of rule. The effect of "flexibility" is the same. I read the works of Viramontes and Hagedorn as exposing the ways that "postmodernist" accounts of the disintegration of the possessive individual elide the histories of colonialism and neocolonialism that are the proper context for this disintegration.

"Flexibility" as a concept has its origins in political economic discussions of late capitalism. It has been widely discussed that late capitalism depends on strategies of "flexible accumulation" and "mixed production," in which Fordist factories are supplemented by other, more informal modes of production, often using gray- or black-market labor organized through feudal, patriarchal, ethnic, or artisanal logics. A developmental conception of capitalism prior to the latter half of the twentieth century maintained that "nonmodern" and informal production processes would eventually be eclipsed, and that Fordism would become the universal production model. Ironically, both management and labor depended on this narrative of capitalist development. Management (such as Ford and Taylor) imagined modernization as producing uniformly happy and compliant workers, while many Marxist scholars and labor organizers argued that the similarity of working conditions under a homogenizing Fordism would render differences of race, ethnicity, gender, and nationality insignificant, and make labor the most important condition of working life, as well as the only significant locus around which to organize. As I argued in chapter 3, this universalizing tendency made the white working class hegemonic (and thus not antagonistic to, but in collusion with capital) insofar as it facilitated the erasure of a variety of heterogeneous formations: both the colonized and racialized populations against which the white working class was defined, and those ethnic white immigrants and rural whites whose incorporation into consumerist domesticity was uneven and contentious. Therefore, insofar as racialized immigrant female labor is the "new proletariat" under globalization, this category is aligned with subaltern formations of previous eras. But the proper antecedent to this "new proletariat" is not so much the white working class as it is those who, as I argued in chapter 3, could not be incorporated into a white working class: colonized and racialized subjects, as well as those "improperly" and incompletely interpellated into consumerist domesticity.

Because this strategy of homogenization was so contradictory and unstable, it has been displaced under late twentieth-century global capital in favor of an emphasis on differentiated modes of accumulation that have proved to be the most profitable. For the past three decades, political economists have been describing a different capitalist strategy, often referred to as "flexible accumulation," where Fordist factories exist alongside more "informal" modes of production. Such production modes include sweatshops organized not through rationalized bureaucracy, but through very personal familial or ethnic ties. In this era, subcontracting has also become a widespread practice, one that allows transnational corporations to avoid liability for illegal and substandard labor practices while more efficiently extracting surplus value through subsistence level wages, the use of child or prison labor, and the violation of environmental, health, and safety standards. Not only do such practices exist, but the largest of transnational corporations depend on them, meaning that within "modern" economies some of the most "nonmodern" of practices proliferate. In this context, the analytic rubric of "flexible accumulation" displaces the earlier developmental narrative by noting that late capital opportunistically uses both "modern" and "nonmodern" modes simultaneously, rather than emphasizing a temporally arranged narrative where the nonmodern is superseded by the modern.

Scholars such as Jameson and Harvey have identified "postmodernism" as the cultural analogue to such political economic practices as "flexible accumulation." In an influential essay, "Postmodernism and Consumer Society," Jameson argues that pastiche, or the random juxtaposition of a variety of styles, eras, aesthetics, and temporalities, is one of the most significant features of postmodernism, the cultural component of a "new type of social life and a new economic order" that became dominant after World War II (1983, 113). Jameson establishes a dominant high modernism—"Abstract Expressionism; the great modernist poetry of Pound, Elliott, or Wallace Stevens; the International Style (Le Corbusier, Frank Lloyd Wright, Mies van der Rohe); Stravinski, Joyce; Proust and Mann" (111–12)—against which postmodernism reacts. Modernism, in this narrative, is limited to an Anglo-American intellectual tradition, and thus we must remember that the postmodern forms that he reads as reacting against this specific mode of modernism compose likewise a very particular tradition that does not encompass all forms of culture. From this intellectual genealogy, Jameson defines pastiche as arising from a state in which "one no longer [believes] in the existence of normal language, of ordinary speech, of the linguistic norm" (114). With the lack of a linguistic norm or, in other words, with the death of the autonomous, coherent, individuated (in other words, propertied) subject, the abolition of "a unique self and private identity," there remains "nothing but stylistic diversity and heterogeneity" (114). Nostalgia replaces history, as styles from all past eras are randomly and equivalently juxtaposed. Harvey reads pastiche as the cultural analogue of capital's use of multiple modes of production in *The Condition of Postmodernity*. In the same way that flexible accumulation disrupts developmental temporality by using "modern" alongside "nonmodern" forms of production, pastiche recycles and recirculates styles from a variety of eras.

Yet this new stage not only does not obviate differences of race and gender, but it depends on them and reproduces them structurally. Indeed, this is exactly what makes flexible accumulation more profitable: it more efficiently uses racialized and gendered difference to enable the hyperextraction of surplus value. Swasti Mitter contends that one must focus on poor racialized women in the global economy because the restructuring of labor has occurred on the basis of race and gender. Unlike the manufacturing labor base in the Fordist era, the majority of the workers in the post-Fordist era are racialized women, usually very young. The new workers are those very workers who were marginalized in the organized labor movements of the past. Transnational corporations seek out labor that has not been the target of earlier organizing efforts, either young women who might stay away from organized labor on the shop floor or workers in family-based sweatshops. As these jobs are shifted from men to women, and from white to racialized workers, they are also shifted from high-wage, permanent work to low-wage, casual work. In this era, post-Fordist capital reproduces "traditional" modes of racialized and gendered exploitation to extract surplus value. Legal scholars Laura Ho, Catherine Powell, and Leti Volpp have noted the ways the entire garment industry is dependent on sweatshops that are ethnically and patriarchally organized. These scholars have demonstrated that immigration laws are constituted to ensure that ethnic or familial structures are intrinsic to the maintenance of a hyper-exploitable, vulnerable workforce of immigrants, mainly women. They note that the "family reunification" structure of current U.S. immigration laws makes immigrants dependent on their family members for residency and citizenship status and limits these women's ability to negotiate their working conditions because they often work for the very relatives who are sponsoring their immigration.

Therefore, for immigrant women, the family or racial/ethnic community is the site where they are incorporated into the labor market and subjected to labor conditioning, rather than the site that protects them from the exigencies of work, as in the modern bourgeois conception of family and the domestic space. Ho, Powell, and Volpp argue that these seemingly "nonmodern" and "un-American" forms of exploitative labor practices that are dependent on familial relationships are indeed exactly what sustains "modern American" corporations, stating that "sweatshops . . . are a home-grown problem with peculiarly American roots" (1996, 385).

Other scholars have demonstrated that sex work, child labor, domestic work, and other so-called informal labor sectors that reproduce racialized and gendered difference enable a variety of "formal" economies. As Rhacel Parreñas has argued, the contemporary era has seen the incorporation of reproductive labor as a crucial site for capitalist accumulation. Parreñas argues that there now exists an "international division of reproductive labor," or in other words, that reproductive labor is outsourced to third world women and immigrant women of color. Structural adjustment programs and foreign debt make nations such as the Philippines dependent on the remittances that overseas contract workers send back to their families, while state and corporate structures in advanced industrial nations make child care and domestic labor a personal and familial concern, making working women dependent on nannies and maids. She therefore demonstrates that global capital is dependent on the wealth generated by reproductive labor done by racialized and third world women.

While racial and gendered exploitation is intrinsic to informal sectors such as domestic work, it is also crucial for the operation of even those modes of production that seem to operate in modern and bureaucratic ways. As Aihwa Ong, Susan Tiano, and activists such as Mary Tong have noted, even the Fordist factories like the maquiladoras along the U.S.–Mexico border or the production plants in export processing zones [EPZs] in Southeast Asia do not produce homogeneous workers exploited under a singular rubric of class, but build patriarchal, racialized, and gendered practices into the structures of factory labor. As Tiano (1994) has noted, the maquiladora sector exploits and exacerbates familial structures of gendered obligation to reproduce a vulnerable labor force of women. Ong (1991) argues that industrial labor relations and local mores are often in collusion in their rearticulation of male and racial superiority. Likewise, rather than evenly "despotic" and repressive labor regimes, there are many new forms of control that often are manifested as the control over a series of spaces, including the shop floor, but also the body, the state, and the public sphere. Tong has documented the ways that sexual harassment, rape, and pregnancy discrimination are a fundamental mode of labor control in these factories. Thus even the Fordist factories in the post-Fordist era depend on so-called "traditional" or "nonmodern" modes of exploitation.

In these many ways, flexible accumulation's strategy of mixing nonmodern and modern forms of production depends on and reproduces racialized and gendered exploitation. We must therefore write back into our analysis of postmodernism as the cultural analogue to post-Fordism an understanding of the inequities of power and hierarchy upon which such "postmodern" cultures are based. In other words, "pastiche" as the random recycling of past styles or modes, when understood in relation to accumulation strategies, is not random or neutral, but is a mode of exploitation that exacerbates racialized and gendered inequities. These inequities create a variety of differentiated relationships to late twentieth-century global capitalism. As such, late twentieth-century capital *cannot* produce a totalizing commodified global culture, as Jameson has argued. Rather, capital produces a variety of differentiated, contradictory formations. Madhu Dubey's notion of "uneven development" is useful here. She writes that "processes of capitalist reorganization have clearly followed a racialized logic of uneven development, sharpening already existing inequalities and polarities" (2003, 25). While Dubey is referring in particular to the political economic restructuring of the U.S. economy that led to deindustrialization and the further impoverishment of African American communities, this notion of uneven development implies that a variety of conditions of racialized and gendered exploitation characterizes late twentieth-century capital. In other words, the conditions that produce racialized and gendered immigration in the United States exist as another example of the uneven development of late twentieth-century global capitalism. For Dubey, these conditions of uneven development signal a different relationship to "postmodernity" for African American culture:

> The concept of uneven development . . . [allows] us to grasp and to conceive of dominant and residual trends as disparate yet systematically linked. By this logic African American life would not be wholly subsumed within

the "cultural dominant" of postmodernism. . . . At the same time, however, African American culture does not form a residual category that develops in complete autonomy from the dominant culture. (24)

In the same vein, racialized immigrant women's culture registers the uneven relationships to late twentieth-century capital's accumulation practices, relationships conditioned by the different circumstances of racialized and gendered labor.

Further, far from only describing modes of exploitation, histories of race and gender also allow for the emergence of organizational strategies and opportunities for struggle that go beyond the rubric of traditional labor organizing modeled on the white working class of the early twentieth century. In particular, these new struggles blur the line between "social movements" and culture. Mitter (1986) argues that globalized capital creates a new female proletariat that is faced with new challenges, but also holds potential for an entirely different kind of labor movement, one that prioritizes differences of race and gender as opposed to the singular class solidarity of earlier labor movements. Likewise, Ong notes that the attempt to judge all forms of resistance along older models of strict class struggle will efface other methods of resistance deployed by the women workers. Ong replaces the concept of class struggle with what she calls "cultural struggle," opening up the definition of struggle to include the daily practices of women who contest *cultural* meanings, values, and goals. Rather than investing in strict distinctions between "culture" and "social movements," we might imagine Viramontes's and Hagedorn's texts as two examples of such "cultural struggles," through which racialized and gendered subjects express the different ways of knowing and narrating subjects and communities that emerge from the uneven conditions of late twentieth-century capital.

These alternative modes of knowing emerge as the colonial mimicry of the neocolonial consumer as articulated through the formal strategy of "pastiche" in *Dogeaters,* and as the expression of transnational migrant labor as a contradictory epistemological formation in the "mundane fantastic" of Viramontes's stories. An analysis that opens up the notion of struggle to include culture allows us to understand that the role of racialized and gendered difference is not only to exacerbate the extraction of surplus value and thus posit capitalism as totalizing. Such an analysis would take up texts like Hagedorn's and Viramontes's in order to displace an economic determinism and positivism that would situate all "true" struggles as occurring in the sphere of the political or the economic. Toward such a goal, we can read such cultural texts as citing the material histories of colonialism, neocolonialism, and transnational labor migration that have been a foundational, if occluded, condition of possibility for twentieth-century global capitalism. Such cultures can be read as counterhegemonic struggles in this new "flexible" era.

Pastiche in *Dogeaters* is not about the random display of past styles, but about the juxtapositions that happen under consumerist neocolonialism. As Lisa Lowe reminds us, central to the formal strategy of *Dogeaters* is "the turn around different kinds of 'seeming,' the cultural, racial, and linguistic admixtures that are the contemporary expression of a history of colonial and commercial encounter in the Philippines" (1996, 118). Referring back to my discussion of Henri Lefebvre's concepts of "induced" and "produced" difference in chapter 3, we can understand "pastiche" in the way that Jameson describes it in *Postmodernity, or the Cultural Logic of Late Capital,* as "the random cannibalization of all the styles of the past, the play of random stylistic allusion" (18), as a form of induced difference, and the "pastiche" of *Dogeaters* as a form of produced difference. I pause here to restate my discussion of Lefebvre's differentiation between what he calls "induced difference" and "produced difference." Lefebvre writes,

> An *induced* difference remains within a set or a system generated according to a particular law. It is in fact constitutive of that set or system. . . . Similarly: the diversity between villas in a suburb filled with villas; or between different "community facilities"; or again, variations within a particular fashion in a dress, as stipulated by that fashion itself. By contrast, a *produced* difference presupposes the shattering of a system; it is born of an explosion; it emerges from the chasm opened up when a closed universe ruptures. (1991, 72)

While the "pastiche" of *Dogeaters* cites consumerism, using its vocabulary of spectacle and desire, it cannot be reduced to merely an effect of consumerism. The mixing together of seemingly disparate styles, narratives, modes of writing, and chronologies is not "random," but registers the particular conditions of neocolonialism. *Dogeaters* presents consumerism as organizing and producing the neocolony, but also as excluding or erasing it. As such, consumerism interpellates subjects and produces desires, but, as we see time and again in this text, these desires often go awry.

Likewise, Viramontes's use of the "mundane fantastic" expresses the contradictions of racialized migrant labor and thus must be understood as emerging from transnational capital. I will situate Viramontes within a tradition of Latin American magical realist writing, but argue that Viramontes's mundane fantastic is, to use Alejo Carpentier's phrase, the "new optic" produced out of, but exceeding the contemporary conditions of, globalized capital.[1] The formal strategy of "The Moths," the mundane fantastic, is a mode in which the occurrence of the magical is always tied to the most banal of circumstances. Neither reductively determinist in its insistence on the material production of racialized and gendered difference, nor glibly dismissive of race and gender as yet another consumer good or demographic to be used and discarded at will, "The Moths" gives us a nonessentializing yet materialist reading practice that can be called the "mundane fantastic."

We cannot read the formal strategies of "pastiche" and "mundane fantastic" in *Dogeaters* and "The Moths" as another form of commodified ahistorical postmodernism, for that would erase the ways these texts resurrect the histories of colonialism and neocolonialism that these forms excavate. These formal strategies point to the slipperiness of language, not as an effect of a general breakdown of meaning in a postmodern era, but as having a particular history: the role and effect of language under repressive neocolonial dictatorships that both insist on and blatantly disregard the dictates of "truth." As in Jameson's discussion of postmodernism, we can understand the lack of faith in language and its ability to convey "truth" as a consequence of the lack of a linguistic norm that accompanied the displacement of the individuated propertied subject. But as Viramontes's and Hagedorn's texts remind us, the very conditions under which this linguistic norm fell apart were those of colonial and neocolonial violence. In other words, because the possessive individual was displaced by multiperspectival bureaucracy precisely to exacerbate the United States' imperialist ventures, we must write in what Jameson's articulation of postmodernism erases: the colonial and racialized violence that accompanied the displacement of the propertied citizen-subject of the U.S. nation-state.

Dogeaters, set in the era of martial law and dictatorship, pointedly reveals the instability of language. Denials, disavowals, and outright fictions abound under a dictatorship, yet unlike the dictates of "fiction," these words have the ability to create reality outright, rather than merely reflecting it mimetically. Thus, Romeo Rosales is not a mere busboy/wannabe-matinee-idol who happens to be in the wrong place at the wrong time; he is opposition leader Senator Avila's assassin, with established ties to guerilla forces. Never mind that Senator Avila's assassins were agents of the government. Never mind that Romeo Rosales wouldn't know the business end of a gun if it hit him in the head, which, actually, it does. Under such a regime, the appeal of the "lies" of consumerism is easy to understand. The ability of the central narrator, Rio, and her cousin Pucha to divorce the lure of consumerism from any hope of gratification is a register of the colonial context, wherein the symbolic structures the real and where lies are more solid and have more consequences and more weight than the truth.

In making consumerism a condition of pleasurable falsity—a lie that is real, in other words—*Dogeaters* describes the continually elicited but never satisfied desire that is colonial consumerism. Throughout the book, Manila is presented as a consumerist paradise/wasteland, through which consumer culture, both U.S. and local, circulates. *Dogeaters* presents the colonized condition as a state of consumerism without means, in which colonized subjects are simultaneously interpellated by and distanced from—economically, culturally, politically—the glamorized images of American life that constantly surround them. From the hustler who names himself after a Las Vegas casino to the busboy who dreams of becoming a movie star only to end up a casualty of martial rule, the denizens of *Dogeaters'* Manila circulate in a world part fantastic, part realist, in which the images of the celluloid screen are more tangible and authentic than life, and the exigencies of life under military rule and neocolonialism are more grotesque, incredible, and queer than anything that could be dreamed up in fiction. In Hagedorn's Manila, the government under military dictatorship inaugurates a clean-up campaign in which people are paid five dollars for every one thousand flies killed and collected (187). The same government ensures that when the mother of a dissident poet disappears, she not only no longer exists, but "has never existed" (154). In this context, one "can no longer tell what's authentic from what's fake," a condition attributed to Severo Alacran, the "King of Coconuts" and the most powerful man in the country, but which applies to anyone (21). As Lowe notes, "The antirepresentational strategies in Hagedorn's text propose an alternative aesthetic to the realist mode, and in that alternative, the text opens space for a different historical subject engaged with that aesthetic" (Lowe 1996, 120). *Dogeaters* achieves the disassembling of the rules of realism through the use of pastiche. In this text, pastiche is the expression of the excesses inherent in consumerism, but in consumerism as the most exact metaphor for neocolonialism. Yet as I have noted, pastiche in *Dogeaters* is not the Jamesonian sense of the empty mimicking of past styles and mannerisms in the absence of a sense of history.[2] Rather, pastiche is the expression of the material remnants of the processes of colonization. Pastiche, or the juxtaposition of diverse, sometimes incongruous styles, genres, temporalities and realities that constitutes the formal strategy of this text, is the formal representation of *Dogeaters'* Manila.

In *Dogeaters,* consumerism is the neocolonial condition par excellence. As such, consumerism in *Dogeaters* cannot be divorced from its colonial history. In the pre–World War II era of official U.S. colonialism, "American" became the disciplinary category par excellence, the radically uninhabitable ideal to which Filipinos were to ascribe. Yet as I noted in chapter 3, the era of U.S. imperialism in the Philippines was also the very moment in which "American" was inextricably bound to "consumer." U.S. territorial imperialism "failed," but its imperial experiment in the Philippines produced the technologies of neocolonialism that made consumerism a *more,* rather than *less,* important category. U.S. neocolonialism became a way of extending the ideal of consumerism as citizenship all over the world. In other words, the U.S. colonial experiment in the Philippines "failed" insofar as the United States became a colonial power at the exact moment when this older form of colonial rule was becoming obsolete. Instead, the United States crafted a newer form of global influence that we call neocolonialism, in which the United States is a world power, while simultaneously disavowing its own ideological influence. This ideological denial requires that U.S. national culture "forgets" its history of territorial rule in the Philippines as this history blatantly gives the lie to U.S. claims of innocence.[3] Yet neocolonial relations of rule simultaneously depend on the very structures that arose from the era of U.S. colonialism: consumerism.

As such, unlike a conventionally postmodern understanding of consumerism, which evacuates it of its history, for *Dogeaters* consumerism is exactly all about history: the history of colonialism and neocolonialism that was precisely narrated through, and mobilized around, consumerism.

A conventionally postmodern understanding of pastiche understands this form as a kind of ahistorical consumerism, where all styles, formal characteristics, eras, or periods are at one's disposal. The varied facades of stores in a shopping mall, each referencing a different era, aesthetic, or style, whether it be the neon, state-fair carnivalesque of a Hot Dog on a Stick or the quaint Victoriana of a Crabtree and Evelyn, are perhaps the most obvious examples of this kind of ahistorical pastiche. This form of consumerism elides the differences between the histories of the referents, rendering the social and historical contexts of state fairs and English apothecaries equivalent and, more importantly, irrelevant, in their missions to sell corn dogs or perfumed soaps. This form of consumerism erases both the history of the consumerist subject, which arose out of white working-class complicity with racialized labor hierarchies in the early twentieh century, and the contemporary "international division of labor," in which workers in export-processing zones all over the world cannot afford to buy the products they make.

While this kind of ahistorical postmodern understanding of consumerism occludes these histories in a totalizing model that evacuates any sense of the crises and contradictions inherent within consumerism, Néstor García Canclini has a more dialectical understanding of how consumerism works in the global era. In *Consumers and Citizens: Globalization and Multicultural Conflicts* (2001), he argues that, under globalization, the functions of citizenship are far from obsolete, but are rather relocated to a transnational context. García Canclini argues that consumerism has replaced many of the functions of citizenship, including a sense of group membership and identity, the creation of a public sphere, and the endowment of a sense of agency. García Canclini's approach to consumerism is helpful because rather than dismissing all forms of consumerism as helplessly and mechanistically determined by capital, he identifies the ways that the new emphasis on consumerism opens up new terrains for the emergence of social formations in contestation with and in excess of global capital. In this way, García Canclini suggests the unstable nature of consumerism.[4]

Dogeaters likewise describes a more complicated relationship to consumerism. In so doing, *Dogeaters* demonstrates that racialized, gendered, neocolonial subjects inhabit and experience even such a seemingly universalizing process as consumerism differently. From its very beginning, the text thematizes colonial consumerism as the simultaneous privileging of and displacement from an American ideal. In the opening vignette, Rio, one of the book's narrators, recalls watching a lush Hollywood film as a pre-adolescent in a Manila theater, accompanied by her older cousin, Pucha. Instead of the pristine artificiality of *All That Heaven Allows,* set against a rural New England winter backdrop, the Avenue Theater smelled of "flowery pomade, sugary chocolates, cigarette smoke, and sweat," and was full of "furtive lovers stealing noisy kisses" (3). Later, in a café, Rio watches her "overripe cousin" responding to a teenage boy who "leers" and makes "kissing sounds with his fat lips," in marked contrast to the epic and ethereal romance of Rock Hudson and Jane Wyman (5). The difference between the tragic love story depicted in the film and Pucha's imminently pragmatic teenage flirtation is further underscored when Pucha informs Rio that the teenage boy is Boomboom Alacran, scion of the wealthiest and most powerful man in the Philippines, declaring, "I don't care if he's a little *gordito,* or *pangit,* or smells like a dead goat. . . . He's cute enough for me" (6). As such, *Dogeaters* presents the movie theater as a heterotopia. The movie theater—a place to watch a film, to retreat with a lover, to escape Manila's tropical heat—is a place where all different kinds of things happen at once, and where the interpellative mechanism of the film is both enhanced and interrupted by its spatial surroundings.

Certainly, this opening vignette introduces the cultural imperialist role of the Hollywood film, as it stages Rio and Pucha's reverence for the lifestyle depicted in *All That Heaven Allows.* This lifestyle is defined by that which Rio and Pucha cannot attain, whether it's the frozen lake and stark trees of a New England winter or the "brash style," "cool indifference," and "casual arrogance of the teenage Gloria Talbott" (3–4). This attitude, and by extension, this lifestyle, Rio narrates, "seem[ed] inherently American, modern, and enviable," a train of associations that collapses the three adjectives almost inextricably. Yet in keeping with its unsettling of the real and the fake, this vignette consistently foregrounds the artificiality of this ideal. Indeed, it is Hollywood's very artificiality that makes it so irresistible, so enjoyable. The character of the President's Wife—a thinly veiled caricature of Imelda Marcos—operates on exactly this principle. Her interview with an American journalist reveals the charm of this artificiality: "'They accuse me of being extravagant but . . . I am a nationalist when it comes to fashion,' she smiles. She has been lying to him cheerfully all morning, and they both know it. He smiles back" (217). In keeping with the way this interview is staged in the novel, as a satisfyingly spectacular performance of untruth, the film is depicted as glamorized artificiality, from the "garish baby blue" of a sky rendered in Cinemascope to the fires stoked by "cellophane," filmed as they are in the mild California climate (3).

Likewise, the text carefully delineates the difference between this ideal and "America." This ideal may be "American, modern, and enviable," but there is no actual correspondence between this ideal and any physical place. The introductory vignette about Rio's experience of "America" via the movies ends with a meditation inspired by a minor character in *All That Heaven Allows:* Jane Wyman's son, named Ned. Rio muses, "Ned Nickerson is the name of Nancy Drew's boyfriend in those books the American Consul's wife gives me the following Christmas. Now, after all these years in America, I have yet to meet a man named 'Ned' or anyone with the surname 'Nickerson'" (6). The imaginary ideal—the "America" that exists in the movies and in mystery novels about intrepid girl detectives—exists in the ideal and nowhere else. Indeed, it is Rio's immigrant condition—ostensibly a process of incorporation and assimilation into U.S. society—that interrupts the mechanisms of identification and interpellation of U.S. neocolonialism.

What is actually more important than a sense of a coherent reality is the variety of subject positions produced by consumer culture. *Dogeaters* stages the ways that consumer culture offers identities in its attempt to incorporate diverse and potentially unruly subjects. Rio and Pucha's subsequent argument about the merits of the film serves as the first example of a mode of subject constitution that pervades the text. Rio's generally condescending attitude toward her cousin ("Although I'm four years younger than Pucha, I always feel older") expresses itself through radically different identifications vis-à-vis the film (4). The "American, modern, enviable" Gloria Talbott is Rio's "feline heroine," but Pucha finds her *"cara de achay,"* that is, with the "face of a servant" (4). When Pucha fails to understand that characters exist textually and not independently, and wonders "what Rock sees in" Jane Wyman's character, Rio responds in her "driest tone of voice" that "it's a love story" (4). Here, Rio's sense of superiority, her sense of self, is developed by her ability to appreciate the offbeat, subtle charms of Gloria Talbott's character, to have more discriminating tastes than her boy-crazy cousin. Similarly, Pucha disdains anything "corny," which is "the worst sin you can commit in her eyes" (4), distancing herself from serialized melodramas like the radio soap opera "Love Letters," favored by Rio's grandmother and the household servants. Consumerism, for Rio and Pucha, is not compelling in its promise of satisfaction or resolution, which are staged as impossible. Consumerism's seduction, to the contrary, lies in the wanting, rather than the getting. Through wanting—more precisely, through wanting specific things—one is formed; what you want makes you what you are. As such, the "America" that Rio and Pucha dream of is not the actual place, but the subject position of the American consumer. To consume means to be American; to be American is to consume. Simultaneously interpellated by and distanced from both of these terms, Rio and Pucha as colonized consumers are both implicated in neocolonial consumerism and in excess of it.

Consumerism is thus the constant staging of the unattainable, through a desire that can never be fulfilled; the point to consumerism as a logic is not to satisfy desires, but to create new ones. In this way, *Dogeaters* recenters colonial experience through its depiction of consumerism. In the Manila of *Dogeaters,* any sense of consumerism as resolution, as attempting to make oneself whole through the fulfillment of desire, seems deluded. That is, attaining a snowy, frozen winter landscape is impossible in Manila, especially as this landscape is so patently constructed out of cellophane and cotton on a Los Angeles soundstage in the first place. Rio and Pucha wholeheartedly desire what they see, while equally understanding that attainment of this desire is impossible. By portraying colonial consumerism as the inhabiting of fundamentally insatiable desires—a consumerism without means—*Dogeaters* presents the colonial condition as not aberrant or perverse, but as an expression of consumerism taken to its logical extension. U.S. consumerism, preoccupied with resolution, is rather the aberration.

In this vein, we can read the character of the "President's Wife" as actually an unlikely heroine of *Dogeaters.* The President's Wife—never explicitly named, but clearly referencing Imelda Marcos—is startling in her consumerist excesses, which are seemingly unchecked by anything resembling restraint or reason. Yet the President's Wife—and Imelda Marcos, as we have already seen—can be read as the ultimate examples of colonial mimicry, in which the colonized subject so faithfully reproduces the colonial demand that the demand itself is exposed as excessive and impossible.[5] In other words, if the logic of consumerism is to never be satiated, no matter how much is accumulated, Imelda's collection of three thousand pairs of shoes (now installed in the above-mentioned Shoe Museum) is the ultimate instantiation of such a logic. If what it means to be American is to be a good consumer, Imelda, as quite possibly the world's best shopper, is more American than Americans.

We can see the character of the President's Wife as a kind of mirror-image to that of Rio. The narrative strategy of *Dogeaters* is to continually invite and then unsettle identifications with its main characters. In particular, Pucha's letter to Rio at the end of the book, which contradicts major elements of Rio's narrative, undermines the reader's trust in Rio, the character previously presented as the most trustworthy. In contrast, the President's Wife is represented as a monstrously excessive and narcissistic creature who is scorned by streetboys and journalists alike, yet can be seen to be exactly the subject of colonial mimicry that *Dogeaters* expresses. The President's Wife, in the reversal of Rio's trajectory, is presented as deeply flawed and unreliable, yet can be read as the canniest neocolonial subject. As Imelda Marcos has reportedly noted, "I have a different way of thinking. I think synergistically. I'm not linear in thinking, I'm not very logical." (Hamilton-Paterson, 206). And neither should she be, as a "properly" neocolonized subject.

For *Dogeaters,* consumerism is the consumption of "symbolic" goods—subjectivities, identities, narratives, images—rather than material ones. As I noted earlier, this registers the material conditions of neocolonial rule and military dictatorship in the Philippines, in which language itself solidifies and becomes reality. As such, *Dogeaters* pointedly underscores the relationship between consumerism and violence. In particular, this text addresses the ways that consumerism manages the neocolony through sexualized violence and the production of sexualized desires, as well as the ways that these desires exceed the mechanisms of neocolonialism.

Violence itself—in particular sexualized violence—is a consumer good, and one of the Philippines' most important exports in the global market of ideas and images. The marketing and consumption of violence is a preoccupation of Hagedorn's, and we can see the evolution of this idea from her earlier work. Hagedorn's poem, "Song of Bullets," published in *The Forbidden Stitch,* the 1989 anthology of Asian American women's writing, is a meditation on the relationship between safety and violence. A litany of terror, this poem recounts the devastated lives of despotic regimes: "Day after day/with less surprise/we sit/ in apartments/and count/the dead" (Hagedorn 1989, 144). The narrator reflects, "Assassins cruise the streets/in obtrusive limousines/sunbathers idle/on the beach" (146). Rather than underscoring the stark difference between a murder and a day at the seashore, this juxtaposition puts the two in the same economy of tourism, as the linked verbs "cruise" and "idle" reduce both activities to a form of leisure. The "obtrusive" nature of the limousines likewise resonates with the image of sunbathers, both objects of conspicuous consumption and visual display, as they shift between occupying the position of consuming subjects (those who own limousines and bask at the shore) and objects of consumption (being consumed as interesting sights by tourists).

The touristic nature of both violence and leisure is further expressed by the earlier citation of a postcard sent to the narrator by friends "[a]lternating between hectic/*social* Manila life & rural wonders/of Sagata" (145). The difference between violence and leisure, between assassins and sunbathers, is reduced to touristic variety, just as the urban and rural aspects of the Philippines become consumerist attractions, a way to create memorable vacations. In asking how the violence in the "third world" is understood in the Western world, Hagedorn suggests that consumerism as a logic is so constitutive that it becomes the lens through which even violence is viewed.

The link between the concerns of this poem and those of *Dogeaters* is made explicitly, as the second section of *Dogeaters* is also entitled "Song of Bullets." In *Dogeaters,* the neocolonial condition is revealed as the simultaneous production of desire, and the ironic enforcement of that desire through violence. Neocolonialism uses both the carrot and the whip: if the glamour alone of *All That Heaven Allows* doesn't seduce you, the violent suppression of any alternative to consumerist assimilation might convince you otherwise. Like the poem, *Dogeaters* continually draws attention to the display of violence, at the exact moment that this violence is displayed. In so doing, *Dogeaters* implies that merely the "revelation" of violence is not enough because occlusion happens at the precise moment that violence is revealed. Watching violence in the "third world" and feeling appalled, shocked, or moralistic is exactly what forms the "first world" viewer as the consumer of such images. As such, when violence is represented in *Dogeaters,* it is represented as a consumer good. A voluptuous Mabuhay Studios movie star, for example, considers making an "experimental art film," a film that "would involve lengthy close-ups of Lolita Luna's vagina, shot by professional cameramen in living color and in a variety of simulated violent settings. . . . Her vagina teased by the gleaming blade of a knife, for example, or perhaps a stubby black pistol" (177). Here, the focus is not so much on violence itself as on the consumption of violence.

As *Dogeaters* shows violence being consumed, it points to the ways that the violence represented in the text is itself a potential consumer good. The rape and disfigurement suggested by Lolita Luna's potential "experimental art film" is later recalled by the depiction of Daisy Avila's brutal torture and rape at the hands of government soldiers in a chapter entitled "The Famine of Dreams," which is included in the "Song of Bullets" section. This reference immediately implies a parallel between Lolita's film and Daisy's torture, between the reader of "The Famine of Dreams" and the discriminating viewer who, the producer assures Lolita, will compose the audience for her film, both of whom respond to "fear as an erotic stimulant" (177). The account of Daisy's torture is further scripted as a consumer good through its juxtaposition with an episode of the radio serial "Love Letters," complete with commercials, in a chapter that epitomizes the "pastiche" style of the text in both form and content. While at first the juxtaposition might seem to highlight the difference between the saccharine, hyper-romantic plot of the serialized radio program and the sadistically violent torture of a beauty-queen-turned-guerilla, we can also see how Daisy's narrative is yet another "Love Letter" to be consumed by a reading public whose thirst for tales of third world barbarity rivals the Gonzaga family servants' devotion to the radio melodramas.

Fittingly, the account of Daisy's torture and rape is staged as a "boy-meets-girl, boy-loses-girl, boy-gets-girl" romance. Staged as if the two are on a date, the narrative begins when Daisy is met by a colonel who "holds her by the elbow in a deferential manner, as if he were a gallant gentleman escorting her to a formal ball" as he leads her into the interrogation room, which is euphemistically called the "'VIP Lounge'—for very important prisoners" (211). The colonel compliments Daisy on her beauty, calls her *"hija,"* an appellation of fondness and familiarity, makes small talk, and then offers her a drink before grilling her about her association with her lover, the guerilla leader Santos Tirador. Finally, as his men brutally rape Daisy, the General "describes the special equipment set up in another room, a smaller room where the General plans to take her after his men are through. 'We can finally be alone,' the General says. He calls her *hija* once again, exclaims at her extraordinary beauty. He promises to make her dance" (216). The metaphors and vocabulary of sentimental heterosexual romance are easily and fluidly transposed to this scene of violent torture, blurring the boundaries between Daisy's "interrogation" and the melodrama playing in the background. To similar effect, both the descriptions of Daisy's torture and the stage directions of the "Love Letters" script are bracketed by parentheses, making Daisy's torture seem the background to the radio program, rather than the other way around. Likewise, while Daisy's torture is narrated as a romance, the out-of-context snippets of the "Love Letters" program do not tell a coherent story, but instead are ominous moments of doom and violence. In demonstrating the inextricable nature of sex and violence, of desire and fear, by presenting both as consumer goods, *Dogeaters* underscores the fact that moralistic shock is an integral part of the pleasure to be gained from this kind of voyeurism. As such, the text presents the neocolonial condition of the Philippines as a kind of colonial mimicry. Rather than being a deviant, violent derivative of "normal" sexuality, the desires depicted in *Dogeaters* are represented as the neocolonial condition par excellence.

In these ways and in countless others, *Dogeaters* recenters the colonial condition as not merely the nonmodern, undeveloped version of a normative U.S. ideal, but as a methodology, an alternative reading strategy, that denaturalizes the totalizing narratives of U.S. imperialism that privilege the United States as the prototype by which all "developing" nation-states are measured, and the American lifestyle as the standard by which all other lives are evaluated. Such a reading strategy is suggested later in the book, as Rio recounts her mother's frequent afternoon sessions with her dressmaker/best friend Uncle Panchito, a *bakla* given to dressing up in Rio's mother's clothing. One of his meticulously arranged outfits prompts Rio's mother to exclaim, "My God—you make a really pretty girl!" (81). Rio recounts, "Panchito was not impressed. 'I am who I am,' he said, with dignity" (81). Rather than accepting the normative assignations of gender, and despite his success (his *prettiness*) within such a system of meaning, Panchito, "not impressed" and not seduced by the praise, demands that he be understood as his own category, rather than as a successful appropriation of a previously existing one. He demands to be understood as some new, heretofore unnamed and incomprehensible subject formation, not a girl. Rather than understanding this demand as the constitution of an essentialized subject, I see Panchito's statement as suggesting a reading practice through which new subject formations can be recognized ("I am who I am"). As Panchito is a new gender formation, *Dogeaters* depicts the colonial consumer as not only an approximation of the "Western" consumer, but as its own formation. In *Dogeaters,* the colonial consumer asks to be recognized as "who it is": the ultimate instantiation of a consumerist capital that is therefore its undoing. The pastiche form we see in *Dogeaters* is thus expressive of the contradictions of the neocolonial condition, rather than expressive of an ahistorical "postmodern" aesthetic.

While we see in *Dogeaters* a form of "pastiche" that marks the peculiarly contradictory position of the colonial consumer, Viramontes's short stories displace realism through a variety of formal strategies. While Viramontes's most-analyzed story, "Cariboo Café" is easily read through a political economic lens because of its overt references to border crossings, immigration, deportation, and military dictatorship, "The Moths," with its seemingly more internal and domestic concerns, lends itself to such readings less readily. Yet I would read both of these stories' displacement of realism as registering the conditions of transnational migrant labor. While "Cariboo Café" is marked by nonlinear narration and shifts in perspective and voice, "The Moths" uses a formal strategy I call the "mundane fantastic," a form akin to magical realism in which the fantastic is always moored to the prosaic and the banal. Both of these formal strategies express an episteme that emerges out of the contradictions of late twentieth-century global capital, a figure for which is the Mexican migrant laborer. In "The Moths," for example, an unnamed Chicana adolescent narrates how it came to be that she nurses her grandmother, who is dying of cancer. "The Moths" is a story in which transnational migrant workers, ostensibly traveling from the "underdeveloped" third world to the "developed" and modern first world, are faced with the lack of access to modern state institutions such as hospitals, and where a terminally ill woman must be cared for by her adolescent granddaughter. These workers, ostensibly traveling from poverty to wealth, are met by conditions of such austerity that the materials of basic sustenance must be grown in one's backyard: the avocados, sweet potatoes, and chayotes (squash) that are a large part of Abuelita's diet. The existence of these contradictions is named through the "mundane fantastic" in "The Moths," which, as much as "Cariboo Café," brings to light social formations that emerge out of the new political and social conditions of late twentieth-century global capital.

While I argue that these stories attest to the inadequacy of realism, I also want to make clear that Viramontes's texts cannot be reduced to a form of postmodernism. These texts instead demonstrate that postmodern critiques of realism are themselves mystifying, insofar as postmodernism obfuscates the conditions of racialization, neocolonialism, and labor migration that subtend the fracturing of these linear, nationalist narratives. Kumkum Sangari, in her compelling essay, "The Politics of the Possible," elegantly differentiates between "a peculiarly western, historically singular, postmodern epistemology that universalizes the self-conscious dissolution of the bourgeois subject" and magical realism, which is expressive of "the cultural heterogeneity of Latin America [which] is at once different from and determined by the 'linear' history of the West, which both nests inside and shapes Latin American history, often by erasure" (1987, 157–58). Likewise, we can see that the formal strategies of the mundane fantastic as a kind of juxtaposition of disparate elements in "The Moths" or the nonlinear narrative style of "Cariboo Café" are quite different from superficially similar formal strategies of an elite postmodern aesthetic tradition as described in my earlier discussion of Jameson, above. "The Moths" is as much an example of late twentieth-century global culture as the postmodern "pastiche" of malls is, yet it is different from consumer culture because it emerges out of the circumstances of production. Likewise, this story attests to the fact that not all culture is entirely commodified by a totalizing consumer culture. Yet as the casual references to commodified consumer items, whether it be Campbell's soup, Vick's VapoRub, or Folger's coffee, bear out, this story does not posit racialized immigrant women's culture as existing somehow autonomously from or purely outside of the sphere of consumerism. Rather, Viramontes's story provides a narrative that makes sense only within the new conditions of global capitalism, yet the aesthetic of Viramontes's text registers the "new optic" that is produced by transnational migrant *labor*'s particular relationship to global capital.

In this discussion, I locate this particular relationship through an analysis of the the U.S.–Mexico border. The U.S.–Mexico border, and the experience of migration across it, manifests a series of contradictions that racialize and exploit Mexican migrant workers. The mundane fantastic thus mediates the contradictions of global capital as manifested in the U.S.–Mexico border region. These contradictions manifest themselves in the simultaneous reconsolidation of national boundaries at the very moment of their seeming dissolution. This contradiction is articulated at the level of race and gender, as the stresses of U.S. nationalism in relation to globalized capital are manifested through a narrative of the illegality of migrant laborers. In contrast to this, Viramontes offers another epistemology that highlights the contradictory state of being that "illegality" confers.

While the mundane fantastic has important resonances and historical links with the Latin American form called magical realism, the mundane fantastic arises from a different set of historical contradictions than those to which magical realism responds. Rather than homogenizing these different formal strategies, I would like to take a moment to explore the specific contradictions that these forms mediate. Kumkum Sangari describes the unevenness expressed formally through magical realism in contemporary Latin American literature as due to the legacies of colonialism and neocolonialism: "The piecemeal assimilation of European (and American) culture is difficult either to reject or to homogenize: first, because in a contradictory way, it is both something that is *owned* as well as something to be *resisted,* and, second, because of an 'uneven' material development that, contrary to the unidirectional laws of 'progress,' enforces the coexistence of primitive agriculture with advanced technology and export economics" (1987, 159). In this vein, we can read Carpentier, who, in his oft-cited essay, "The Baroque and the Marvelous Real," argues that the use of what he calls the marvelous American real (*lo real maravilloso americano*) by Latin American writers and artists arises from the particular conditions of Latin American history, geography, and culture. Carpentier thus distinguishes between the marvelous real and a seemingly similar European movement, surrealism, which, he argues, places unreal or fantastical elements amidst realist scenes in a deliberate, inorganic manner. Carpentier writes, "[T]he marvelous real that I defend and that is our own marvelous real is encountered in its raw state, latent and omnipresent, in all that is Latin America" (1995a, 104). Defining the "marvelous" as that which is strange and unexpected, he notes that Latin America far exceeded the understanding of rationalized Europe at the moment of conquest:

I find that there is something beautifully dramatic, almost tragic, in a sentence written by Hernán Cortés in his *Cartas de Relación* [Letters from Mexico] addressed to Charles V. After attempting to tell the king what he has seen in Mexico, he acknowledges that the Spanish language is too narrow to identify so many new things and says to Charles V: "As I do not know what to call these things, I cannot express them." And of the native culture, he says, "There is no human tongue that can explain its grandeurs and peculiarities." In order to understand and interpret this new world, a new vocabulary was needed, not to mention—because you can't have one without the other—a new optic. (105)

For Carpentier, the marvelous real marks an episteme or way of knowing—a new vocabulary and a new optic—that is radically different from that of European enlightenment rationalism because of the differences in the material conditions that produced it. Yet, as José David Saldívar (1991) notes, for Carpentier the material conditions that produce the marvelous real are not within some idealized and essentialized precolonial past, but arise exactly out of the interaction between Europe and Latin America. In other words, the marvelous real is the "new optic" born out of the violence of colonization. In the above passage, Carpentier notes the way that European colonization produces the conditions for the marvelous real (Cortes's presence in the New World), yet cannot provide a vocabulary adequate to the encounter (Cortes's inability to describe what he finds there). The marvelous real, for Carpentier, is the excess that European colonization instigated, but cannot account for.

In particular, the marvelous real exists in dialectical contradiction to Enlightenment reason and humanism. In another essay, "On the Marvelous Real in America" (1995b), Carpentier traces an intellectual and historical genealogy of the marvelous real, which is the "other" to the European reason and humanism that legitimated colonialism. Carpentier gives the example of "in the days of the French Revolution—long live Reason and the Supreme Being!—the Campostellan Francisco Menéndez would walk through the land of Patagonia searching for the enchanted city of the Caesars" (1995b, 87). The marvelous real, in other words, is that which is repressed by the rational ("Reason") and the humanistic ("Supreme Being"), and which returns, as the repressed tends to do, sometimes as "veritable monsters" (83). In exposing the monstrous quality, the grotesque alongside the beautiful, Carpentier defies the impulse to romanticize or essentialize the marvelous real.[6]

Carpentier's understanding of the "marvelous real" as both produced and organized by, but in excess of, colonialism resonates with my understanding of the formal strategy of Viramontes's stories. I argue that this marvelous real might look like the mundane fantastic if the context of its production were not the Latin America born out of its history of colonization, but rather that of racialized migrant labor along the U.S.–Mexico border.

In reading Viramontes this way, I extend arguments by scholars of Viramontes who focus on the ways they provide alternative subjects and narratives to the nation-state. Saldívar, Carl Gutiérrez-Jones, Leticia Magda Garza-Falcón, and Barbara Harlow identify national subjects as they are produced through the institutions of citizenship, juridical and legal discourse, journalism, and detention and imprisonment.[7] Sonia Saldívar-Hull, on the other hand, does not explicitly posit "The Cariboo Café" as a displacement of the narratives of the nation-state, but in reading the story as a critique of white feminism, Saldívar-Hull implies that such feminisms unwittingly reproduce the logics of universality and equivalence that characterize the nation-state.[8] These scholars situate Viramontes's work as exceeding the abstract political subject of the nation-state and in so doing, they wrest Viramontes from multiculturalist readings, which would attempt to read these stories as expressing "cultural" differences ultimately resolvable to a pluralist nation-state. In this way, they highlight nationalism's current role under global capital.

In keeping with these arguments, I contend that Viramontes's stories register the contradictions of the U.S.–Mexico border, contradictions that mark the new role of the U.S. nation-state in relation to capital. In this era, the United States is itself a flexible and differentiated formation; it is manifested in a form of "pastiche" in that it is simultaneously nationalist and extra-nationalist. U.S. nation-state form in the late twentieth century, in other words, mixes temporalities insofar as it is made up of state forms from both the nineteenth and the twentieth centuries.

Starting in the 1970s, as I have noted, transnational corporations shifted to a mode of accumulation that freed them from national economies. This new phase of capitalism, which is marked by a new international division of labor, the increasing transnationalization of corporate power, and a new labor force of racialized women, has required scholars to rethink a variety of concepts, including the role of the nation-state. As many have argued, we have seen the restructuring, rather than the dissipation, of the nation-state under globalization, which has meant both the weakening of national boundaries and the increase in repressive state militarism. In contradiction to Masao Miyoshi's claim that the nation-state is now entirely controlled by transnational corporations (TNCs), it is possible to argue that this era sees a new set of contradictions between state and capital. While national boundaries weaken to allow for the movement of goods, labor, and capital, nation-states have an interest in being politically strong, consolidated, and hegemonic, so they can dictate the terms of the global restructuring of capital to their own benefit. That is, capitalism needs military power to protect its interests in areas where increasingly repressive labor regimes stir up resentment and insurrection among workers. Likewise, as Douglas Dowd notes, U.S. capitalism uses the military to soak up the products (in the form of excess goods and labor) of the inevitable overaccumulation that always threatens capitalism. We can thus see how dependent capitalism is on a nationalist militarism.

The United States is not exempt from such contradictions. The United States' contradictory negotiations of the postwar reorganization of capital have formed and reformed the U.S.–Mexico border since the 1970s. As theorists of the U.S.–Mexico border have often noted, the remarkable escalation of militarization and surveillance along the border has occurred at the same time that other policies—most notably the North American Free Trade Agreement (NAFTA) of 1994—have made the border more permeable and North America more integrated than it has ever been (Andreas 2000, x). The U.S.–Mexico border, a space under a regime of hypersurveillance, is arguably the most militarized in the world, as the United States expends hundreds of millions of dollars a year to try to maintain the integrity and impermeability of its national boundaries. Timothy Dunn has argued that the U.S. Border Patrol utilizes what is known as low-intensity conflict (LIC) doctrine along the U.S.–Mexico border, which rivals the Middle East and Latin America in the level of militarization. However, we can also see the ways in which the very permeability of national boundaries—the passage of NAFTA and the restructuring of capital across national boundaries—enables the United States to extend a global hegemony based on a mix of state intervention and economic "free" enterprise. In response to the increased mobility of capital, state polices have tended toward making the flow of goods, capital, and information across the border more fluid and unimpeded. Yet simultaneously, a deeply rooted history of white nativism and anti-immigrant hysteria stemming from the eighteenth and nineteenth centuries surfaced, causing people to blame the economic recessions not on capital reorganization and transnational corporate policies, but on Mexican immigrants, who were ostensibly taking American jobs while draining the United States of its scarce social service and welfare resources.[9] Such hysteria coalesced in 1994, when California passed the anti-immigrant referendum item Proposition 187, which denied public education, social services, and public health services to undocumented immigrants. This same era saw the increased militarization and surveillance of the border. By the early 1990s, the U.S. state had implemented such measures as a steel fence along the border, massive enforcement programs such as Operation Blockade/Hold the Line in the El Paso/Cuidad Juarez area in 1993 and Operation Gatekeeper in the San Diego/Tijuana area in 1994, the use of sophisticated technology such as infrared sensors, and the doubling of the INS staff and budget. As Joseph Nevins has demonstrated, these measures did not noticeably limit the actual number of undocumented immigrant workers, but they did make the border crossing more risky and dangerous (2002, 127–28). As Mike Davis notes, "Realists, of course, understand that a cheap labor flux without the necessary quotient of fear and uncertainty imposed by illegality might cease to be cheap labor" (Nevins 2002, x). We can see that the U.S. state, in response to the demands of transnationalizing capital, is now both hypernationalist (in its strict control and policing of the border) and extranationalist (in the permeability of the border to capital, information, labor, and goods).

Although seemingly contradictory, this simultaneously hypernationalist and extranationalist state form has an ideological force that allows it to present itself as naturalized, uncontradictory, and even common sense, as can be seen in a Web site attempting to recruit those exiting the military for the Border Patrol. "You Can Leave the Military without Leaving the Challenge Behind" underscores the militaristic aspects of the Border Patrol, "an organization with one of the best reputations in all of law enforcement." Unabashedly nationalist, the Web site invokes a variety of romantic narratives to present Border Patrol work as exciting and masculine:

Out here there's nothing to get in your way. . . . This is rigorous outdoor work, often in isolated areas and under extreme weather conditions. . . . Many opportunities are available for bike patrol, marine patrol, and horse patrol and with all-terrain vehicles (ATVs).[10]

The notion of an empty untamed land connoted by such phrases as "out here" and "isolated areas" resonates with the frontier mythology long associated with the U.S. Southwest, while the reference to bikes, boats, horses, and ATVs makes the Border Patrol sound surprisingly similar to summer camp. The adolescent fantasy is extended when high-tech gadgetry is coupled with this frontier image, as in the section entitled "The Latest Tools to Get the Job Done Right":

> Border Patrol Agents work with some of the most technologically advanced equipment in law enforcement, including infrared scopes, low light television systems, and detection systems involving seismic metallic and infrared sensors, and a unique computerized identification and tracking system. Advanced technology and automation have freed agents from tedious paperwork. The result—more time spent on important patrol duties.

The resulting image is that of a high-tech cowboy, a masculine fantasy of unfettered mobility implied in phrases like, "Out here there is nothing to get in your way." The question of what exactly would "get in one's way" is answered by the promise that "advanced technology and automation have freed agents from tedious paperwork." In other words, petty bureaucracy and pointless legality won't disturb the Border Patrol's fundamental mission: "the prevention, detection, and apprehension of those illegally entering the United States, as well as for intercepting drug smugglers and others who mean to invoke harm on our country." This image disturbingly resurrects the history of the paramilitary Texas Rangers, who originally enforced the newly drawn border by lynching and slaughtering countless Mexicans and Chicanos living along the Rio Grande, as well as more recent incidents of the murder of undocumented immigrants at the hands of the Border Patrol, making one wonder what exactly these "important patrol duties" are.[11] The addition of the phrase, "others who mean to invoke harm on our country" to the original Web site after jurisdiction over the INS was transferred from the Department of Justice to the newly created Department of Homeland Security after September 11, 2001, creates a link between a variety of criminalized subjects, as undocumented immigrants, drug traffickers, and terrorists (the ostensible, unspoken, "others" referenced in the site) are taxonomized as threats to a presumably coherent national body.[12] The hypermilitaristic rhetoric with the implied threat of violence renders particularly ironic the cultural pluralist invocation at the end of the Web site, which lists one of the qualifications for being a Border Patrol officer as a desire for "interacting with people of other cultures."

In this way, the narrative of this Web site certainly reproduces nationalist identifications and reinforces nationalist boundaries. Yet the construction of an unfettered masculinity also produces an extranationalist, imperialist subject that cannot itself be contained by these borders. The representation of the state as bureaucracy certainly adds to this construction; evidently, being a part of the Border Patrol means upholding the principles of American democracy while simultaneously remaining unconstrained by such principles; it is their duty to protect the state, yet they must not be limited by the state's useless paperwork, such as laws, perhaps. The emphasis on surveillance technologies likewise projects an omniscient gaze that, like that of Dos Passos's *U.S.A.,* is not limited to the borders of the nation-state. This militarized subject is thus both nationalist and extranationalist, insofar as the U.S. nation-state now goes beyond its own borders. We can thus see that the U.S. nation-state itself displaces strictly nationalist identifications even as it produces them. Yet such a seemingly contradictory and unreal state is presented as common sense and rational.

Through Viramontes's texts, we can see the ways that transnational migrant labor is constituted through the simultaneity of the national/extranational and the mobile/immobile, and is thus characterized by a form of flexibility as well, but through a very different relationship to U.S. capital and its various violences. In the section that follows, I read the use of shifting perspective and nonlinear narration in another of Viramontes's stories, "Cariboo Café," as situating a relationship between the violent conditions of transnational labor migration and the inadequacy of realism to narrate those conditions. I do so to link the explicit critique found in "Cariboo Café" to the more implicit one of "The Moths." In reading "Cariboo Café" this way, I follow Michael Murashige (1995), who argues that the fragmented subject of "Cariboo Café" is constituted by the spatialized race relations of urban, transnational Los Angeles, which render linear, chronological histories impossible and inadequate. Murashige attributes the "distrust for narration to tell the whole story" (112) that characterizes the formal style of "Cariboo Café" to Viramontes's understanding of the "problematic nature of narrating space." "Rather than providing the reader with an interpretive position from which to view her 'subjects,'" Murashige says, "Viramontes

suggests that narrations of these individuals will always 'displace' their subjects and mystify the social unity of production and accumulation within
which they labor and struggle" (84).[13]

The layered and fractured narrative structure and the shifts in narrative
voice in "The Cariboo Café" juxtapose the stories and perspectives of three
characters thrown together by circumstance: a young undocumented Mexican immigrant girl, Sonya, accidentally locked out of her house after school
with her younger brother Macky; a washerwoman from an unnamed Latin
American country distraught by the loss of her disappeared son; and the
working-class owner of the run-down café where they all meet. How the
washerwoman comes to misrecognize Macky as her son, how she ends up
"kidnapping" him and Sonya, how the cook at the café takes recourse in the
repressive apparatuses of the state by turning the woman in, and how
the washerwoman is ultimately killed in a confrontation with the police are
the basic elements of this story, which is told in fragmented, layered ways.

"Cariboo Café" explicitly comments on the "flexible" uses of language
under a repressive neocolonial regime, particularly in a scene where the
washerwoman goes to the military compound where she believes her son
is being held. The conversation between the washerwoman and the soldier,
"barely a few years older than Geraldo," is an exercise in the blackest absur-
dist comedy (73). The soldier claims that her son is not in the detainment
camp, but if he was, he deserved to be because he was probably a guerilla,
even though he was only five years old. In this scene, language is both
essential and superfluous. The actions of a dictatorship must be narrated,
but under a military dictatorship, they will do whatever they want in any
case. The intensity of a dictatorship's insistence on an absolute idea of
"truth" is matched only by the blitheness with which it violates this truth.

The violence of a U.S.-backed military dictatorship in Latin America is
explicitly linked to the militarism of "la polie" and "la migra" within the
United States. At the moment of her death at the hands of the police in
the kitchen of the Cariboo Café, the washerwoman "misrecognizes" the
police as the army that took her son. Although this can be read as evidence
of the washerwoman's madness, the story emphasizes the militarized, violent state policing of migrant workers, or, as Viramontes writes, "displaced
people" (65). In the very first paragraph of the story, we learn one of the
most important edicts of Sonya's existance: that "the police, or 'polie' as
Sonya's popi pronounced the word, was La Migra in disguise and thus

should always be avoided" (65). Sonya later sees the father of a friend being taken away in a police car. The owner of the Cariboo Café turns in undocumented workers hiding in his bathroom to the INS but guiltily maintains, "I didn't expect agents putting their hands up and down their thighs" (72). As such, while the description of the mis-uses of language is in the context of the military dictatorship in the unnamed Latin American country, the story links the violence of military dictatorship and the state violence that helps maintain the vulnerable, exploitable status of racialized immigrant labor.

In such a context, the line separating what is true and what is untrue, who is reliable and who is not, begins to blur. What can be read as the use of "unreliable" narrators—the seeming madness of the washerwoman, the naiveté of the young Sonya, the obviously defensive self-validation of the owner of the Cariboo Café—are examples of the "unreal." This, as well as the use of multiple narrators, the shifts in perspective and voice, and the disjunctures in time and space demonstrate the limits of realism as a mode of representation. The fantastic can be as terrifying as the unbelievable sight of small children put to work sorting dismembered body parts, as disorienting as a situation in which sending a son on an errand to buy a mango is sending him to his doom, as grim as a junkie overdosing in a bathroom. All of these moments express the limits of realism. In a way, we can read "Cariboo Café" as using a "mundane fantastic" style as well. The formal style of "Cariboo Café" implies a real that is unbelievable. As such, I would argue that "Cariboo Café" is not a realist text, even in its seemingly most realist moments. As Sangari notes, "[I]f the furthest reaches of imaginary construction alone can equal the hideous deformations of the real, then marvellous realism must exceed mimetic reflection in order to become an interrogative mode that can press up on the real at the point of maximum contradiction" (1987, 163). In other words, by presenting the real as fantastical, "Cariboo Café" comments on the ability of language to represent that which is almost too horrible to be imagined, while commenting on a reality so terrifying that it exceeds the capabilities of language.

"Cariboo Café" thus displaces realism by providing an alternative formal and linguistic structure that surfaces from the conditions of transnational labor migration. While "The Moths" does not as explicitly reference the repressive state apparatus of the border patrol as "Cariboo Café" does, I would argue that its use of the mundane fantastic can likewise be read as a commentary on realism's tendency to obfuscate the contradictions of global capital. The austerity and lack of access to state institutions, the prosaic and monotonous nature of menial labor—the very things that the "mundane fantastic" highlights—are repressive conditions enforced through violence. They imply a whole array of apparatuses of violence that structure transnational labor migration. Yet the mundane fantastic also expresses the cultural logic of the border, an episteme that is formed by, but not limited to, state and economic violence. These stories register the ways that late twentieth-century global capital is not totalizing or comprehensive, no matter how cleverly it uses difference and diversity.

The mundane fantastic is itself an expression of the "flexible" mode of late twentieth-century global culture in that seeming opposites exist simultaneously. However, in articulating a different relationship to the "flexibility" of the neocolonial nation-state, this formal strategy bespeaks the ruptures in global capital's seemingly totalizing logic. In this story, the occurrence of the magical is always tied to the most banal of circumstances. Two moments in the text, both referencing the title of the story, exemplify this formal strategy. Early on in the story, the narrator recounts an episode in which her hands grew outlandishly outsized, a kind of punishment for disrespectfully expressing skepticism about her grandmother's home remedies. Her grandmother's cure for this fantastical deformity was to rub them back to size with a concoction of "dried moth wings and Vicks" (Viramontes 1995, 27). This seemingly unreal and magical moment, where the narrator experiences "the strangest feeling. Like bones melting. Like sun shining through the darkness of your eyes" (27) is firmly tied to the mundane. To perform a seemingly magical act, the grandmother uses the most prosaic of ingredients: Vick's VapoRub, an inexpensive and common drugstore remedy.[14] The second moment comes at the end of the story, when "the moths came" after her Abuelita's death: "Small gray ones that came from her soul and out through her mouth fluttering to light, circling the single dull light bulb of the bathroom" (32). The juxtaposition of the moths and the "single dull light bulb" demonstrates the mundane physicality of the moths, which behave as any moths would, and which exist alongside the austerity that characterized her grandmother's existence. The moths, though presumably a physical manifestation of the grandmother's soul, are themselves not described in aestheticized prose; they are merely "small, gray." As Carpentier notes, the fantastic is not always (or ever) pleasant, beautiful, or comforting.

These moments of the mundane fantastic are not romanticized in the story as transcendent or utopic. These moments mark Abuelita dying of cancer at home, with no access to medical care, nursed by a fourteen-year-old girl. The mundane fantastic exists in her neighborhood, where the closest market, Jay's, is a corner store where "the tomatoes were always soft and the cans of Campbell soups had rusted spots on them" (30). Likewise, we see that the narrator's stretched-out hands were re-formed or reformed to do work: gardening and nursing. The narrator's mother first sends the narrator to Abuelita's house to help with the tasks of gardening. Rather than being a feminine and decorative activity, as flower gardening is, gardening for the narrator is a sustenance activity because she helps tend to the garden vegetables that her Abuelita eats. Later, her mother sends her to nurse her Abuelita as she dies of cancer. These are particularly inflected, not neutral, forms of work; these are forms of gendered, raced, and classed work. While refusing to romanticize immigrant workers, the mundane fantastic equally insists that such a condition creates circumstances that exceed realism's ability to narrate them. The mundane fantastic insists on both elements, the mundane and the fantastic, as the only way to describe the alternative mode of knowing and being of transnational migrant labor.

As such, the mundane fantastic proves that the simultaneous coexistence of seemingly contradictory elements is not only possible, but is its own formation, a new optic; to borrow Uncle Panchito's formulation, "[I]t is what it is." In presenting us with the mundane fantastic, "The Moths" gives us a reading strategy for the entire story. The text's consistent formal technique is the juxtaposition of seeming opposites, and the presentation of a mode of being and knowing that exists exactly in the interstices of these opposites, as can be seen in the following passage:

There comes a time when the sun is defiant. Just about the time when moods change, inevitable seasons of a day, transitions from one color to another, that hour or minute or second when the sun is finally defeated, finally sinks into the realization that it cannot with all its power to heal or burn, exist forever, there comes an illumination where the sun and the earth meet, a final birth of burning red orange fury reminding us that although endings are inevitable, they are necessary for rebirths, and that when that time came, just when I switched on the light in the kitchen to open Abuelita's can of soup, it was probably then that she died. (31)

This passage, arguably the climactic moment, exemplifies the mundane fantastic style of the entire text. Using sunset—the moment when day and night, sky and earth meet and coexist—as the setting, the narrator meditates on the moment of her grandmother's death as simultaneously a moment for "rebirth." Yet the sun itself is not unitary, but also inhabits the space between two opposites: "its power to heal or burn." Finally, sunset is not only a mythic, magical time of transition, but is also, quite appropriate to the prosaic tenor of the story, a time when it gets dark and electric lights must be switched on so the practical task of heating up cans of soup can be performed. The mundane fantastic thus expresses a way of reading and understanding the world that marks the particular epistemology of racialized and gendered immigrant laborers.

These examples of the mundane fantastic, like the "pastiche" of *Dogeaters,* eschew the economic determinism of political economy that reduces everything to an epiphenomena of capitalism and also the ahistorical, nonmaterialist understanding of difference that is the hallmark of postmodernism. When the dominant episteme itself is a critique of homogeneity and abstraction, these formal strategies must express a "different kind of difference." The mundane fantastic of "The Moths" and the pastiche of *Dogeaters* are new formations, new optics, and thus they are examples of the alternative practices and knowledges that disrupt and disorganize the homogenizing and totalizing tendencies of late twentieth-century global capital. Racialized immigrant women's culture, like *Dogeaters* and "The Moths," let us know that such new optics do indeed exist. As such, they mark the ways that new forms of struggle always arise from new circumstances of exploitation.

EPILOGUE

In this book, I have addressed an important shift in U.S. capital, from its national phase to its global phase, but through an examination of the new formations—women of color feminism and racialized immigrant women's culture—that emerge to mark the crises of each phase. I have traced the shift from nationalist modes of universality, in the form of the possessive individual, to transnational modes, in the form of a commodified fetishization of diversity. As I have argued, these modes of universality occlude the modes of racialized and gendered difference on which they depend, and are thus rife with contradiction. Women of color feminism and racialized immigrant women's culture situate culture as the site where these occluded knowledges arise, to name the process of erasure at the moment of recovery.

I ended my discussion of the post–World War II logic of flexibility that I identified as a key interpretive paradigm for understanding our contemporary moment. Within the logic of flexibility, however, we can delineate two different phases. The first, characterized by what is now known as multiculturalism and neocolonialism, has very recently been replaced by an ironic performative understanding of racialized and gendered difference and a new recombitant state formation that flexibly and simultaneously represents itself as using brute force, yet insists on a neocolonial disavowal of global influence.

Perhaps the most obvious example comes in the form of the United States' blatantly hypocritical actions during the war in Iraq, which officially began in 2003 and is ongoing as I write this in 2005. On the one hand, the U.S.

state openly defies international opinion in pursuing war with Iraq and explicitly calls attention to its military might in terminology like "shock and awe." Yet on the other hand, the U.S. state calls the entire action "Operation Iraqi Freedom," hypocritically covering its actions with a veneer of humanitarianism—a tried-and-true strategy of neocolonial legitimation. This model demands that we reconceptualize and rename the operations of state rule. That is, if the definition of a neocolonial state is a state that is a world power but must disavow its global influence, what is the United States now? Is the state no longer neocolonial? Or is the state using strategies of neocolonialism such as the management of consent through the disavowal of power when it wants, alongside blatantly aggressive militarism? I would maintain that the state is now *flexibly* neocolonial. In other words, much as race and gender become commodified forms of difference to be put on or taken off, the state puts on and takes off its various historical incarnations at will. In this way, I would argue that the contemporary U.S. state operates through the use of a kind of pastiche.

This new state formation may render previous strategies and modes of organization less effective than before. For example, during the strictly neocolonial period, one strategy of intervention against the state was that of revelation. If the state was operating in a hypocritical manner and denying its international role, one way to undermine this was to reveal or render explicit the symbiotic relationships between state and capital in exacerbating unequal international relationships and creating a hierarchy of nations. Yet if one of the U.S. state's strategies of rule is exactly to broadcast this inequality, and to use its own strength as a weapon of intimidation, such a strategy of revelation seems beside the point.

Yet the historical incarnations that the current "flexible" state accesses and references simultaneously—whether it be the repressive genocidal state, the paranoid cold war state, the occlusive neocolonial state—are all incarnations that are themselves dependent on ideologies and material histories of race and gender. As such, even these incarnations have their contradictions. Therefore, rather than reading this turn of events with fatalism, understanding this as the triumph of a capitalist/imperialist juggernaut, we might see this as the new terrain of struggle, the new conditions against which the next set of strategies, critiques, and alternative epistemological formations will emerge. For if there is anything that can be learned from women of color feminism and racialized immigrant women's culture, it is that all relations of rule are constituted out of their own sets of contradictions and foreclosures, which occasion new forms of brutality and injustice, but also provide the vocabulary for new sites and strategies of struggle, contestation, and emergence.

ACKNOWLEDGMENTS

I began my graduate career in the fall of 1992, just months after an epistemic shift in the theorizing of race, gender, and globalization had occurred with the advent of the Los Angeles riots. Entering graduate school, I found myself in the uncertain but energizing position of laying aside many of my previous assumptions and engaging in the study of race and gender with different priorities and goals. Although this book may not seem to have much to do with that moment, it is very much shaped by it. If, as the L.A. riots starkly demonstrated, a common and analogous exclusion from power was not to be the ground from which to forge alliances among people of color, where could we turn for another mode of theorizing coalition? In the wake of one crisis, I reached back to another: women of color feminism as the epistemic crisis of a seemingly triumphant U.S. nationalism, as a usable tradition for imagining alliance based on, rather than exclusive of, difference and particularity.

Along the way, I was the recipient of all manner of support, and there is very little that gives me more satisfaction and joy than this opportunity to thank my friends and colleagues for their generosity. Working on the intersections of race and gender has allowed me to work with some of the most brilliant, responsible, and talented people in the world. Anything I have been able to accomplish has been because of their help, and the flaws and omissions in this book are due entirely to my own lapses in ability or judgment.

I began thinking about race comparatively while in the master's program in Asian American studies at UCLA. I'd like to thank the chair of my thesis committee, King-Kok Cheung, as well as the other members, Jinqi Ling and Valerie Matsumoto. Portions of this manuscript have been revised from my dissertation. I thank the members of my dissertation committee, chaired by Lisa Lowe: Rosemary George, George Lipsitz, Rosaura Sánchez, Shelley Streeby, and Lisa Yoneyama. While writing my dissertation, I had support from the Civil Liberties Public Education Fund's National Fellowship Program and the University of California–San Diego University Predoctoral Humanities Fellowship. I thank Cathy N. Davidson, Carol Rigsby, Thomas J. Ferraro, and the anonymous readers at *American Literature* for their careful and thoughtful reading of a previous publication of portions of chapter 2.

My gratitude goes to those who have composed my intellectual community throughout graduate school and thereafter: Helen Jun, Min-Jung Kim, Saundra Liggins, Jodi Melamed, Demian Pritchard, and Laura Ruberto. I also thank Mary Tong, Cynthia Rich, and June Brashares from the Support Committee for Maquiladora Workers, which is with me in spirit if no longer as an existing organization. Their dedication to their work inspires me to mine.

I thank the members of Ruby's Reading Group: Roderick Ferguson, Gayatri Gopinath, Chandan Reddy, Maurice Stevens, Ruby Tapia, Victor Viesca, and Danny Widener. I am grateful to learn from these scholars, whose work is among the most brilliant and necessary interventions being produced today.

While at Princeton University, I was part of a writing group of Asian Americanist women junior faculty from the greater New York area. I thank in particular Juliana Chang, Shirley Lim, Mary Lui, Sanda Lwin, Mae Ngai, Lok Sui, and Sandhya Shukla. Knowing that these dedicated and intelligent—not to mention chic—women are at the forefront of Asian American studies gives me great hope for the field. At Princeton, I thank Donna Jones, Noliwe Rooks, Michael Wood, and Emily Belcher.

I was the fortunate recipient of a University of California President's Post-Doctoral Fellowship, which allowed me necessary time away from teaching to work on this manuscript. My kind and generous mentor for this program was Emory Elliott. During my fellowship year, I was invited to sit in on a faculty seminar at the University of California-Riverside Center for Ideas and Society, which Emory directs. The members of this faculty seminar, led by Lisa Lowe, gave me immensely useful feedback on my manuscript. I'd like to thank them now, particularly Savvina Chowdhury, Steve Cullenberg, Katherine Kinney, Glen Mimura, and Leti Volpp.

At the University of Wisconsin at Madison, I thank foremost the members of my reading group: Leslie Bow, Shilpa Davé, Victor Jew, Lisa Nakamura, and Michael Peterson. Many people in Madison have provided intellectual, institutional, and moral support and thus have made an immeasurable difference in my life here; I thank Mary Beltran, Ned Blackhawk, Nan Enstad, Camille Guerin-Gonzalez, Ryan Hertweck, Mary Layoun, Dana Maya, Rhacel Parreñas, Birgit Rasmussen, Cherene Sherrard, Sean Teuton, Ethelene Whitmire, and Kay Yandell.

I was invited to present portions of this manuscript at conferences, where the feedback I received was invaluable to my writing process. I am grateful to scholars at Ewha University in Seoul, Korea, who invited me to present at their Crossing Boundaries conference and their Locating Feminist Studies conference, both in the fall of 1999. I thank the Center for Advanced Feminist Studies at the University of Minnesota–Twin Cities, particularly Jennifer Pierce and Juliana Pegues, for inviting me to present my work at their summer institute, "Gender, Migration, and Global Change: Feminist Perspectives on the Political and Cultural Economy of Immigration" in 2003. I thank the organizers of the Comparative Study of Race, Ethnicity, and Indigeneity Conference at Cornell University in 2004, particularly Shelley Wong and Viranjini Munasinghe, as well as commentators Leslie Adelson and Ricardo Laremont for their careful readings of my work.

My gratitude and admiration go to my editor at the University of Minnesota Press, the talented, ethical, responsible Richard Morrison. I also thank the two readers of my manuscript, whose rigorous and generous comments helped me immensely in my revisions.

I thank my mother, Sung Ja Hong, and my father, Dai Soon Hong, for their patience and support. I also thank my lovely and talented sisters, Christine Hong and Judy Hong; they are successful at whatever they put their hand to, and I am proud to know them. I acknowledge my grandfather, Kim Jung Jin, and my grandmother, Cho Byung Sook, who died within six months of each other as I was finishing this manuscript. I especially wish that I could have celebrated the completion of this book with my grandfather, who was the first person to show me what it was to have a life of the mind. He was a learned and scholarly man, and I can't help but think that I ended up doing what I do because of his influence and example.

I thank my partner, Victor Bascara, my best and most constant interlocutor.

Finally, nothing I can say could ever do justice to Lisa Lowe, who has been and continues to be the most wonderful teacher, mentor, and friend a girl could ever want. For as long as I've known her, Lisa has always generously centered my work and my projects, which have been ever sustained by her unwavering faith in my ability to pursue the complex and the nuanced. Lisa has been my model for what an ethical, rigorous, and politically committed scholar should be, and to her go my greatest thanks.

NOTES

INTRODUCTION

1. As manufacturing in the post-Fordist era became increasingly decentralized and scattered all over the globe, scholars theorized that, with the advent of communications technologies, managerial functions would likewise be decentralized. To the contrary, top-level control and management of the industry have become concentrated in a few leading financial centers: global cities. These global cities become the sites of great wealth, populated by managerial and professional workers. Yet the fact that these new finance sectors of the economy can accumulate profit at vastly superior rates than traditional economic sectors also exacerbates conditions of inequity. Sassen argues that while traditional economies may "be essential to the operation of the urban economy and the daily needs of residents, their survival is threatened in a situation where finance and specialized services can earn superprofits. Going informal or subcontracting to informal enterprises is often one solution" (1998, xxiv). Informal economies, staffed by racialized labor or immigrant labor rendered cheap and vulnerable through racist immigration policies, therefore proliferate further in the global city, which is marked by an increased gap between rich and poor. The transition from nationally organized city to global city reconfigures urban spaces. Global cities are often the sites with the greatest disparities in income and wealth, inequalities that manifest spatially: "[T]he downtowns of global cities and metropolitan business centers receive massive investments in real estate and telecommunications while low-income city areas are starved for resources" (xxvi).

2. See Ruth Gilmore's essay "Globalization and U.S. Prison Growth" (1998–99), where she argues that in post-industrial California, African Americans are no longer incorporated as *labor* but as *raw material* for the prison-industrial complex.

3. See Karen Hossfield (1994), who documents the fact that managers of production plants for the high-tech industries in the Bay Area explicitly recruit racialized and gendered labor. She quotes a white male production manager and hiring supervisor in a

Silicon Valley assembly shop, who said, "I have a very simple formula for hiring. You hire right, and managing takes care of itself. Just three things I look for in hiring: small, foreign, and female. You find those three things and you're pretty much automatically guaranteed the right kind of work force. These little foreign gals are grateful to be hired—very, very grateful—no matter what" (66).

4. Masao Miyoshi (1993) uses the example of the effects of transnational capital to propose that the power of the nation-state is declining and will eventually become obsolete. He suggests that current forms of nationalism are merely "a nostalgic and sentimental myth" and that nation-states hold no actual power in and of themselves, but are rather the puppets of the transnational corporations.

5. While an exhaustive discussion of long wave Marxist theory is not possible here, I would like to trace an abbreviated genealogy, focusing on a few of the major texts of this avenue of inquiry. Ernest Mandel's *Late Capitalism* resurrected interest in long wave theory among postwar Marxist scholars, who used such studies to argue for the imminent demise of capital. Immanuel Wallerstein's concept of the "world system" takes up Marx's idea of the division of labor and applies it on a global scale, thus introducing the idea of the international division of labor. Wallerstein's analysis articulates a singular world history of capital, stretching from the sixteenth century to the present, in which the world can be divided up into core, periphery, and semiperiphery regions, each with their own particular function. Thus, the rise of capital and the modern world was occasioned not only by class formation in Europe, but through a hierarchical organization of regions of the world, which benefited unevenly from the development of capital. Wallerstein's is a very important critique of the systems of exploitation and inequity that render certain regions wealthy at the expense of others. However, Wallerstein's global view tends to homogenize the relationships between regions, and is not concerned with accounting for more localized processes that might contradict his broader analysis or for histories of struggle against modes of capital. We can see a similar tendency toward a "total" critique in Giovanni Arrighi's *The Long Twentieth Century* (1994). Building on Marx and Wallerstein, Arrighi situates the ascendance of U.S. capitalism in the twentieth century within a longer history of capitalism. He posits a pattern of overlapping cycles of capitalist growth, expansion, and decline as the center of capitalist accumulation moved from Genoa in the mid-1300s to the early 1600s, to the United Provinces from the late 1500s to the late 1700s, to the United Kingdom from the mid-1700s to the early twentieth century, to the United States from the late nineteenth century to the present. Arrighi argues that each capitalist cycle meets its inevitable end as it goes through a world historical version of Marx's general formula of capital (MCM'), which Arrighi argues not only describes localized capitalist investments, but provides a historical narrative for the development and decline of whole capitalist cycles. In other words, each capitalist cycle has an MC period, in which money capital (M) is turned into commodity capital (C) in a fixed combination that will lead to profit. In the U.S. example, Arrighi posits the Fordist period as the MC period. Yet investing money capital in commodity capital means "concreteness, rigidity, and a narrowing down of options" (5) and thus is only attractive as a means for further eventual

liquidity. Arrighi notes that all capitalist cycles have a point of financial rebirth and expansion (the CM' period), and that eventually, a great deal of money capital does not even need to proceed through the commodity form, and accumulation occurs through entirely financial operations (Marx's MM'). Arrighi suggests that the post-Fordist, late twentieth-century moment is the CM' and MM' moment of the U.S. cycle of accumulation. Arrighi takes up Marx's notion in *Capital* that capitalism has inherent or immanent contradictions, citing Marx's contention that "the real barrier of capitalist production is capital itself" and saying that capitalist formations overcome these inherent barriers "only by means which again place these barriers in its way on a more formidable scale" (quoted in Arrighi 1994, 245). We can see the same developmentalist tendencies in Arrighi's work. While we see that individual cycles of capital inevitably decline as the inherent contradictions of capital catch up to them, each cycle is succeeded by the next, more expansive and powerful phase. The logical conclusion of this developmentalist history—in other words, the only way to narrate capital's ultimate decline—is to narrate an end to history. The question of Arrighi's book is, indeed, whether that end is nigh. Arrighi notes that while the U.S. cycle of accumulation has not yet ended, an analysis of recent developments in Asian capital demonstrates that the relationship between U.S. and Asian capital does not exactly follow previous relationships between waxing and waning world powers. He asks whether this relationship indicates the crisis point of U.S. capital, or if indeed, whether "the structures of U.S. capitalism constitute the ultimate limit of the six centuries-long process through which capitalist power has attained its present, seemingly all-encompassing scale and scope?" (19). In his epilogue, Arrighi argues that there are indeed signs that such a stage of ultimate decline—in other words, signs that capital cannot overcome the barriers of overaccumulation—has begun.

6. See, for example, Blackwell (2000).

7. In some ways, the attempt to delineate between primary and secondary work about women of color feminism is contrary to women of color feminism's often self-conscious project of undermining the theorist/object dichotomy. Thus, the discussion that follows is not meant to arbitrarily impose such a dichotomy. Rather, the following scholars *study* women of color feminism as a genealogy of intellectual and political thought and *produce* women of color feminism as a simultaneous project. An important strand of the analysis of women of color feminism emerges as a response to white, Western feminism. Norma Alarcón's essay, which I also discuss in the introduction, is perhaps the best of these interventions. Alarcón helpfully situates women of color feminism's critique of white feminism's investments in Enlightenment subjectivity. Please also see my discussion of Alarcón's essay in the body of this introduction. Rachel Lee's essay, "Notes from the (Non)field: Teaching and Theorizing Women of Color" (2002), investigates several recent studies of women of color feminism to stage a productive critique of the institutionalization of women's studies within university settings; she notes that women of color feminism courses end up merely being the tokenized corrective to women's studies curricula, rather than fundamentally restructuring such curricula to take race seriously into account. Lee argues that women's studies curricula

must be reorganized to situate women of color feminism as a starting point for a rigorous and varied series of research and teaching agendas. Chela Sandoval's *Methodology of the Oppressed* (2000) takes up women of color feminism as an example of "differential consciousness," which she describes as "mobile," as not having its own innate or essential characteristics, but being rather a "theoretical and methodological device for retroactively clarifying and giving new meaning to any other" (44). Another set of studies reads women of color feminism through a materialist history of colonialism and transnational capital. These are the studies to which I am most indebted. Chandra Mohanty's landmark essay, "Cartographies of Struggle" (1991) outlines the ways that third world women's feminism is necessitated by the globalization of capital, which replicates and extends colonial domination. Mohanty lays out a nonessentializing basis for the solidarity of "third world women." Noting that the "third world" is defined through "geographical location as well as particular sociohistorical conjunctures," Mohanty includes in her definition of the third world the racialized people of the United States (Mohanty, Russo, and Torres 1991, 2). She brings attention to the ways that a third world women's feminism and its historiography necessarily perform an intersectional critique of unidimensional progressive discourses (that is, of white feminism, third-world nationalist, and socialist discoures, which would insist on the possibility of looking only at one level of exploitation at a time). Emphasizing that an "imagined community" of third-world feminists has its basis in situated oppositional struggles, rather than in biology or an ossified notion of an essential culture, Mohanty warns against the freezing of "third world women" as objects of study, as outside history. Mohanty, writing with M. Jacqui Alexander, extends this discussion in the introduction to their coedited collection, *Feminist Genealogies, Colonial Legacies, Democratic Futures.* Please see my discussion of this volume in the body of this introduction. In Roderick Ferguson's chapter, "Something Else to Be: *Sula, The Moynihan Report,* and the Negations of Black Lesbian Feminism," from *Aberrations in Black,* he situates the emergence of women of color feminism as a negation of black nationalism's investments in heteropatriarchal norms, produced in this era as a discourse of pathological black matriarchy by such studies as Daniel Moynihan's infamous *The Negro Family.* Ferguson further demonstrates the ways that "black matriarchal deviance justified and promoted the regulatory practices of the state and the exploitative practices of global capital as the U.S. nation-state began to absorb women of color labor from the United States and the third world as part of capital's new regimes of exploitation" (2004, 111).

8. This is also the title of a 1974 book by activist Barbara Deming.

1. THE POSSESSIVE INDIVIDUAL AND SOCIAL DEATH

1. See Saxton's discussion in *The Indispensable Enemy: Labor and the Anti-Chinese Movement in California (1995, 258–67)* in which he demonstrates that white working-class identity in the U.S. West was constituted around movements of Chinese exclusion. See also Roediger's "White Slaves, Wage Slaves, and Free White Labor" in *The Wages of Whiteness* (1999, 65–93) in which he discusses the ways in which the discourse of "slavery" was appropriated by working-class whites to distance themselves from African

American slaves, and thus occlude, rather than facilitate, the possibility of cross-race labor solidarities.

2. Many ethnic studies scholars have long pointed out that "white" is a race, and therefore, that the process by which subjects become white can also be called "racialization." I do reserve the use of the terms "racialized" and "racialization" to indicate the process by which certain racial categories are constructed through differentiation and disidentification. When I discuss the different, but related histories of the production of whiteness, I call it "whiteness" rather than "racialization." This is not to imply that whiteness is not a race, but to establish a nomenclature that distinguishes between these different processes.

3. All subsequent references to the *Second Treatise* will be from the edition edited by MacPherson.

4. See Mailloux, "Rhetorical Hermeneutics as Reception Study" (1996).

5. Bernard De Voto took particular exception to the "extemporized burlesque" of the last section, which he read as a "defacement of [Twain's] purer work" (312). Lionel Trilling and T. S. Eliot both defend the ending on various aesthetic grounds. Leo Marx's comprehensive statement of the case against the ending critiques on political grounds the ways the ending mars the purpose of the book and detracts from the importance of the mission of the book, which for him is the quest for Jim's freedom.

6. See Leslie Fiedler, who argues that Huck's desire to escape from women's "sivilizing" influence produces Huck as a homoerotic character.

7. This is not to suggest, however, that the thoughts and ideas of Booker T. Washington, the living historical person, can be limited to this autobiography. Many scholars have argued that Washington was a complex, even manipulative man, who quite deliberately wrote this autobiography to have certain effects and functions, rather than as a straightforward, transparent account of his life. William T. Andrews notes, "More analytical assessments of Washington . . . enhanced by extensive investigations of his private papers in recent years, have unveiled a considerably more complex figure who carefully cultivated an image of the plain-spoken altruist for public consumption while operating behind the scenes as a savvy, sometimes ruthless political infighter" (1996, vii). In "Strategies and Revisions for Self-Representation in Booker T. Washington's Autobiographies," Donald Gibson notes that although Washington says he was inspired to take on his last name by George Washington, it's probably more likely that Washington took the last name of his stepfather, also named Washington. I thoroughly agree with these scholars, who caution against conflating the actual historical personage and the character "Booker T. Washington" that he creates in his autobiography. In this analysis, I read "Booker T. Washington" as the character of a text, *Up from Slavery*. Likewise, I agree with Andrews (2002) that we can read *Up from Slavery* for moments where Washington uses irony subversively to ridicule white racism. Yet because my reading is about racialized historical and material particularities that fundamentally cannot be resolved to a universal form, arguing for authorial intentionality is not the purpose of this reading.

8. See "Defining the American Standard of Living" in Glickman 1997, and "White Women, Hygiene, and the Struggle for Respectable Domesticity" in Shah 2003.

9. Barbara Epstein argues that in the industrializing Northeast United States, the agrarian familial system, in which white women were direct producers of necessary household goods, was gradually replaced by an industrialized, urbanized setting where production occurred more and more in factories. As such, the white woman's role in the middle-class family shifted from production to consumption, and domesticity became the feminized counterpart to male participation in the public sphere of citizenship.

2. HISTORIES OF THE DISPOSSESSED

1. This is not to imply, of course, that agricultural property was never a significant form of property dispossession for African Americans. As Oliver and Shapiro note, in the Reconstruction period, African American fortunes seemed to be tied to yeomanry and farming—the possibility of self-sufficiency enabled by "forty acres and a mule" (1995, 13–15). The racist effects of the Homestead Act of 1866, which overwhelmingly gave land grants to whites, again thematize the impossibility of ownership for African Americans. Morrison's preoccupation with home ownership instead indicates the critique of racialization through private property, which encompassed both the moment of production of the text and the setting of the novel.

2. See Rolf 1994.

3. Donald C. Goellnicht's article, "Transplanted Discourse in Yamamoto's 'Seventeen Syllables,'" reads the haiku written by the protagonist's mother as representing both the fall in class standing that the mother experienced in her move from Japan to the United States and the inability of the second-generation protagonist to maintain and replicate the "pure" Japanese culture of her mother. In "'Seventeen Syllables': A Symbolic Haiku," Zenobia Baxter Mistri argues that the story itself is written much like a haiku, packing meaning into a multiply layered story.

4. See Susan Koppelman's introduction (1985, 161–62) to Yamamoto's anthologized story, "Seventeen Syllables."

5. See Kim 1999.

6. See Cheung, "Double-Telling" (1994). In this article, she also argues that Japanese cultural norms require various strategies of communication and indirection. See also Yogi, "Legacies Revealed: Uncovering Buried Plots in the Stories of Hisaye Yamamoto" (1994).

7. Because of Morrison's great popularity, there is a body of scholarship on Morrison's texts addressed to the general reading public. Much of this work tends to be summative; see, for example, Furman (1996), Kubitschek (1998), and Peach (1995). For a useful collection of essays about Morrison and African American literary studies, see Gates and Appiah (1993). See, in particular, Valerie Smith's essay, "'Circling the Subject': History and Narrative in *Beloved*," in which Smith uses the text to examine why the actual suffering body of the slave cannot be transparently "represented," yet must somehow be constantly remembered and articulated. Smith argues that *Beloved*'s strategy is not to attempt to "represent" the suffering of the slave body, but instead to "[humble] contemporary readers before the unknown and finally unknowable horrors the slave endured" (354). See also Mobley (1993), whose article situates Morrison's novels

in the literary tradition of slave narratives, which Mobley calls "the genre that began the African-American literary tradition in prose" (357). Mobley notes that slave narratives record and remember the conditions of slavery in order to disrupt a contemporaneously existing system of slavery. While *Beloved* also remembers slavery, it is for a different purpose—to "disrupt the cultural notion that the untold story of the black slave mother is, in the words of the novel, 'the past something to leave behind'"—and must therefore be different in form (358). Min-Jung Kim's analysis of *Sula, Song of Solomon,* and *Paradise* in her dissertation (1999) argues that Morrison's novels critique discourses of the liberal democratic state and capitalism: "the nuclear family, bourgeois domesticity, economically defined gender roles, propertied subject, separate spheres" (viii). Kim's focus in her analysis is the critique of cultural nationalist ideologies, which would impose an artificial homogeneity on complex community formations by privileging an oppositional subjectivity. In her analysis of *Sula,* Kim reads the novel's unconventional use of conventional "women's" themes (bonds between women, mother/daughter relationships, etc.) to argue that the "aberrant social units" described by Morrison are not uniformly liberating to all of their members, and that rather, Morrison depicts these social relations as varied and differentiated. Kim argues in her analysis of *Song of Solomon* and *Paradise* that "Morrison presents alternative ways to transcend the condition of marginality: i.e., of creating meaningful identities without defining oneself solely in opposition to an oppressive force." Kim notes the striking similarities between assimilation and cultural nationalism as responses to racism, despite the fact that these positions are often considered binary opposites.

8. Donald Gibson (1993) situates Morrison within a tradition of African American writing beginning with the slave narrative, arguing that in placing the "Dick and Jane" story at the beginning of the novel, Morrison subverts the usual relationship of authentication that structured the slave narrative. Gibson uses this example, among others, to argue deconstructively that Morrison's text is composed of contradicting yet mutually dependent "texts and countertexts." Michael Awkward (1993) situates Morrison within a twentieth-century African American literary tradition, arguing that Morrison takes Ralph Ellison and James Baldwin to task for glamorizing rape, and instead finds Zora Neale Hurston as more of an antecedent for Morrison. Susan Willis's article (1993) stresses the importance of understanding the historical moment described by *The Bluest Eye.* She argues that the novel is about the development of neighborhoods, a historic phenomenon unique to the 1940s and unique to the Midwest of Morrison's setting. For critical discussions of Morrison's critique of standards of beauty, see Christian (1993), Terrell (1993), Guerrero (1997), and Heinze (1993).

9. For a discussion of the Japanese American community's responses to the Alien Land laws, see Ichioka (1984). For an exhaustive discussion of the ways Chinese immigrants in the nineteenth century dealt with the state through the judicial system, see McClain, *In Search of Equality* (1994b).

10. A series of acts in the nineteenth century, such as the Foreign Miners Tax and various restrictions on Chinese laundries, for example, severely constricted the ability of Chinese immigrants to operate businesses. See Chan 1991, 46.

11. By "formal" I mean the legal granting of citizenship, which ostensibly gives the same rights to every citizen. "Substantive" rights of citizenship take into account the social inequalities of class, race, and gender that make the formal rights of citizenship more accessible to some citizens than to others. See Bendix (1977).

12. See California, State of (1913; 1921).

13. Harris here is quoting powell 1990 (364, 374).

14. In discussing citizenship as an important valance of racialization for Asian Americans and segregation as an important valance of racialization for African Americans, I do not mean to suggest that Asian Americans did not experience segregation and that African Americans did not struggle over issues of citizenship. There has been a long tradition of struggle by African Americans over citizenship rights that were denied to them, even after the enactment of the Fourteenth and Fifteenth Amendments. Also, segregation has long been a fact of life for Asian Americans, as evidenced, for example, by Chinatown ghettoes in many cities that have existed since the nineteenth century and are now becoming homes to new Asian immigrants.

15. The conventional markers of the end of de jure segregation are *Brown vs. Board of Education* in 1954 and the Civil Rights Act of 1964. But also pertinent to this discussion is the 1948 Supreme Court ruling that states could not enforce restrictive covenants, though private parties could still enter into them and county officials could record them.

16. I use "discipline" in the Foucauldian sense; that is, to indicate the ways that subjects are formed in relation to the state, but not through overt mechanisms seen as exterior to the subject. Foucault writes, "The chief function of the disciplinary power is to 'train,' rather than to select and to levy; or, no doubt, to train in order to levy and select all the more. . . . Discipline 'makes' individuals; it is the specific technique of a power that regards individuals both as objects and as instruments of its exercise" (1975, 170).

3. BAD WORKERS, WORSE CONSUMERS

1. The importance of surveillance to colonial regimes predates U.S. imperialism, as Mary Louise Pratt (1992) notes in her study of eighteenth- and nineteenth-century European travel writing. She argues that travel writing and the science of natural history, which arose alongside the genre, created what she calls "the seeing man," whose cataloging gaze over the landscape produced and reinforced his uni-directional and totalizing power over it. Benedict Anderson discusses three mechanisms of surveillance, the census, the map, and the museum, which he says "profoundly shaped the way in which the colonial state imaged its dominion—the nature of the human beings it ruled, the geography of its domain, and the legitimacy of its ancestry" (1991, 164).

2. See my discussion of Vicente Rafael's work (1993) in this chapter.

3. For a discussion of the "management revolution" of the late nineteenth and early twentieth centuries, see Alfred Chandler (1977), who contextualizes this shift in the history of traditional management before this era, and in effect writes the history of the ascendancy of the manager and the invention of the middle-manager. Chandler details how the "multi-unit" business enterprise, by which he means corporations divided into

simultaneously functioning cells, was not necessary until the railroad and telegraph, which demanded coordination on a national level. This level of administrative coordination necessitated the "new subspecies of economic man—the salaried manager" (484).

4. We can see the ways this era holds the seeds of our own: the shift from a producer-based economy in the nineteenth century to the current consumer-based one happened in this early twentieth-century era, when workers were simultaneously both producers and consumers. A fitting measurement of this shift can be seen in a promotion offered by many Ford dealers in 2003 celebrating the hundredth anniversary of the Ford Motor Company: the Five Dollars a Day deal. Yet unlike the original Five Dollar Plan, this deal is aimed not at workers, but consumers: this deal is a lease incentive in which one can purchase a Ford motor vehicle for five dollars a day. Ironically, many of the subcontractors currently supplying parts to Ford operate overseas production facilities in which their workers do not make five dollars a day.

5. Middle-class subjects were interpellated as consumers through newly minted modes of surveillance, which presented buying as a form of voting. As Roland Marchand describes, at the moment in the 1920s when General Motors overtook Ford in sales, it had established a consumer research division. By 1939, this organization had a staff of thirty-seven and expenditures of $300,000 per year (Marchand 1998, 107). Through questionnaires and letters sent directly to car owners, General Motors solicited consumer input on new features and other preferences. While this proved to be impractical as an actual means of soliciting design innovation, simply because the public often could not agree on what it wanted, it proved to be an effective means of producing subjects with consumerist identities that were born when they were hailed by or "recognized by a great corporation" (109). These consumerist identities were again presented as the preeminent form of empowered citizenship, as General Motors proclaimed the company to be run "OF THE PEOPLE, FOR THE PEOPLE, BY THE PEOPLE," and likened filling out a form to voting in an election.

Of course, as the previous examples demonstrate, this mode of "citizenship" was not universal; it was marked as quintessentially American, whether through references to revered American documents like the Gettysburg Address or through unceasing representations of the modern American self and family as consumers. "Americanization" in this era meant being formed as consumers. In her study of Jewish and Italian immigrant women in New York at the turn of the twentieth century, Elizabeth Ewen revises pluralist notions of Americanization as assimilation to a cultural norm by showing how Americanization meant incorporation into U.S. capitalism, which was in this era "the initiation of people into an emerging industrial and consumer society" (1985, 15). Yet she astutely argues that this process happened not only to immigrants, but to the entire nation as the economy shifted from a producer to a consumer society. In other words, nonimmigrants had to undergo "Americanization" and learn to be consumers as well.

6. An extensive and rigorous body of scholarship exists on the history of consumption in the United States. For a succinct yet thorough overview, see Strasser, "Consumption" (1996). Stuart Ewen's study, *Captains of Consciousness,* is a pioneering work that details the ways that advertising produced new conceptions of the self and gender

identities (the New Woman) and relationships (the family ideal). In *Buy Now, Pay Later: Advertising, Credit, and Consumer Durables in the 1920s* (1991), Martha Olney comprehensively examines the "consumer durables revolution" of the 1920s, in particular the synergy of a newly established credit economy and the expansion of advertising in constructing a consumer-based, rather than a producer-based, economy. Daniel Horowitz's *The Morality of Spending* (1985) delineates the ways that a puritanical suspicion of spending and adherence to austerity had to be displaced in the World War II era as consumerism became a way of life for most Americans. There have also been several edited collections about the rise of consumerism in the United States, the best of which are *Getting and Spending* (1998), edited by Strasser, McGovern, and Judt; *Consuming Desires* (1999), edited by Rosenblatt; and *The Culture of Consumption* (1983), edited by Fox and Lears. See also specific texts cited in the body of this chapter.

7. Marz insightfully notes the ways that *U.S.A.* records "the extinction of the private voice, the invasion of the private space" (1980–81, 398). My reading of *U.S.A.* notes many of the same formal characteristics of the text as Marz's, in particular the privileging of the spatialized, fragmented nature of the subject in *U.S.A.* and the ways that the characters of the text are unlike the traditional characters of novels. I differ from Marz in that he mourns the passing of this privatized individual, and valorizes *U.S.A.* inasmuch as it records this fragmented subject in order to critique it and thus restore some vestiges of privacy and individuation.

8. See Ludington (1977) and Vanderwerken (1977)

9. Quoted in Sanders 1976, 81.

4. CONSUMERISM WITHOUT MEANS

1. Yet in using Carpentier's formulation to clarify the "mundane fantastic," I am not merely "adding" Viramontes to the intellectual tradition Carpentier describes, and in which he imagines himself. Indeed, while I find Carpentier's description of the genesis of the marvelous real in the epistemic violence and productivity of colonial encounter to be a compelling narrative, it is not the case that such epistemic shifts produce similar results in different eras, or that these results can be sutured together into a particular tradition. Thus, the conditions under which the marvelous real of the colonial era developed are different from those of Carpentier's setting, and from those of Viramontes. Likewise, the differences in these "new optics" cannot be leveled.

2. Although a less totalizing sense of his description of the postmodern as limited and specific is missing in Jameson's 1983 essay, "Postmodernism and Consumer Society," in *Postmodernism, Or the Cultural Logic of Late Capitalism,* Jameson concedes, "I am far from feeling that all cultural production today is 'postmodernism.' . . . The postmodern is, however, the force field in which very different kinds of cultural impulses—what Raymond Williams has usefully termed 'residual' and 'emergent' forms of cultural production—must make their way" (1991, 6).

3. Many scholars have argued this very important point—that an amnesia around the United States' colonial history is a necessary ideological foundation for U.S. neocolonialism. See Campomanes (1995) and Kaplan (2003).

4. George Lipsitz has a similar argument about commodified transnational culture in *Dangerous Crossroads* (1994), which examines a variety of popular musical forms. Lipsitz argues that the mobility of popular music across national borders presents both peril and potential simultaneously. The very same circuits of capital that bring low-wage jobs, military repression, and dependence to formerly colonized nations are also the means for distributing cultural forms that focus international attention on the struggles of the people of these nations. Lipsitz avoids both the glorification and the pessimistic dismissal of transnational consumer culture by stressing the importance of taking up the challenge presented by the increasing globalization of culture.

5. Homi Bhabha writes, "Mimicry is thus the sign of a double articulation; a complex strategy of reform, regulation, and discipline, which 'appropriates' the Other as it visualizes power. Mimicry is also the sign of the inappropriate, however, a difference or recalcitrance which coheres the dominant strategic function of colonial power, intensifies surveillance, and poses an immanent threat to both 'normalized' knowledge and disciplinary powers" (1994, 86).

6. There is quite a body of work on magical realism in Latin American, Caribbean, and U.S. literature. Most periodizations of the intellectual genesis of this concept begin with Franz Roh's original use of the term to describe European surrealism. Alejo Carpentier's influential essays applied this concept to Latin American literature, insisting on the difference between European surrealism and the American marvelous real. Angel Flores's 1955 essay departed from Carpentier's, emphasizing the aesthetic qualities of magical realism, the goal of which was to transcend the material conditions of impoverishment under which many Spanish and Latin American writers worked: "The conditions of life are so difficult that they are unable to devote the time and travail required for all memorable achievements, with the result that their output is heterogeneous, often careless" (1995, 111). Rather, he said, the use of magical realism by "meticulous craftsmen," influenced by European literary masters of the form like Kafka, produces the "transformation of the common and the everyday into the awesome and the unreal" (114). Such craftsmanship, Flores contends, finally makes Latin American literature as good as the best European literature. Luis Leal's 1967 essay took exception to Flores's Eurocentrism, insisting that Latin American magical realism expressed reality, rather than transcended it: "In magical realism, the writer confronts reality and tries to untangle it, to discover what is mysterious in things, in life, in human acts" (1995, 121). Zamora and Faris's edited collection, *Magical Realism: Theory, History, Community* (1995) is an excellent resource, and these early essays on magical realism, as well as more contemporary works, are reprinted there. Scholars of Afro-Caribbean literature and culture have also contested the role of magical realism, specifically as a corrective to universalizing notions of Negritude. One such contestation involved Haitian novelist Jacques Stephen Aléxis and his nationalist manifesto, "Of the Marvellous Realism of the Haitians" (1956), in which he argued that magical realism was a subset of social realism, a progressive, scientific mode of art produced for the achievement of national liberation. Magical realism registered the conditions of Haitian "underdevelopment," but more important, it was the means for imagining a way out of such impoverishment.

Caribbeanist Michael Dash insightfully locates Aléxis's argument as countering Negritude's "negativity of pure protest" (1974, 66). While Negritude conceived of an enslaved past so violent that nothing had survived, Dash said Aléxis's conception insisted that "colonization and slavery did *not* make things of men but in their own way, the enslaved peoples might have in their own imagination so reordered their reality as to reach beyond the tangible and concrete to acquire a new re-creative sensibility which could aid in the harsh battle for survival" (66). Yet it is important to note that Aléxis's vision of the project of marvellous realism was programmatically nationalist, to the extent that he ends his essay with a four-point description of its objectives, the first being "[singing] the beauties of the Haitian motherland." The two most comprehensive studies of literary magical realism available in English are by Roberto González Echevarría and Amaryll Chanady. González Echevarría prefers the term "Baroque" to "magical realism," which is dismissed in his exhaustively coedited compendium, *The Cambridge History of Latin American Literature* (1996), as an imprecise term that, unfortunately in his view, has quite a bit of influence, having sold many Spanish and Latin American novels in the world marketplace. In *Celestina's Brood* (1993), González Echevarría traces a literary tradition of baroque texts in Spanish and Latin American literature, noting that the Baroque is the only Spanish literary tradition not rejected by Latin American artists. He attributes this to the syncretic, inclusive nature of the Spanish baroque (in particular, the poetry of Luis Góngora y Argote), which lent itself well to the self-definition of Latin American artists and writers (1993, 195–97 passim). Chanady's study, *Magical Realism and the Fantastic: Resolved vs. Unresolved Antimonies* (1985), is an attempt to systematically define these terms to make them less nebulous and more useful. Chanady notes that while both the fantastic and the magical realist modes employ clearly developed codes of the natural and the supernatural (the antimonies of her title), in magical realism the natural and the supernatural coexist or resolve, enabling the fantastic elements to maintain or even highlight the contradictions. I read Chanady's use of the term "resolved" not as describing a teleological resolution, but as referring to magical realism's integrative treatment of supernatural elements within the text. For work on English-language magical realist literature, see Linguanti, Casotti, and Concilio's anthology (1999). There have been some studies of magical realism in U.S. ethnic literature, the best being "Postmodern Realism" by José Saldivar (1991). See also Catherine Bartlett's essay (1986), which argues that Chicano literature should not be placed within an Anglo-American literary tradition, but rather a Latin American one. See also Roland Walter (1993), who examines four Chicano authors to delineate the ways they rely on Latin American forms of magical realism, but also have an independently Chicano aesthetic.

7. José David Saldívar (1997) posits Viramontes's work as a corrective to the limitations of "the national perspective in American Studies," noting the centrality of Chicano/a literature in articulating the "multifaceted migrations across borders" that more accurately describe the contemporary context of American neocolonialism, deindustrialization, and transnational capital, and in creating alternatives to the linear narratives of the nation (1997, 3, 1). In particular, Saldívar maintains that "The Cariboo Café" constitutes "liminality" as a "permanent social reality," rather than as a transitory and

temporary state (104). The undocumented migrants in the story never "come into full cultural or legal citizenship" and thus are never fully incorporated into a national narrative of development, the telos of which is assimilation into the abstract citizen-subject (99). This kind of liminal subject is conveyed through the "fractured form" of the story, its disruption of linear, chronological time, its displacement of unified narratives and narrators (103). Carl Gutiérrez-Jones posits "The Cariboo Café" as constructing an alternative to the juridical subject. In *Rethinking the Borderlands: Between Chicano Culture and Legal Discourse* (1995), Gutiérrez-Jones argues that the centrality of criminalization to Chicano racialization makes Chicano literature a privileged site for the construction of alternatives to the juridical subject constructed by the nation-state's legal discourses. Gutiérrez-Jones argues that "The Cariboo Café" constructs just such an alternative through its intervention into form. Gutiérrez-Jones says that "resisting the monological authority of the law, the story presents multiple distinct voices, which are significantly not resolved into a judgmental closure by either an omniscient narrator or a reflective character" (121). For Leticia Magda Garza-Falcón, the story displaces the complicity of journalism and the media in articulating national subjects. In *Gente Decente: A Borderlands Response to the Rhetoric of Dominance* (1998), Garza-Falcón critiques the complicity of journalism and media reportage in the construction of a hegemonic history. She argues that discourses produced through the mechanisms of journalism and law replicate the flattening, reductive function of language. Citing the language theories of Raymond Williams, Garza-Falcón argues that "language constitutes the 'practical, constitutive activity' and often works reductively. It is necessary to recognize this reductive character of the linguistic sign, just as we recognize that news reports shrink the events they relate" (200). Garza-Falcón says that in contrast to the narratives of journalism, which is one way that "reality is defined by those in a position of authority to define it" (201), Viramontes's "The Cariboo Café" expands the story, emphasizing the great variety and complexity of the lives of working-class immigrants. Barbara Harlow argues in her essay, "Sites of Struggle: Immigration, Deportation, Prison, and Exile" (1991), that the nation-state uses these four institutions to maintain national borders as sites of racialization and gendering. Yet the sites of state control are the very sites in which women of color articulate alternatives to the state. Harlow reads "Cariboo Café" in exactly this way. Noting the ways the story draws together subjects who transgress national boundaries in different ways—undocumented Mexican children and a Latin American in exile—Harlow argues that in "The Cariboo Café," "borders become bonds among peoples, rather than the articulation of national difference and the basis for exclusion" (152). In this way, "The Cariboo Café" constructs an understanding of subjects who come together around difference; who form communities not through the wholeness of narratives of identification, but around displacement, dispossession, and difference. Harlow implies that "Cariboo Café" necessarily eschews the linear temporality and the unitary narrative voice of national culture because the histories of those who are disciplined by, and thus disrupt and transgress, national borders cannot be articulated through the forms of national culture: "Much as these refugees transgress national boundaries, victims of political persecution who by their very international mobility challenge the ideology of national borders and its agenda of depoliticization in the interest of hegemony, so too the story refuses to respect the boundaries and conventions of literary time and space and their disciplining of plot genre" (142).

8. Sonia Saldívar-Hull contextualizes "The Cariboo Café" within a discussion of the limits of white feminism in her book, *Feminism on the Border* (2000). She argues that the story imbues the killing of the undocumented washerwoman with immense significance, as the interweaving of narrative voices creates multiple contexts for this story. One of the contexts is the labor exploitation, criminalization, and disenfranchisement that constitute the histories of undocumented immigrants in the United States. Another is the legacy of U.S. imperialism and neocolonialism that led to the restaurant owner's son's death in Vietnam and that backs the authoritarian Salvadoran government responsible for the disappearance of the washerwoman's son. As the story attests that all of these social and political contexts are relevant to a woman's grief over her son, it articulates a historical materialist theory of Chicana feminism that refuses and refutes the universalizing tendencies of white feminism.

9. For a detailed analysis of the emergence of white anti-immigrant nativism in California from the 1970s to the 1990s, see "The Ideological Roots of the 'Illegal,'" in Joseph Nevins's *Operation Gatekeeper: The Rise of the "Illegal Alien" and the Making of the U.S.–Mexico Boundary* (2002). For a comprehensive history of the beginnings of white anti-immigrant nativism in California, see Tomás Almaguer's *Racial Fault Lines* (1994).

10. See www.immigration.gov/graphics/workforcareers/bpcareer/exiting.htm. Last consulted January 2005.

11. In an article in the *Christian Science Monitor*, Mike Nicley, deputy chief of the Border Patrol in Washington, says, "Unfortunately, violence along the border is a part of the job. . . . If Border Patrol agents [come into contact with] more migrants, there are going to be more violent encounters." See *The Christian Science Monitor*, "Violence up as Border Bristles with Guns," June 19, 2000.

12. Certainly, after September 11, definitions of national boundaries, as well as citizenship, have changed dramatically. Leti Volpp (2002) argues that "citizen" is now defined against "terrorist," a category that constitutes a new racial formation that borrows from older Orientalist tropes, but is a new historical formation in the post–9/11 era. She ends her essay by noting the inability of legal discourse to "know" the noncitizen—in particular, the hundreds, perhaps thousands of Arabs taken into custody by the INS, but whose numbers and presence are undetectable because the Patriot Act does not require disclosure.

13. See also Raúl Villa (2000), who makes a similar argument with Viramontes's story "Neighbors."

14. But how banal is it, really? The container of Vick's VapoRub that sits in my medicine cabinet has a line of fine print at the bottom informing me that the contents were made in Mexico. It seems to me equally unreal and unbelievable that this small plastic jar of translucent jelly traveled hundreds, perhaps thousands of miles across the most militarized as well as the most trafficked border in the world, specifically to relieve my congestion. How did the world come to be that this could happen?

WORKS CITED

Alarcón, Norma. 1990. "The Theoretical Subjects of *This Bridge Called My Back* and Anglo-American Feminism." In *Making Face, Making Soul = Haciendo Caras: Creative and Critical Perspectives by Feminists of Color,* ed. Gloria Anzaldúa. San Francisco, Calif.: Aunt Lute Foundation Books.

Alexander, M. Jacqui. 1994. "Not Just (Any)Body Can Be A Citizen: The Politics of Law, Sexuality, and Postcoloniality in Trinidad and Tobago and the Bahamas." *Feminist Review* 48:5–23.

Aléxis, Jacques Stephen. 1956. "Of the Marvellous Realism of the Haitians." *Présence Africaine* 8–10 (June–November): 245–71.

Almaguer, Tomás. 1994. *Racial Fault Lines: The Historical Origins of White Supremacy in California.* Berkeley and Los Angeles: University of California Press.

Anderson, Benedict. 1991. *Imagined Communities: Reflections on the Origin and Spread of Nationalism.* Rev. ed. London: Verso.

Andreas, Peter. 2000. *Border Games: Policing the U.S.–Mexico Divide.* Ithaca, N.Y.: Cornell University Press.

Andrews, William T. 1996. Preface to *Up from Slavery: Authoritative Text, Contexts, and Compositional History Criticism,* ed. William T. Andrews. New York: W.W. Norton and Co., 1996.

———. 2002. "Bookerese: Performing Blackness in *Up from Slavery.*" Keynote address presented at the Multi-Ethnic Studies of Europe and the Americas Conference, Padua, Italy, June 26–29.

Anzaldúa, Gloria. 2002. "Foreword, 2001." In Moraga and Anzaldúa 2002, xxxiv–xxxix.

Arrighi, Giovanni. 1994. *The Long Twentieth Century: Money, Power, and the Origins of Our Times.* London: Verso.

Awkward, Michael. 1993. "'The Evil of Fulfillment': Scapegoating and Narration in *The Bluest Eye.*" In Gates and Appiah 1993, 175–209.

Bartlett, Catherine. 1986. "Magical Realism: The Latin American Influence on Modern Chicano Writers." *Confluencia* 1, no. 2 (Spring): 27–37.

Bendix, Reinhard. 1977. "The Extension of Citizenship to the Lower Classes." In *Nation-Building and Citizenship: Studies of Our Changing Social Order,* 89–126. Berkeley and Los Angeles: University of California Press.

Bhabha, Homi. 1994. "Of Mimicry and Man: The Ambivalence of Colonial Discourse." In *The Location of Culture,* 85–92. New York: Routledge.

Blackwell, Maylei. 2000. *Geographies of Difference: Mapping Multiple Feminist Insurgencies and Transnational Public Cultures in the Americas.* PhD diss., History of Consciousness, University of California, Santa Cruz.

Bonacich, Edna, and Richard P. Appelbaum. 2000. *Behind the Label: Inequality in the Los Angeles Apparel Industry.* Berkeley and Los Angeles: University of California Press.

Bordwell, David, and Kristin Thompson. 2001. *Film Art: An Introduction.* 6th ed. New York: McGraw-Hill.

Brodhead, Richard. 1993. *Cultures of Letters: Scenes of Reading and Writing in Nineteenth-Century America.* Chicago: University of Chicago Press.

Brown, Gillian. 1990. *Domestic Individualism: Imagining Self in Nineteenth-Century America.* Berkeley and Los Angeles: University of California Press.

Calderon, Hector, and José David Saldívar, eds. 1991. *Criticism in the Borderlands: Studies in Chicano Literature, Culture, and Ideology.* Durham, N.C.: Duke University Press.

California, State of. 1913. Alien Land Law of 1913 (Webb-Heney Bill). *Statutes of California* 1913, Chapter 113, 206–8.

———. 1921. Alien Land Law of 1920. *Statutes of California* 1921, lxxxiii–lxxxvi.

Campomanes, Oscar. 1995. "The New Empire's Forgetful and Forgotten Citizens: Unrepresentability and Unassimilability in Filipino-American Postcolonialities." *Hitting Critical Mass* 2, no. 2 (Spring): 145–200.

Carby, Hazel. 1987. *Reconstructing Womanhood.* New York: Oxford University Press.

Carpentier, Alejo. 1995a. "The Baroque and the Marvelous Real." In Zamora and Faris 1995, 89–108.

———. 1995b. "Marvelous Real in America." In Zamora and Faris 1995, 76–88.

Chan, Sucheng. 1991. *Asian Americans: An Interpretive History.* Boston, Mass.: Twayne Publishers.

Chanady, Amaryll Beatrice. 1985. *Magical Realism and the Fantastic: Resolved vs. Unsolved Antimonies.* New York: Garland.

Chandler, Alfred D. 1977. *The Visible Hand: The Management Revolution in American Business.* Cambridge, Mass.: Belknap Press.

Cheung, King-Kok. 1994a. "Double-Telling: Intertextual Silence in Hisaye Yamamoto's Fiction." In Yamamoto 1994, 161–79.

———. 1994b. Introduction. In Yamamoto 1994, 3–16.

Chin, Frank, Jeffery Chan, Lawson Inada, Shawn Wong, eds., 1974. *Aiiieeeee! An Anthology of Asian American Writers.* Washington, D.C.: Howard University Press, 1–58.

Christian, Barbara. 1993. "The Contemporary Fables of Toni Morrison." In Gates and Appiah 1993, 59–99.

Christian Science Monitor. 2000. "Violence up as Border Bristles with Guns." June 19. Http://csmweb2.emcweb.com/durable/2000/06/19/p3s1.htm (last consulted September 9, 2003).

Cohen, Lizabeth. 1992. *Making a New Deal: Industrial Workers in Chicago, 1919–1939.* Cambridge: Harvard University Press.

———. 1998. "The New Deal State and the Making of Citizen Consumers." In Strasser, McGovern, and Judt 1998, 111–26.

Coletta, Paolo E. 1967. "'The Most Thankless Task': Byron and the California Alien Land Legislation," *Pacific Historical Review* 36:163–87. Reprinted in McClain 1994a.

Combahee River Collective. 1979. "Why Did They Die? A Document of Black Feminism." *Radical America* 13, no. 6 (October/November): 41–50.

———. 1981. "A Black Feminist Statement." In Moraga and Anzaldúa 1981, 210–18.

Cox, James M. 1995. "Attacks on the Ending and Twain's Attack on the Conscience." In *The Adventures of Huckleberry Finn: A Case Study in Critical Controversy,* ed. Gerald Graff and James Phelan, 105–12. Boston, Mass.: Bedford.

Crowther, Samuel. 1926. "Henry Ford: Why I Favor Five Days' Work for Six Days' Pay." *World's Work* 52 (October): 613–16.

Dash, Michael. 1974. "Marvellous Realism: The Way Out of Negritude." *Caribbean Studies* 13, no. 4: 57–70.

Davidson, Cathy. 1986. *Revolution and the Word: The Rise of the Novel in America.* New York: Oxford University Press.

Davis, Angela. 1997. "Reflections on Race, Gender, and Class in the U.S.A." In *The Politics of Culture in the Shadow of Capital,* ed. Lisa Lowe and David Lloyd, 303–23. Durham, N.C.: Duke University Press.

———. 1981a. "Rape, Racism, and the Myth of the Black Rapist." In *Women, Race, and Class,* 172–201. New York: Random House.

———. 1981b. *Women, Race, and Class.* New York: Random House.

Deming, Barbara. 1974. *We Cannot Live without Our Lives.* New York: Grossman Publishers.

Denning, Michael. 1996. *The Cultural Front.* London: Verso.

DeVoto, Bernard. 1932. *Mark Twain's America.* Cambridge, Mass.: Houghton Mifflin.

Dos Passos, John. 1996. *U.S.A.* New York: Library of America.

Dowd, Douglas Fitzgerald. 1974. *The Twisted Dream: Capitalist Development in the United States Since 1776.* Cambridge, Mass.: Winthrop Publishers.

Dubey, Madhu. 2003. *Signs and Cities: Black Literary Postmodernism.* Chicago: University of Chicago Press.

Dunn, Timothy. 1996. *The Militarization of the U.S.–Mexico Border, 1978–1992: Low Intensity Conflict Doctrine Comes Home.* Austin: University of Texas Press.

Eliot, T. S. 1950. Introduction to *The Adventures of Huckleberry Finn.* New York: Canticleer Press.

Ewen, Elizabeth. 1985. *Immigrant Women in the Land of Dollars: Life and Culture on the Lower East Side, 1890–1925.* New York: Monthly Review Press.

Ewen, Stuart. 1976. *Captains of Consciousness: Advertising and the Social Roots of Consumer Culture.* New York: McGraw Hill.

Ferguson, Edwin. 1947. "The California Alien Land Law and the Fourteenth Amendment." *California Law Review* 35: 61–90.

Ferguson, Roderick A. 2004. *Aberrations in Black: Toward a Queer of Color Critique.* Minneapolis: University of Minnesota Press.

Fiedler, Leslie. 1948. "Come Back to the Raft Ag'in, Huck Honey!" *Partison Review* 15: 664–711.

Flores, Angel. 1995. "Magical Realism in Spanish American Fiction." In Zamora and Faris 1995, 109–18.

Foley, Barbara. 1979. "History, Fiction, and Satirical Form: The Example of Dos Passos's *1919." Genre* 12 (Fall): 357–78.

———. 1980–81. "The Treatment of Time in *The Big Money:* An Examination of Ideology and Literary Form." *Modern Fiction Studies* 26, no. 4 (Winter): 447–67.

Foucault, Michel. 1975. *Discipline and Punish: The Birth of the Prison.* New York: Pantheon Books.

———. 1986. "Of Other Spaces." *Diacritics* 16, no. 1 (Spring): 22–27.

———. 1991. "Governmentality." In *The Foucault Effect: Studies in Governmentality,* ed. Graham Burchell, Colin Gordon, and Peter Miller, 87–104. Chicago: University of Chicago Press.

Fox, Richard Wightman, and T. J. Jackson Lears, eds. 1983. *The Culture of Consumption: Critical Essays in American History, 1880–1980.* New York: Pantheon Books.

Furman, Jan. 1996. *Toni Morrison's Fiction.* Columbia: University of South Carolina Press.

García Canclini, Néstor. 2001. *Consumers and Citizens: Globalization and Multicultural Conflicts.* Minneapolis: University of Minnesota Press.

Garza-Falcón, Leticia Magda. 1998. *Gente Decente: A Borderlands Response to the Rhetoric of Dominance.* Austin: University of Texas Press.

Gates, Jr., Henry Louis, and K. A. Appiah. 1993. *Toni Morrison: Critical Perspectives Past and Present.* New York: Amistad Press.

Gibson, Donald. 1993. "Text and Countertext in *The Bluest Eye.*" In Gates and Appiah 1993, 159–74.

———. 1996. "Chapter One of Booker T. Washington's 'Up From Slavery' and the Feminization of the African American Male." In *Representing Black Men,* ed. Marcellus Blount and George P. Cunningham, 95–110. New York: Routledge.

Gilmore, Ruth Wilson. 1998–99. "Globalization and U.S. Prison Growth: From Military Keynesianism to Post-Keynesian Militarism." *Race and Class* 40, no. 2/3: 171–87.

Glenn, Evelyn Nakano. 1983. "Racial Ethnic Women's Labor: The Intersection of Race, Gender, and Class Oppression." *Review of Radical Political Economics* 17:86–108.

Glickman, Lawrence B. 1997. *A Living Wage: American Workers and the Making of Consumer Society.* Ithaca, N.Y.: Cornell University Press.

Goellnicht, Donald C. 1994. "Transplanted Discourse in Yamamoto's 'Seventeen Syllables.'" In Yamamoto 1994, 181–94.

González Echevarría, Roberto. 1993. *Celestina's Brood: Continuities of the Baroque in Spanish and Latin American Literatures.* Durham, N.C.: Duke University Press.

González Echevarría, Roberto, and Enrique Pupo-Walker, eds. 1996. *The Cambridge History of Latin American Literature.* Cambridge, England: Cambridge University Press.

Guerrero, Ed. 1997. "Tracking 'The Look' in the Novels of Toni Morrison." In *Toni Morrison's Fiction: Contemporary Criticism,* ed. David L. Middleton, 27–41. New York: Garland Publishing.

Gutiérrez-Jones, Carl. 1995. *Rethinking the Borderlands: Between Chicano Culture and Legal Discourse.* Berkeley and Los Angeles: University of California Press.

Hagedorn, Jessica. 1989. "Song of Bullets." In *The Forbidden Stitch: An Asian American Women's Anthology,* ed. Shirley Geok-lin Lim, Mayumi Tsutakawa, and Margarita Donnelly, 144–46. Corvallis, Ore.: Calyx Books.

———. 1990. *Dogeaters.* New York: Penguin.

Hamilton-Paterson, James. 1999. *America's Boy.* London: Granta Books.

Harlow, Barbara. 1991. "Sites of Struggle: Immigration, Deportation, Prison, and Exile." In Calderon and Saldívar 1991, 149–63.

Harris, Cheryl. 1993. "Whiteness as Property." *Harvard Law Review* 106, no. 8 (June): 1710–91.

Harris, Miriam Lynell. 1997. "From Kennedy to Combahee: Black Feminist Activism from 1960 to 1980." PhD dissertation, University of Minnesota.

Harris, William H. 1982. *The Harder We Run: Black Workers Since the Civil War.* New York: Oxford University Press.

Hartmann, Saidiya. 1997. *Scenes of Subjection: Terror, Slavery, and Self-Making in Nineteenth-Century America.* London and New York: Oxford University Press, 1997.

Harvey, David. 1990. *The Condition of Postmodernity.* Cambridge, England: Basil Blackwell.

Hedin, Raymond. 1979. "Paternal at Last: Booker T. Washington and the Slave Narrative Tradition." *Callaloo* 2, no. 7 (October): 95–102.

Heinze, Denise. 1993. *The Dilemma of "Double Consciousness": Toni Morrison's Novels.* Athens: University of Georgia Press.

Ho, Laura, Catherine Powell, and Leti Volpp. 1996. "(Dis)assembling Women Workers' Rights along the Global Assemblyline: Human Rights and the Garment Industry." *Harvard Civil Rights Civil Liberties Review* 31, no. 2 (Summer): 383–414.

Hohri, William Minoru. 1988. *Repairing America: An Account of the Movement for Japanese American Redress.* Pullman: Washington University Press.

Hooker, Clarence. 1997. *Life in the Shadows of the Crystal Palace 1910–1927: Ford Workers in the Model T Era.* Bowling Green, Ohio: Bowling Green State University Popular Press.

Horowitz, Daniel. 1985. *The Morality of Spending: Attitudes toward the Consumer Society in America, 1875–1940.* Baltimore: The Johns Hopkins University Press.

Hossfield, Karen. 1994. "Hiring Immigrant Women: Silicon Valley's 'Simple Formula.'" In *Women of Color in U.S. Society,* ed. Maxine Baca Zinn and Bonnie Thornton Dill, 65–94. Philadelphia: Temple University Press.

Ichioka, Yuji. 1984. "Japanese Immigrant Response to the 1920 California Alien Land Law." In *Agricultural History* 58, no. 1: 157–78. Reprinted in McClain 1994a.

Jacoby, Sanford M. 1985. *Employing Bureaucracy: Managers, Unions, and the Transformation of Work in American Industry, 1900–1945.* New York: Columbia University Press.

James, Henry. 1990. "Daisy Miller: A Study." In *Heath Anthology of American Literature,* vol. 2, ed. Paul Lauter, 551–89. Lexington, Mass.: D.C. Heath and Company.

Jameson, Fredric. 1983. "Postmodernism and Consumer Society." In *The Anti-Aesthetic: Essays on Postmodern Culture,* ed. Hal Foster, 111–25. Seattle: Bay Press.

———. 1991. *Postmodernity, or the Cultural Logic of Late Capital.* Durham, N.C.: Duke University Press.

Kanigel, Robert. 1997. "Taylor-made." *Sciences* 37, no. 3 (May): 18.

Kaplan, Amy. 2003. *The Anarchy of Empire in the Making of U.S. Culture.* Cambridge: Harvard University Press.

Keeling, Kara. 2001. "'Let's Eat Pomegranates': 'Eve's Bayou,' the Black Femme, and the Limits of Visibility." Paper presented at the American Studies Association Annual Conference, Washington, D.C.

Kennedy, Lawrence. 1992. *Planning the City Upon a Hill: Boston Since 1630.* Amherst: University of Massachusetts Press.

Kim, Elaine. 1994. "Hisaye Yamamoto: A Woman's View." In Yamamoto 1994, 109–18.

Kim, Min-Jung. 1999. "Renarrating the 'Private': Gender, Family, and Race in Zora Neale Hurston, Alice Walker, and Toni Morrison." PhD dissertation, University of California, San Diego.

Koppelman, Susan. 1985. *Between Mothers and Daughters: Stories across a Generation.* Old Westbury, N.Y.: The Feminist Press at CUNY.

Kubitschek, Missy Dehn. 1998. *Toni Morrison: A Critical Companion.* Westport, Conn.: Greenwood Press, 1998.

Lasch, Christopher. 1977. *Haven in a Heartless World.* New York: Basic Books.

Leal, Luis. 1995. "Magical Realism in Spanish Literature." In Zamora and Faris 1995, 119–24.

Lee, Jim. 2004. *Urban Triage: Race and the Fictions of Multiculturalism.* Minneapolis: University of Minnesota Press.

Lee, Rachel. 2002. "Notes from the (Non)field: Teaching and Theorizing Women of Color." In *Women's Studies on Its Own: A Next Wave Reader in Institutional Change,* ed. Robyn Wiegman, 82–105. Durham, N.C.: Duke University Press.

Lefebvre, Henri. 1991. *The Production of Space.* Oxford and Cambridge: Basil Blackwell.

Linguanti, Elisa, Francesco Casotti, and Carmen Concilio. 1999. *Coterminous Worlds: Magical Realism and Contemporary Post-Colonial Literature in English.* Amsterdam, Holland: Rodopi.

Lipsitz, George. 1994. *Dangerous Crossroads: Popular Music, Postmodernism, and the Poetics of Place.* London: Verso Press.

———. 1995. "The Possessive Investment in Whiteness: Racialized Social Democracy and the 'White' Problem in American Studies," *American Quarterly* 47, no. 3 (September): 369–87.

Locke, John. 1980. *Second Treatise of Government*. Ed. C. B. MacPherson. Indianapolis, Ind.: Hackett Publishing Company, Inc.

Lorde, Audre. 1984. *Sister Outsider: Essays and Speeches*. Trumansburg, N.Y.: Crossing Press.

Lowe, Donald. 1982. *History of Bourgeois Perception*. Chicago: The University of Chicago Press.

Lowe, Lisa. 1996. *Immigrant Acts: On Asian American Cultural Politics*. Durham, N.C.: Duke University Press.

Ludington, Townsend. 1977. "The Ordering of the Camera Eye in *U.S.A.*" *American Literature* 49 (November): 443–46.

MacPherson, C. B. *The Political Theory of Possessive Individualism: Hobbes to Locke*. Oxford: Clarendon Press, 1962.

Mailloux, Steven. 1996. "Rhetorical Hermeneutics as Reception Study: Huckleberry Finn and 'The Bad Boy Boom.'" In *Reconceptualizing American Literary/Cultural Studies: Rhetoric, History, and Politics in the Humanities,* ed. William E. Cain, 35–56. New York: Garland.

Mandel, Ernest. 1975. *Late Capitalism*. London: NLB.

Marchand, Roland. 1998. "Customer Research as Public Relations: General Motors in the 1930s." In Strasser, McGovern, and Judt 1998, 85–110.

Marx, Karl. 1978. "On the Jewish Question." In *The Marx-Engels Reader, Second Edition,* ed. Robert Tucker, 26–52. New York: W.W. Norton and Co.

Marx, Leo. 1953. "Mr. Eliot, Mr. Trilling, and Huckleberry Finn." *The American Scholar* 23 (Autumn): 423–39.

Marz, Charles. 1980–81. "*U.S.A.*: Chronicle and Performance." *Modern Fiction Studies* 26, no. 4 (Winter): 398–415.

Massey, Douglas S., and Nancy Ann Denton. 1993. *American Apartheid: Segregation and the Making of the Underclass*. Cambridge: Harvard University Press.

McClain, Charles, ed. 1994a. *In Search of Equality: The Chinese Struggle against Discrimination in Nineteenth-Century America*. Berkeley and Los Angeles: University of California Press.

———. 1994b. *Japanese Immigrants and American Law*, vol. 2 of *Asian Americans and the Law*. New York: Garland Publishing.

McGovern, Charles. 1998. "Consumption and Citizenship in the United States, 1900–1940." In Strasser, McGovern, and Judt 1998, 37–58.

Meyer, Stephen. 1981. *The Five Dollar Day: Labor Management and Social Control in the Ford Motor Company, 1908–1921*. Albany: State University of New York Press.

Mistri, Zenobia Baxter. 1994. "'Seventeen Syllables': A Symbolic Haiku." In Yamamoto 1994, 195–202.

Mitter, Swasti. 1986. *Common Fate, Common Bond: Women in the Global Economy*. London: Pluto Press.

Miyoshi, Masao. 1993. "A Borderless World? From Colonialism to Transnationalism and the Decline of the Nation-State." *Critical Inquiry* 19 (Summer): 726–51.

Mobley, Marilyn Sanders. 1993. "A Different Remembering: Memory, History, and Meaning in *Beloved.*" In Gates and Appiah 1993, 356–65.

Mohanty, Chandra, and M. Jacqui Alexander. 1997. *Feminist Genealogies, Colonial Legacies, Democratic Futures.* New York: Routledge.

Mohanty, Chandra Talpade. 1991. "Cartographies of Struggle: Third World Women and the Politics of Feminism." In Mohanty, Russo, and Torres 1991, 1–47.

Mohanty, Chandra Talpade, Ann Russo, and Lourdes Torres, eds. 1991. *Third World Women and the Politics of Feminism.* Bloomington: Indiana University Press.

Moraga, Cherríe. 2002. "Foreword, 2001." In Moraga and Anzaldúa 2002, xv–xxxiii.

Moraga, Cherríe, and Gloria Anzaldúa, eds. 1981. *This Bridge Called My Back: Writings by Radical Women of Color.* Watertown, Mass.: Persephone Press.

———, eds. 2002. *This Bridge Called My Back: Writings by Radical Women of Color,* 3d ed. Berkeley, Calif.: Third Woman Press.

Moretti, Franco. 1987. *The Way of the World: The Bildungsroman in European Culture.* London: Verso.

Morrison, Toni. 1970. *The Bluest Eye.* New York: Plume Books.

Murase, Mike. 1978. "Ethnic Studies and Higher Education for Asian Americans." In *Counterpoint: Perspectives on Asian America,* ed. Emma Gee. Los Angeles: UCLA Asian American Studies Center, 205–23.

Murashige, Michael. 1995. "Race, Resistance, and Contestations of Urban Space." PhD dissertation, University of California, Los Angeles.

Nevins, Joseph. 2002. *Operation Gatekeeper: The Rise of the "Illegal Alien" and the Making of the U.S.–Mexico Boundary.* New York: Routledge.

Nietzsche, Friedrich. [1887] 1967. *On the Genealogy of Morals.* Trans. Walter Kaufman and R. J. Hollingdale. New York: Vintage.

Oliver, Melvin, and Thomas Shapiro. 1995. *Black Wealth, White Wealth: A New Perspective on Racial Inequality.* New York and London: Routledge.

Olney, Martha A. 1991. *Buy Now, Pay Later: Advertising, Credit, and Consumer Durables in the 1920s.* Chapel Hill: University of North Carolina Press.

Ong, Aihwa. 1991. "The Gender and Labor Politics of Postmodernity." *Annual Review of Anthropology* 20: 279–309.

Parreñas, Rhacel. 2002. "Migrant Filipina Domestic Workers and the International Division of Reproductive Labor." *Gender and Society* 14, no. 4 (August): 560–80.

Patterson, Orlando. 1982. *Slavery and Social Death.* Cambridge: Harvard University Press.

Payne, Charles. 1995. *I've Got the Light of Freedom: The Organizing Tradition and the Mississippi Freedom Struggle.* Berkeley and Los Angeles: University of California Press.

Peach, Linden. 1995. *Toni Morrison.* New York: St. Martin's Press.

Pizer, Donald. 1980–81. "The Camera Eye in *U.S.A.:* The Sexual Center." *Modern Fiction Studies* 26, no. 4 (Winter): 417–30.

———. 1988. *Dos Passos's U.S.A.* Charlottesville: University Press of Virginia.

Pomeroy, William. 1970. *American Neo-Colonialism: Its Emergence in the Philippines and Asia.* New York: International Publishers.

powell, john a. 1990. "New Property Disaggregated: A Model to Address Employment Discrimination." *University of San Francisco Law Review* 24 (Winter): 363–83.

Pratt, Mary Louise. 1992. *Imperial Eyes: Travel Writing and Transculturation.* London: Routledge.

Rafael, Vicente. 1993. "White Love: Surveillance and Nationalist Resistance in the U.S. Colonization of the Philippines." In *Cultures of United States Imperialism,* ed. Amy Kaplan and Donald Pease, 185–218. Durham, N.C.: Duke University Press.

Reddy, Chandan. 2005. "Asian Diasporas, Neo-Liberalism, and the Critique of Gay Identity: Re-viewing the Case for Homosexual Asylum in the Context of 'Family Rights.'" *Social Text* 23, no. 3/4 (October): 101–19.

———. 1998. "Home, Houses, Non-identity: Paris Is Burning." In *Burning Down the House: Recycling Domesticity,* ed. Rosemary George, 355–79. Boulder, Colo.: Westview Press.

Roediger, David. 1999. *The Wages of Whiteness.* Rev. ed. London: Verso Press.

Rolf, Robert T. 1994. "The Short Stories of Hisaye Yamamoto, Japanese American Writer." In Yamamoto 1994, 89–108.

Rosenblatt, Roger, ed. 1999. *Consuming Desires: Consumption, Culture, and the Pursuit of Happiness.* Washington, D.C.: Island Press.

Rubenstein, Roberta. 1993. "Pariahs and Community." In Gates and Appiah 1993, 126–58.

Ruffins, Faith Davis. 1998. "Reflecting on Ethnic Imagery in the Landscape of Commerce, 1945–1975." In Strasser, McGovern, and Judt 1998, 379–406.

Saldívar, José David. 1991. "Postmodern Realism." In *The Columbia History of the American Novel,* ed. Emory Elliott, 521–41. New York: Columbia University Press.

———. 1997. *Border Matters: Remapping American Cultural Studies.* Berkeley and Los Angeles: University of California Press.

Saldívar-Hull, Sonia. 2000. *Feminism on the Border: Chicana Gender Politics and Literature.* Berkeley: University of California.

Sanders, David. 1976. "Interview with John Dos Passos." In *Writers at Work: The "Paris Review" Interviews,* 4th series, ed. George Plimpton, 89–100. New York: Viking.

Sandoval, Chela. 2000. *Methodology of the Oppressed.* Minneapolis: University of Minnesota Press.

Sangari, Kumkum. 1987. "The Politics of the Possible." *Cultural Critique* 7 (Fall): 157–86.

Sassen, Saskia. 1998. *Globalization and Its Discontents: Essays on the New Mobility of People and Money.* New York: New Press.

Saxton, Alexander. 1995. *The Indispensable Enemy: Labor and the Anti-Chinese Movement in California.* Berkeley and Los Angeles: University of California Press.

Shah, Nayan. 2001. *Contagious Divides: Epidemic and Race in San Francisco's Chinatown.* Berkeley and Los Angeles: University of California Press.

Short, Kayann. 1994. "Coming to the Table: The Differential Politics of *This Bridge Called My Back.*" *Genders* 19: 3–44.

Smith, Valerie. 1993a. "'Circling the Subject': History and Narrative in *Beloved*." In Gates and Appiah 1993, 342–55.

———. 1993b. "Song of Solomon: Continuities of Community." In Gates and Appiah 1993, 274–83.

Strasser, Susan. 1996. "Consumption." In *Encyclopedia of the United States in the Twentieth Century*, vol. 3, ed. Stanley I. Kutler, 1017–36. New York: Charles Scribner and Sons.

Strasser, Susan, Charles McGovern, and Matthias Judt, eds. 1998. *Getting and Spending: European and American Consumer Societies in the Twentieth Century*. Cambridge: Cambridge University Press.

Sturken, Marita. 1997. *Tangled Memories: The Vietnam War, The AIDS Epidemic, and the Politics of Remembering*. Berkeley and Los Angeles: University of California Press.

Taylor, Fredrick Winslow. 1947. "Shop Management" and "Principles of Scientific Management." In *Scientific Management*, 17–207 and 5–144. New York: Harper & Brothers.

tenBroek, Jacobus, Edward N. Barnhart, and Floyd W. Matson. 1954. *Prejudice, War, and the Constitution: Causes and Consequences of the Evacuation of the Japanese Americans in World War II*. Berkeley and Los Angeles: University of California Press.

Terrell, Lynne. 1993. "Storytelling and Moral Agency." In Gates and Appiah 1993, 3–25.

Thompkins, E. Berkeley. 1970. *Anti-Imperialism in the United States: The Great Debate, 1890–1920*. Philadelphia: University of Philadelphia Press.

Tiano, Susan. 1994. *Patriarchy on the Line: Labor, Gender, and Ideology in the Mexican Maquila Industry*. Philadelphia: Temple University Press.

Trilling, Lionel. 1950. *The Liberal Imagination*. New York: Viking.

Turner, Frederick Jackson. 1894. *The Significance of the Frontier in American History*. Madison: Wisconsin State Historical Society.

Twain, Mark. 1990. "The Adventures of Huckleberry Finn." In *Heath Anthology of American Literature*, ed. Paul Lauter, vol. 2, 243–428. Lexington, Mass.: D.C. Heath and Company.

United States Border Patrol. 2003. "You Can Leave the Military Without Leaving the Challenge Behind." http://www.immigration.gov/graphics/workfor/careers/bpcareer/exiting.htm. Last consulted September 13, 2003.

United States Department of the Census. 1905. *Census of the Philippine Islands*, 4 vols. Washington, D.C.: Government Printing Office.

Vanderwerken, David L. 1977. "*U.S.A.*: Dos Passos and the 'Old Words.'" *Twentieth Century Literature* 23 (February): 195–228.

Villa, Raúl Romero. 2000. *Barrio-Logos: Space and Place in Urban Chicano Literature and Culture*. Austin: University of Texas Press.

Viramontes, Helena Maria. 1995. *The Moths and Other Stories*. Houston: Arte Público Press.

Volpp, Leti. 2002. "The Citizen and the Terrorist," *UCLA Law Review* 49 (June): 1575–92.

Wallerstein, Immanuel Maurice. 1976. *The Modern World System: Capitalist Agriculture and the Origins of the European World-Economy in the Sixteenth Century.* New York: Academic Press.

Walter, Roland. 1993. *Magical Realism in Contemporary Chicano Fiction.* Frankfurt, Germany: Vervuert.

Wardley, Lynn. 1991. "Reassembling Daisy Miller." *American Literary History* 3, no. 2 (Summer): 232–54.

Washington, Booker T. 1996 [1901]. *Up from Slavery: Authoritative Text, Contexts, and Compositional History Criticism,* ed. William T. Andrews. New York: W.W. Norton and Co.

Westbrook, Robert B. 1983. "Politics as Consumption: Managing the Modern American Election." In *The Culture of Consumption: Critical Essays in American History, 1880–1980,* ed. Richard Wightman Fox and T. J. Jackson Lears, 143–73. New York: Pantheon Books.

Williams, Patricia. 1991a. *The Alchemy of Race and Rights.* Cambridge: Harvard University Press.

———. 1991b. "On Being the Object of Property." In Williams 1991a, 216–38.

Williams, Raymond. 1977. *Marxism and Literature.* Oxford: Oxford University Press.

Willis, Susan. 1993. "Eruptions of Funk: Historicizing Toni Morrison." In Gates and Appiah 1993, 308–29.

Yamamoto, Hisaye. 1988. *Seventeen Syllables and Other Stories.* Ed. King-Kok Cheung. Latham, N.Y.: Kitchen Table: Women of Color Press.

———. 1988. "Yoneko's Earthquake." In Yamamoto 1988, 46–56.

———. 1994. *Seventeen Syllables/Hisaye Yamamoto.* Ed. King-Kok Cheung. New Brunswick, N.J.: Rutgers University Press.

———. 2001. "A Fire in Fontana." In *Seventeen Syllables and Other Stories,* 150–57. Revised and expanded edition. New Brunswick, N.J.: Rutgers University Press.

Yogi, Stan. 1994. "Legacies Revealed: Uncovering Buried Plots in the Stories of Hisaye Yamamoto." In Yamamoto 1994, 143–60.

Zamora, Lois Parkinson, and Wendy B. Faris, eds. 1995. *Magical Realism: Theory, History, Community.* Durham, N.C.: Duke University Press.

INDEX

abstract space, xiv–xv, 75, 81, 99, 103; articulation of, 71; bureaucracy and, 72; capitalism and, 70; difference and, 80; production and, 110; surveillance and, 78; violence and, 70

accumulation, xxiii, 116; capital, xxiii, 28, 29, 114; cycles of, 153n5; differentiated modes of, 112; flexible, 108, 111, 113, 115; social unity of, 138

Adventures of Huckleberry Finn, The (Twain), xiii, 5, 9, 13, 21, 23, 68, 75; bonds in, 17; and *Daisy Miller* compared, 14–15; impact of, 12, 16; and *Up from Slavery* compared, 26

African Americans, xxi, xxvii; characterization of, 37; devaluation of, 12; Japanese Americans and, 36, 54; literary tradition of, 157n7; material circumstances of, 56; normative subject and, 37; property rights over, 28; racialized/gendered history of, 40

African American women: devaluation of, xvii, xxxii, 57; "properly" formed, 57; racialization of, xxxii; threat to, xxxiii, 49

agency, 67, 70, 104; consumerism as, 89; personal, 89, 90; political, 89; valorization of, 68

Aiiieeeee!: on Yamamoto, 38

Alarcón, Norma, xxix, 153n7

Alexander, M. Jacqui, xx, xxii, 154n7

Aléxis, Jacques Stephen, 161–62n6

Alhambra, 51, 52

alienation, 76, 84, 85, 93, 94, 95; consumerism and, 90; natal, 28–29

Alien Land laws, 32, 41, 43, 44, 45; Japanese Americans and, 35, 157n9; people of color and, 42

Allen, William, 92

All That Heaven Allows, 122, 123, 126

Americanization, 87, 88, 89, 159n5

"American Standard of Living," 44, 45, 48, 49, 91, 92

Anderson, Benedict, 15, 158n1

Anderson, Charley, 96, 100, 101, 104, 105

Andrews, William T.: on Washington, 155n7

anti-Chinese sentiment, 91–92

anti-immigrant sentiment, 134, 135, 164n9

Anti-Imperialism League, 91

anti-Japanese sentiment, 38, 43–44

Grace Kyungwon Hong is assistant professor of Asian American studies and women's studies at the University of California, Los Angeles.